Life, Love and Economics

GAVIN SINCLAIR • ROBERT W. TAYLOR • DEE E. CUTTELL

PURDUE UNIVERSITY

Pearson
Custom
Publishing

Cover photo of the Federal Reserve Building, Washington, D.C., PhotoDisc, Inc.

Printed in the United States of America

10 9 8 7 6 5 4 3

This manuscript was supplied camera-ready by the author(s).

Please visit our website at www.pearsoncustom.com

ISBN 0–536–60338–3

BA 990721

PEARSON CUSTOM PUBLISHING
75 Arlington Street, Boston, MA 02116
A Pearson Education Company

Table of Contents

Introduction   What is Economics?   **5**

Chapter 1   Jason Looks for a Job: The GDP Chapter   **7**

Chapter 2   Watching a Soccer Game: The Economics of Society Chapter   **15**

Chapter 3   Samantha Looks for a Job: The Unemployment and Growth Chapter   **25**

Chapter 4   Jason and Samantha Meet: The Car Buying Chapter   **31**

Chapter 5   Jason Wants a Honda: The International Economics Chapter   **39**

Chapter 6   Rent or Buy? The Housing Chapter   **45**

Chapter 7   The First Date: The Paycheck and Financial Planning Chapter   **53**

Chapter 8   Politics: The Conservatives Versus Liberals Chapter   **63**

Chapter 9   Samantha Buys a House: The Real Estate Chapter   **71**

Chapter 10   A Visit to WLU: The Monetary Policy Chapter   **79**

Chapter 11   Another Lecture at WLU: The Fiscal Policy Chapter   **91**

Chapter 12   Marriage: The Financial Planning for Couples Chapter   **99**

Chapter 13   Family Decisions: The Utility Chapter   **109**

Chapter 14   The Promotion: The Managerial Economics Chapter   **119**

Chapter 15   The International Assignment: The Economics of LDCs Chapter   **131**

Chapter 16   Planning to the End: The Funeral and Estate Planning Chapter   **143**

Chapter 17   The Decision: The Entrepreneurship Chapter   **151**

Chapter 18   The Next Generation: The Welfare Economics Chapter   **161**

Conclusion   The Essential Economic Principles in Life   **165**

Glossary   Key Terms   **169**

Index   **177**

Appendix   Written Assignments   **A-1**

Introduction
What is Economics?

The Organization of this Book

Life, Love, and Economics covers the basics of economics. After this short introduction, we launch into the fictional story of Samantha and Jason. We meet Samantha and Jason as they are finishing college. We then trace their steps through life and try to understand the economic issues they face as they start new jobs, buy cars and houses, and eventually marry and have children. We summarize the key principles of economics in the last chapter of the book, and we will show how these principles have surfaced repeatedly in the life stories of Samantha and Jason. Economics is an extremely relevant and applied subject.

This book also includes a complete glossary at the back of the book. If you come across a term that you do not understand, check the glossary. Key terms are summarized at the end of each chapter.

What is Economics?

Everybody wants more. People want more time, more money, and more stuff. Unfortunately, resources are limited. There are only 24 hours in a day. Everyone has a limited amount of money, although some people's bank accounts are more limited than others. There are limited natural resources like gas, coal, and diamonds.

The way we allocate our scarce resources to try to satisfy our unlimited wants is called economics. When you decide how to spend your money, you are making an economic choice. You are trying to decide how to maximize your satisfaction with the amount of money that you have available. A company makes economic choices when it makes staffing or investment decisions. The company is allocating its limited resources to get the maximum satisfaction. The U.S. government makes decisions on tax laws or government spending to maximize the satisfaction of the people (or to get more votes for the politicians!). Once again, we see decisions to allocate resources for maximum satisfaction.

There is naturally quite a difference between an individual deciding whether to spend money on a movie ticket or a new shirt, a business deciding whether to hire 10 new employees or buy a new piece of equipment, and the U.S. government deciding to send emergency relief to hurricane victims or to build a new road. All of these examples involve allocating scarce resources for maximum benefit, however, so it is all economics. Economics is about choices.

And now . . . Samantha and Jason!

The next 18 chapters take an interesting approach to economics through the fictional story of Samantha and Jason. We will cover the important issues of economics in a way that shows how these topics are relevant and important for everyone. In the concluding chapter of the book, we will summarize the essential economic principles in life.

Key Economic Terms – Introduction

Economics
Unlimited wants
Scarce resources

Chapter 1
Jason Looks for a Job: The GDP Chapter

Jason Cooley, a major in retail management, tapped his pencil against his desk. This stuff made no sense to him. The professor was babbling on about who-knows-what. He began thinking of the party that he was going to tonight.

"Jason?" the professor asked, "Jason?"

"Uh . . . what?" Jason answered, waking up from his trance.

"Can you tell us the answer to this problem?"

"Uh, I'm afraid not, sir."

The professor scowled at him and asked someone else the question.

Jason made a mental note to pay more attention in class. The latest grade sheet suggested that he was almost failing Economics 101. He wished that he hadn't waited so long to take this class. He was a senior now. It was the fall semester, and he would be graduating (hopefully) next semester.

"Of course," Jason thought, "even if I get past Econ 101 and graduate, I still don't have any job leads." He was a little discouraged. He had sent out 25 résumés a month ago, and he had not gotten a single response yet. Of course, he hadn't done any campus interviews yet, which is where a person usually gets the action.

Jason began playing with his pencil again, half listening to the lecture. He studied the words engraved on his pencil, *Bloomington University*. "This class is so hard!" Jason thought. "How could anyone pass it?"

After the class finally ended, Jason headed back home, totally worn out. Lots of homework tonight. He would have to skip the party. He sighed.

Just as he was walking up the sidewalk to his house, he saw his Uncle Mitchell waving to him. He now remembered that Uncle Mitchell had come for the homecoming game tomorrow.

"Hello, Jason! How's school been?"

"Oh, just fine."

"Well that's good! And how's the job search? Did you follow up on the leads that I gave you?" It seems like Uncle Mitchell knew everyone. He had been a senior executive in a Fortune 500 company, and now he owned a car dealership.

"I sent in my résumé to everybody you suggested. I haven't heard anything yet," Jason replied.

"C'mon boy, I'm going to take you out to dinner!"

"Well, Uncle Mitchell, I'd love to, but I have all this homework."

"Nonsense!" his uncle said. "This won't take that long! Get in!" Uncle Mitchell was used to giving orders, and he usually got his way.

Jason, against his will, climbed into Uncle Mitchell's car. They dodged through college students on bikes until they stopped in front of a little restaurant.

"I remember I used to go to this place when I was in college," his uncle exclaimed, looking around. "Of course, the place has changed a little since then."

His uncle went in and Jason followed. A waitress wearing too much make-up came up to them.

"How many?" she asked, flashing them a smile.

"Two." Jason's uncle said.

"Follow me."

She led them to a table by a window. Jason took off his coat and sat down.

"So, Jason, how have your grades been?"

"Oh no," Jason thought to himself. But he put on a smile and said, "Oh, pretty good, except for Economics 101."

"Economics 101? I believe I had that class! It had nothing to do with real life, but I could say that about many of my college classes."

"You bet!" Jason agreed.

They stared at the menus for a while. There was an uncomfortable silence.

"So, Uncle Mitchell, I've been worrying about what kind of job I am going to find," Jason said, trying to strike up a conversation.

"Why are you worried?" asked Uncle Mitchell. "This is a great time to be graduating and looking for a job."

"Why do you say that?" asked Jason.

"The current national and global economic conditions have created a seller's market. You, the new graduate, are the seller; and the companies, institutions and governments that need people are the buyers," Uncle Mitchell explained.

"You make me sound like a piece of meat," Jason complained.

"Sorry about that," Uncle Mitchell said. "But this is business. You don't know how hard it is to get good people right now."

"I've just been worried about an employer wanting me. I never considered that employers are worried about getting enough people," Jason said.

"These are tough times to be an employer. I can never get enough good people for my car dealership," Uncle Mitchell responded.

"Is it always like this?" Jason asked.

"Not at all," Uncle Mitchell replied. "But GDP is really growing right now and there are not enough workers to go around."

"They mention GDP in my Econ class, but to tell you the truth, I don't really know what that is," Jason confessed.

"The problem with college," Uncle Mitchell philosophized, "is that you take classes before you know what is important to know. GDP is an important idea, but it gets lost in all the stuff that's not important. Let me tell you what you really need to know about GDP.

"GDP stands for Gross Domestic Product. GDP is essentially a measure of economic activity. When we think about how well our country is doing, one of the first economic statistics that we look at is Gross Domestic Product. Have you ever heard about the economy being in a 'recession'?" asked Uncle Mitchell.

"Sure," responded Jason, "that means the economy isn't doing too good."

"That's true," said Uncle Mitchell. "More specifically, it means that GDP, after adjusting for inflation (and we'll talk more about inflation in a minute), has gone down two quarters in a row. In other words, there was less economic activity for two quarters in a row. That's not good. When GDP goes down, that means that companies are producing less. If companies are producing less, they are employing fewer people. It can be hard to get a job during a recession."

"How in the world can the government measure GDP? What does it include? I can't even keep track of the checks that I write," said Jason.

"Well, Gross Domestic Product is the value of the final goods and services produced in the country in a year. Since we are measuring final goods and services, it makes it a little easier to calculate, but it is still a big job and the government needs to use estimates in some places," Uncle Mitchell replied. "There are a couple of ways to look at it. One way is to look at the consumption side, which would count all the spending by consumers, businesses, government, and the net spending by foreigners. Another way to look at it is the total income earned by people in the United States. After all, one person's spending is another person's income."

"How to you figure?" Jason asked.

"Take this restaurant, for example. If we added up all the money spent by the customers, it would exactly equal the income of the restaurant. One person's spending is another person's income."

"You said that GDP is the final value of the goods and services produced in the country in a year. What exactly do you mean by 'final value'?" asked Jason.

"Let's take my shirt as an example," said Uncle Mitchell. "To make this shirt, somebody had to grow some cotton."

"Actually, someone had to buy the seeds first. Is the cost of the seed part of GDP? It's sort of like a final product," interjected Jason.

"Hold on a second. You are right, the cotton grower did have to start with seed, but that is not part of GDP," said Uncle Mitchell. "Furthermore, the man sells the cotton to a shirt manufacturer, and the cost of the cotton doesn't count in GDP either. By 'final product', that means the product is actually purchased and used by the ultimate consumer. Once the cotton is turned into a shirt, and I buy the shirt at my local *Sears* store, then the price of the shirt becomes part of GDP," Uncle Mitchell finished the story.

"You shop at *Sears*!" laughed Jason. "Have you ever heard of *Old Navy*?"

"I will ignore your lack of respect for your elders and continue my story," responded Uncle Mitchell, smiling.

"You mean there is more?" asked Jason. "I didn't know I was coming to dinner for an economics lesson."

"Since you're obviously not paying attention in Econ 101, I think I had better tell you what you are going to need to know in the real world," said Uncle Mitchell.

Just then the waitress came to take their order.

"If I order water, does that count in GDP?" asked Jason.

"Of course not," said Uncle Mitchell, "unless they are going to charge for the water. If something doesn't cost money, it's not counted in GDP. Order a steak, and that will be counted in GDP."

"Okay," Jason said, and Jason and Uncle Mitchell placed their order.

"What about the waitress?" Jason asked.

"Pretty cute, except for the lipstick on her teeth," Uncle Mitchell replied.

"No," said Jason, "I mean does the money she earns go into GDP?"

"If that is your interest in a pretty girl, I think you have bigger problems than economics," Uncle Mitchell teased. "But to answer your question, that is where 'services' come in. I said GDP is the final value of all goods and services. In this case, the steak dinner is a 'good', and it will be counted in GDP. Goods are things that you can touch:

cars and televisions and steak dinners. The waitress, the cook, the manager are all 'services', and the money they earn is part of GDP."

"What if I buy a steak and the supermarket and cook it at home?" Jason asked.

"I don't think I would want to see you cook. But if I follow your question, the price that you pay for the steak at the supermarket is counted in GDP, but your free labor in cooking the meat is not counted."

"This gets complicated. Why do we go to all this trouble to figure out GDP? After all, once we count it, it's already happened anyway," complained Jason.

"The only way I could answer your question about whether you will be likely to get a job or not is because I keep track of GDP. I know when economic activity is strong. I need that information to figure out how many new cars to have on my lot, to help me figure out how much money I will need to offer to attract new employees, and so forth. For government decision makers, it is even more important to keep track of GDP. I don't want to totally spoil your dinner with all this economic talk, but GDP is something that the Federal Reserve follows closely to decide on interest rate changes. Congress also follows GDP to make decisions on government spending and tax policy," Uncle Mitchell said.

"Well, you're right about one thing. Let's not get into all that right now, especially the stuff about the Federal Reserve. Let's just say you've convinced me that GDP is a very important measure, because it tells how the U.S. economy is doing. I do have one last question on GDP, however," said Jason.

"You are a glutton for punishment," said Uncle Mitchell.

"In class I heard the professor mention GNP. Is that the same as GDP?" asked Jason.

"For our purposes, they are close enough. GNP stands for Gross National Product. In the past there was more attention on GNP, which is the value of all the goods and services produced by Americans or American companies around the world. With all the multinational companies now, GNP is a little more difficult to interpret. GDP, or Gross Domestic Product, is the value of the final goods and services produced in the United States by anybody, and GDP doesn't count anything going on outside of the U.S. People have decided that GDP is a more meaningful measure, but the differences in the GNP and GDP are pretty small anyway. And since you want to keep talking about GDP, there is one other important thing that I forgot to mention," said Uncle Mitchell. "Has your economics professor talked about the difference between 'real' GDP and 'nominal' GDP?"

"That's very possible," replied Jason, "but I probably wasn't paying attention."

"Fair enough. Let me ask you this. Do you know what inflation is?" asked Uncle Mitchell.

"I think I finally know an answer to one of your questions," Jason replied proudly. "Inflation is when you used to be able to buy a cheeseburger for 50 cents, and now they cost a dollar," Jason explained. "It's like the same thing costs more money each year."

"That's the general idea," agreed Uncle Mitchell. "Inflation means rising prices. So how do you account for that in your GDP calculation? Does GDP double just because a cheeseburger costs twice as much as it used to?"

"I guess so," said Jason. "Is that why GDP is usually going up except for in a recession?"

"Wrong!" Uncle Mitchell said. "How would it help me to know how many cars to have on the lot if GDP is just going up because of inflation? If anything, more inflation means that people will have less money to spend on cars, so they will end up buying fewer cars. That's why we have 'nominal GDP' and 'real GDP'. Nominal GDP just adds up the value of the goods and services without trying to account for inflation. Real GDP adjusts for inflation so you know whether economic activity is really going up or whether it is just inflation."

"How do they calculate inflation?" asked Jason.

"Government economists pick a typical market basket of all the things that people buy, and they keep track of the prices of those typical items. One popular price index is called the Consumer Price Index, or CPI, which keeps track of goods and services that are purchased by consumers. Other well-known indices are the Producer Price Index, or PPI, which measures the prices of goods and services purchased by producers, and the GDP deflator, which is the index actually used to calculate real GDP. If prices for goods and services in the GDP deflator market basket increase by 10%, then the value of nominal GDP is reduced by 10% to come up with real GDP. Real GDP is the number that most people care about," said Uncle Mitchell.

"Pretty clever," said Jason. "They've thought of everything. How do they know what items go into the market basket?"

"That is another subject for a different night. Basically they try to keep the market basket updated based on what people buy. You read about arguments about what should be included from time to time, but they try to keep things updated for new products that come out and changes in what people buy. It doesn't make that much difference. The important thing is to make sure you are looking at real GDP, because that takes out the distortion of inflation," said Uncle Mitchell.

"And there is one last thing to remember about GDP," added Uncle Mitchell. "GDP tends to move up and down, sometimes in cycles. You shouldn't get too excited about the normal fluctuations. Consumption spending tends to vary, and investment spending by businesses can make big swings up and down. There are some economic forecasters that try to predict GDP, but they generally don't do a very good job. It is better to look for the longer-term trends of GDP to understand how the economy is going and not get caught up in the short-term variations. The short-term fluctuations can be more confusing than helpful."

The waitress brought the steaks. This time Jason looked at her teeth rather than wondering if her tip would be included in GDP.

"So, are we going to beat West Lafayette University this weekend?" asked Uncle Mitchell, changing the subject. "That quarterback they have is awesome."

"Hey wait a minute," said Jason. "All this talk about GDP has made me forget my original question. Do you think I will ever get a job?"

"I don't talk this much about economics at work," said Uncle Mitchell. "Okay, I'll give you a complete answer if you promise we can drop this economics discussion and talk about the game."

"It's a deal," Jason agreed.

"Okay, here it is all at once. Don't interrupt. Presently, business is good. There is strong demand for products and services, and a willingness to buy right now. That situation pressures companies and business to produce more to meet the demand. Companies and businesses have to increase their effort, which translates to a need for more output. Increasing output requires more people and more equipment. Such an increase may occur by using more efficient machines and creating new processes designed by engineers and technicians. The increased output will not usually sell itself; therefore, there is a need for more infrastructure. Marketing, customer service, and sales people are in demand, for example. These people and others are needed so that the products and services demanded make their way to the ultimate consumer efficiently.

"Okay," said Jason. "I follow."

"I said no interruptions! To continue . . .," said Uncle Mitchell, clearing his throat. "Clearly this is not rocket science. However, there are pitfalls and warning signs that unchecked growth is not always desirable. For example, if consumer demand steadily increases, this can cause demand-pull inflation, meaning the inflation is caused by an increase in demand.

"The strong consumer demand can make it difficult for companies to hire more workers so they can make enough product. This will drive up people costs, and larger salaries translate to higher company overhead costs. You can easily visualize the next step. Margins, or the profits for the sale of goods and services, will generally be protected. Therefore, if costs rise and margins are not allowed to suffer, then the only alternative is to raise prices. This causes cost-push inflation, meaning the inflation is caused by increases in the company's costs.

"By the way, Jason, is inflation good or bad?" Uncle Mitchell asked.

"It's bad, of course. Everyone knows that," Jason answered confidently.

"That's what most people think," agreed Uncle Mitchell, "but it's not true. Let's say you owe somebody money. If we start to have high inflation, your pay will go up because of the inflation, and it will be easier to pay off your debt. Inflation helps some people and hurts others. If you owe money, inflation can help you. If you have loaned people money, inflation can hurt you.

"The big problem with inflation is that it helps some people and hurts others, and some prices go up and others do not. Inflation distorts the economy. If you anticipate high inflation, do you want to loan people money at a low interest rate?" Uncle Mitchell asked.

"I guess not. If I did loan somebody some money, I would probably want a high interest rate to make up for the inflation," Jason said, starting to figure out how things worked.

"That's right," said Uncle Mitchell. "That's very good. So people will charge a higher interest rate to make up for the possible inflation. What if the inflation never materializes? Then you are charging people higher interest rates for no good reason. Nobody will want to borrow money from you because your interest rates are too high. Inflation can really distort people's decisions, especially if inflation rates are unpredictable.

"But back to your situation. Most of those companies I suggested that you send résumés to are in the hiring mood. The companies themselves are doing their share to keep the consumer ball rolling. Presently, it makes sense for many existing companies to expand and for new companies to be created. In many cases it is the availability of cheap money. What I mean by cheap money is that banks and lending institutions will make loans at very low interest rates today. It is kind of like buying a car. When interests rates for car loans are low, people believe they can buy because the monthly payments are affordable. The same is true for a company that is borrowing to build new plants, buy new equipment, or hire expensive people like you.

"Now, having said all that; I warn you that this process is constantly monitored by the authorities. This is accomplished by the Federal Reserve Bank, or as they are commonly called, 'the Fed'."

"I thought we weren't going to talk about the Fed tonight," laughed Jason.

"We weren't," Uncle Mitchell said. "But you have me on a roll. The Fed's responsibility is to keep inflation under control and at the same time create a climate where business and the economy may prosper. The Fed accomplishes their goal principally by influencing interest rates. When the Fed senses businesses are willing to invest in themselves to promote growth and increased productivity, there is generally no reason to change policy. However, if the Fed believes that there is a chance that inflation, those rising prices, is moving towards 4, 5 or 6%, in any given year they may take action to slow borrowing by raising interest rates, thus slowing business expansion. Take the car buying example again. If your rate of interest goes up, so does your monthly payment. At some point the new car becomes too costly, so you continue to drive your 1989 Ford Escort. It is not that different for a company. If borrowing money is too costly, then they won't do it, thus slowing growth. That usually results in a loss of people and reduced costs. Inflation will fade, and we begin anew.

"Today as you approach graduation, we see the Fed telling business and industry to continue their expansion and growth but be careful. The current wave of business optimism is the perfect scenario for you and your fellow graduates. It is quite likely that you will have the luxury of choosing from several employment opportunities. Consumer confidence is high and corporate profits are favorable. As I mentioned before, you are the seller and it's a seller's market."

Jason listened. That was actually pretty good advice. Much better than he was getting in his Economics 101 class. "Thanks, Uncle Mitchell. You've helped me a lot."

"Glad I could assist you."

"Well," Jason said, getting up, "I've got to head back. I still have a lot of homework waiting."

"What happened to our discussion about football?" asked Uncle Mitchell.

"Bloomington University by 10," replied Jason.

"Care to put a little money on that?" Uncle Mitchell asked. "I'll take West Lafayette University, and I don't even want your points."

"Traitor!" said Jason.

"Just because I graduated from Bloomington University doesn't mean I'm stupid. Especially when money is involved."

"Okay, $10. But in the unlikely event that I lose, I don't have to pay you until I get my first real paycheck. You're the one who is practically guaranteeing me that I'll get a job."

"It's a deal. And if you don't get a job, you can work for me washing cars."

"Thanks a lot. It's good to know that I have a fallback position after spending six years in college getting my B.S. degree," said Jason.

"Want a ride?" asked Uncle Mitchell.

"Sure."

They went out to the parking lot. Jason felt a lot better about his job prospects now, and he might even end up passing Econ 101. Uncle Mitchell dropped him off. "See you at the game tomorrow," Uncle Mitchell said. "I'll root for Bloomington, but if they lose, at least I'll get $10 from you."

"I don't think so," Jason said confidently.

Key Economic Terms – Chapter 1

Gross Domestic Product (GDP)
Recession
Federal Reserve (the Fed)
Gross National Product (GNP)
Real GDP
Nominal GDP

Inflation
Cost-push inflation
Demand-pull inflation
Consumer Price Index (CPI)
Producer Price Index (PPI)
GDP Deflator
Interest rates

Chapter 2
Watching a Soccer Game: The Economics of a Society Chapter

The game didn't go too well for Bloomington University. West Lafayette University beat them 72-6, largely on the strength of six touchdown passes by WLU's star quarterback, Sketch Wind. After the game, Jason and Uncle Mitchell stopped by Jason's house.

"Time to pay up," Uncle Mitchell said to Jason.

"After my first paycheck," Jason replied. "That was the deal. And I still can't believe that you would bet against Bloomington University."

"I was only trying to teach you that betting is wrong," counseled Uncle Mitchell. "Hey, look. One of those ESPN greatest games." Uncle Mitchell motioned to a soccer game on the television.

"This must be an old one," said Jason. "It's black and white."

"No," said Uncle Mitchell. "It's a 1972 soccer game that was played in China. It only looks black and white because the game is being played in a communist country, and everyone has pretty drab clothes."

"You mean they force people to wear boring clothes in China?" Jason asked.

"No, that is just what type of clothes were produced in China in 1972. They didn't think other colors were necessary. The government decided they would produce drab clothes, so that's all people had to wear," Uncle Mitchell explained.

"Why did they do that?" Jason asked.

"That's how China decided to set up their economic system. There are three basic questions that all societies have to answer:

1. What to produce
2. How to produce
3. Who gets it

"China, the United States, Canada, and every other country in the world need to answer these three questions. They just all answer the questions a little differently."

"What are the different ways they can answer it?" Jason asked, somewhat intrigued by this conversation. He had always thought of the communists as bad and the United States as good. He never thought about how all countries have to answer the same basic questions.

"There are three basic ways to make these decisions. One is the command system such as communism. In this case, a single person or committee decides what will be produced, how it will be produced, and who will get the end products.

"Another way to answer these questions is through the market system, such as a capitalistic system. The U.S., for example, uses largely a market system. This system works on price and profit, supply and demand. If a restaurant is good, people will go there for dinner, and the restaurant will make money and thrive. If the restaurant is bad or poorly managed, the restaurant will lose money and eventually go out of business. The market system rewards success and punishes failure.

"The third way to answer these questions is through tradition. You just do it the way that it has always been done.

"In most societies, there is a blend of these three systems. In the United States, for example, the decision to operate a restaurant is usually the result of market forces like supply and demand. But the command system also enters the picture. The Board of Health will periodically inspect the restaurant, and if they feel the restaurant is a danger to human health, they can shut down the restaurant–regardless of how successful the restaurant may be. Government regulation adds aspects of the command system to our otherwise market-driven economy.

"Tradition also plays a role. Some people go to really bad restaurants because they have gone there for 20 years, and it has become part of their routine.

"If you look at other countries across the world, you see different combinations of the market, command, and tradition systems. In the communist countries, the command system answers more of the three key questions: What to produce, how to produce, and who gets it. But there are still elements of the market system and tradition in communist countries."

"Can I ask a stupid question?" asked Jason.

"I would like to say there are no stupid questions, but in your case, I'll just answer yes," Uncle Mitchell joked.

"What exactly is supply and demand?" Jason asked.

"Sleeping through Economics 101 again, eh?" Uncle Mitchell said.

"The professor puts up a lot of graphs, but I never understand what he is talking about," Jason replied. "Do you still remember this stuff?"

"Actually, the basics are pretty simple. Do you have a piece of paper?" Uncle Mitchell asked. Jason left and came back with a pile of napkins.

"This is the best I could find," Jason said sheepishly.

"It figures," Uncle Mitchell said. "But this will do." He took out the first napkin and started drawing.

"Let's say we are looking at the market for big screen televisions, something that you guys could use, by the way," Uncle Mitchell said as he tried to catch a peek at the soccer game across the room.

"The first step in supply/demand analysis is to create a demand schedule and a supply schedule. Let's start with a demand schedule, which shows how many of something people are willing and able to buy at different prices. If the price of something goes up, people want less of it. If the price of something goes down, people want more of it.

"For example, if the price of big screen televisions is $1,500, not many people will buy the product. There will be some high income people who are not scared off by the $1,500 price tag and probably some people who love getting the latest electronic device, but the total quantity demanded will not be very large. Let's say we did a market survey and found the annual quantity of big screen televisions that people are willing and able to buy at a price of $1,500 is 100,000 units in the United States. If we dropped the price to $1,000, maybe we would sell 500,000 units, because more people will think it is worth it to buy a big screen television at that price. If the price of big screen televisions was only $500, even more people will buy one. Even poor college students might decide they can afford a big screen television. Let's say we do a market study and at a price of $500, the annual quantity of big screen televisions demanded is 900,000 units in the United States.

If we put all of these numbers into a table, that table is called a demand schedule. Here, let me show you." Uncle Mitchell wrote the following table on the first napkin.

Table 1
Demand Schedule for Big Screen Televisions

Price	Quantity Demanded
$1,500	100,000
$1,000	500,000
$ 500	900,000

"We could also put the same information on a graph. This graph would be called the demand curve for big screen televisions." Uncle Mitchell wrote a graph on the next napkin.

Figure 1
Demand Curve

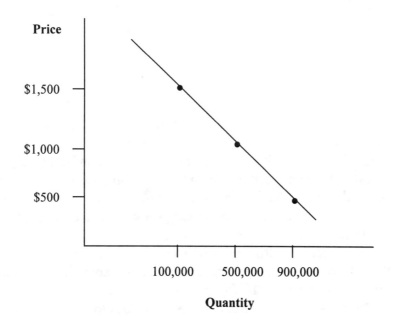

"Does that curve look familiar?" Uncle Mitchell asked Jason.

"It sure does," Jason said. "That's what my econ professor keeps putting up on the board. But this time I understand it."

"Notice that in creating our demand curve, we only talked about price and quantity demanded," Uncle Mitchell continued. "We did not say anything about advertising, for example, even though advertising could have a huge effect on the sales of big screen televisions. If we decide to spend a lot of money advertising big screen televisions, the quantity that people will buy at a given price would probably go up at all prices. The demand curve with extra advertising would shift right. A change in price causes a movement along the demand curve. A change in anything else, like advertising, shifts the demand curve." Uncle Mitchell wrote the next curve on another napkin.

Figure 2
Demand Curve

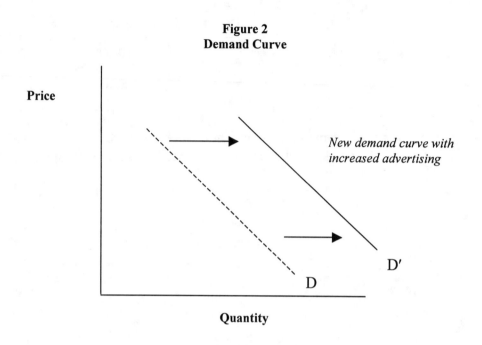

"I get it," said Jason. "My econ professor always makes a big deal about the difference between demand and quantity demanded. I thought he was just being picky."

"Not really," said Uncle Mitchell. "A change in quantity demanded means a movement along a single demand curve, meaning the only thing we change is price. For example, if a person will buy one candy bar at a price of 50 cents but two candy bars if the price of each candy bar is 40 cents, we are talking about a difference in quantity demanded. The only thing that has changed is the price.

"A change in demand means shifting the whole curve, which means changing something other than price, such as advertising or consumer income. For example, let's say a person buys one candy bar every Friday for 50 cents. One day, the person gets a big raise. On the Friday following the big raise, the person decides to buy two candy bars for 50 cents each because he or she has more income. This is a shift in demand, because the increase in income has made the person willing to buy more candy bars at the same price.

"We can derive a supply curve in the same way," Uncle Mitchell continued, "but this time we ask suppliers what quantity they would be willing and able to sell at different prices. At $1,500, suppliers can make a good profit, so they are willing to sell 1,000,000 units. They might even like to sell more, but perhaps they might run out of production capacity or workers beyond 1,000,000 units. Remember, we only want to know the quantity they are ready and willing to sell. At a price of $500, the suppliers are not too anxious to produce big screen televisions. Perhaps they are willing to sell 10,000 units just to keep their plants running, and many of the individual producers would probably choose to make none. At $1,000, they are willing to sell some number in-between. I'll pick 500,000 to make the graph easier to understand."

"What do you mean?" Jason asked.

"You'll see in a minute. Just trust me for now. So now we can create a supply schedule with these numbers." Uncle Mitchell wrote a table on the next napkin.

Table 2
Supply Schedule for Big Screen Televisions

Price	Quantity Demanded
$1,500	1,000,000
$1,000	500,000
$ 500	10,000

"We can put the same information on a supply curve," Uncle Mitchell explained. "I am picking the numbers to give us straight lines, but the lines don't have to be straight."

Figure 3
Supply Curve

"We can shift the supply curve by changing something other than price," Uncle Mitchell said, drawing on the next napkin. "If the cost of production goes down, for example, the big screen television producers will make a higher profit at every price. They will be willing to sell more big screen televisions at all prices, which shifts the supply curve to the right.

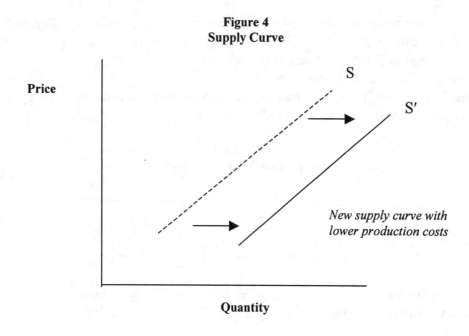

Figure 4
Supply Curve

New supply curve with lower production costs

"The real fun comes when we put the supply and demand curve on the same graph," Uncle Mitchell said, quickly scribbling another graph. "Combining the original supply and demand curves on the same graph results in an equilibrium price of $500 and an equilibrium quantity of 500,000 units. At a price of $500, the quantity that consumers are will buy exactly equals the quantity that producers will sell."

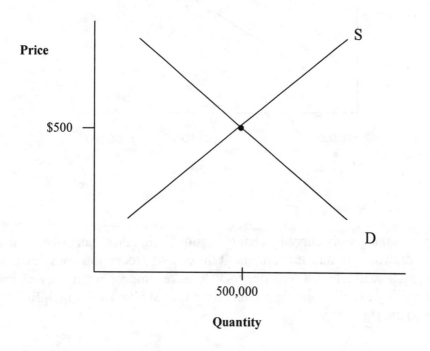

Figure 5
The Market for Big Screen Televisions

"So that's why you chose the numbers that you did," Jason observed.

"Right, I wanted to make it work out," Uncle Mitchell confessed. "But we could have chosen any numbers. Wherever the curves intersected would have been the equilibrium point."

"What if companies priced their big screen televisions for $600? Or $400? What happens then?" asked Jason.

"If companies priced their big screen televisions for $600," Uncle Mitchell patiently explained, "we would have a surplus in the market, because suppliers would want to sell more units than consumers are willing to buy. If firms priced their big screen televisions for $400, we would have a shortage in the market, because consumers would want to buy more units than producers are willing to sell. You could show that on the graph too," Uncle Mitchell said, drawing two more lines on the previous graph.

Figure 6
The Market for Big Screen Televisions

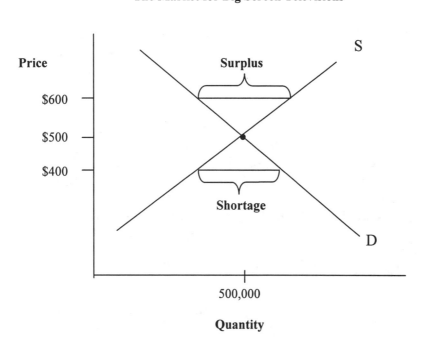

"Under a market system, as soon as it becomes clear that there is a shortage or surplus, people will change their prices so the quantity that consumers are willing to buy equals the quantity that producers are willing to sell. A shortage or surplus only arises when a person is unwilling to change their price or if government regulation prevents the free movement of prices.

"If that wasn't exciting enough," Uncle Mitchell, "things get even better when we shift the supply or demand curve. What happens if we take the original situation, and then a new technology is introduced which lowers production costs? The demand curve stays in the same place, but the supply curve shifts to the right. This results in a lower equilibrium price and a higher equilibrium quantity.

Figure 7
The Market for Big Screen Televisions

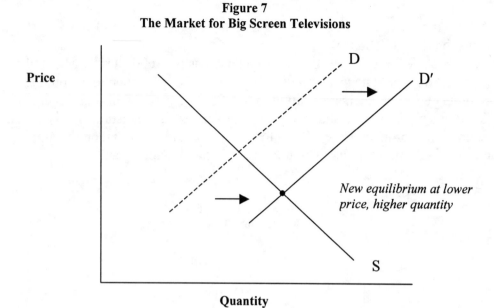

"You can try out all kinds of scenarios using supply/demand analysis. It is one of the most powerful tools of economic analysis," Uncle Mitchell concluded.

"Wow, that was great," Jason said. "I learned more with these napkins than I learned in class all semester."

"Glad to help," said Uncle Mitchell. "But you still owe me $10."

Key Economic Terms – Chapter 2

Market system
Command system
Tradition
Supply
Demand
Supply/demand analysis
    (see following page)
Demand schedule

Demand curve
Quantity demanded
Supply schedule
Supply curve
Quantity supplied
Equilibrium price
Equilibrium quantity
Surplus
Shortage

Key Economic Terms – Chapter 2 (continued)

Supply/demand analysis

Price determination through supply and demand is much easier to learn if you follow this step-by-step approach. For each of the situations below:

- For what product is this the supply and demand?
- Note the change (What happened to cause a market change?)
- If the government or a controlling agency deliberately changed the price of **this** product, it is a **command change.** If it did not, it is a **market change.**
- Label the axes and the lines.
- Remember some things change supply, some demand, and some neither (in this introductory book, never both).

If the change is a result of a market change:

- Decide who is directly and immediately affected by the change given in each example; producers or consumers.
- If producers are affected first, supply changes, if consumers; demand.
- Is supply or demand increased, decreased or not changed?
- Draw the new supply or demand curve if appropriate (increased, to the right; decreased, to the left) and the new price and quantity. Label each.
- Report changes in supply, demand, price, and quantity from this change.

If a command system changed the product price:

- Neither supply nor demand changes–just the price changes.
- Draw in the new price line.
- Draw quantity lines down from the intersections of the new price line with the supply and demand curves.
- Label the quantity from the supply line "Amount available".
- Label the quantity from the demand line "Amount wanted".
- Show the surplus or shortage.
- Report no changes in supply or demand, the change in price, and clearly indicate changes in both quantities available and wanted as a result of this price change.

Chapter 3
Samantha Looks for a Job: The Unemployment and Growth Chapter

Somewhere in the same state, Samantha Fletcher was walking back to her apartment. She had spent most of the afternoon in the computer lab, checking out the web sites of prospective employers. She was a senior at West Lafayette University majoring in education, but it didn't look like there were many teaching jobs available. It was looking like she would be going to graduate school or taking a job outside of education.

Samantha was a good student, scoring mostly A's. She didn't have much of a social life, but she didn't care. WLU people were smart, and she was more interested in good grades than going to parties.

The crisp autumn air blew her hair back. She hugged her books to her chest. After looking at a computer screen all afternoon, she just wanted to finish her homework, eat dinner, and get some sleep.

She walked up the steps of her apartment. She opened her door to hear the sound of a hair dryer.

"Hi Samantha!" Susie, her roommate's best friend, stuck her head outside the bathroom door. Susie was way too hyper, and Samantha didn't like her very much. "Do you want to go to a party tonight with me and Christina?" Susie turned off the hair dryer.

"Actually, I just wanted to drop off my books, and then I need to get going." Samantha changed her plans just to get out of the apartment. She hoped that Susie wouldn't ask any more questions.

Susie put on a frown. "Oh, that's too bad. Oh well, see you around!"

"Yeah, see you." Samantha dropped her books on her bed and left, slamming the door.

Back outside. Now what could she do? Maybe she would have an early dinner. She started walking across the campus to her favorite pizza place.

"Samantha? Samantha Fletcher?"

Samantha looked over. "Professor Dowers! How are you?"

Dr. Dowers, her old economics professor, was sitting down on a bench. Samantha stopped to sit next to him. "Pretty good," answered Professor Dowers, "except I've got to teach the freshman again this year. Whine, whine, whine. That's all they do." He was kidding, because he really loved his students.

"I wasn't whiny when I was a freshman!"

"Well, there are a few exceptions. You were a very good student," Professor Dowers said seriously. A pause. "So, how has life been treating you?" Professor Dowers asked.

"Just fine. I'm only getting one B this semester."

"That's good. Any problems?"

"Well, I'm worried about getting a job. I'm an education major, but there are not many teaching positions available. I'm looking for a sales or customer service job."

"Well, this is a great time to be looking for a job," Professor Dowers said with his usual positive attitude. "GDP is up, and unemployment is down."

"It seems like there are so many unemployed people around though," Samantha observed. "How do I know I won't end up like one of them?"

"Well, just because they aren't working doesn't mean they are unemployed," Professor Dowers reminded her. "Remember, unemployment means looking for and not finding work. A lot of people who don't have jobs aren't even looking for work, so they don't count as unemployed. You know, like my seven-year-old niece or my 82-year old uncle. In fact, about half of the people in the United States are neither employed or unemployed. They are not employed and not looking for a job."

"That was a definition from your class," said Samantha. "But that doesn't make me feel much better. I *am* looking for a job. I just don't know if I will find one. Maybe I should have majored in engineering."

"There's no need to be rash," said the professor. "If you remember my class, there are five reasons for unemployment, and I don't think you are going to fit any of those reasons."

"Please go through them," asked Samantha. "Maybe that will cheer me up." She was also hoping that her roommate's friend would be gone by the time the professor went through the reasons.

"Okay," said the professor. "The first reason for unemployment is called cyclical unemployment. Cyclical unemployment means there is a temporary drop in spending in the economy, less is being produced, so producers cut back and people are laid off. Let's say a person has a job building a house. If interest rates rise so nobody can afford to build new houses, that person is going to be laid off. The unemployment is caused by a bad economy. That certainly isn't the case right now, so you are not going to be unemployed because of cyclical unemployment."

"Plus I don't think I will be going into home construction," joked Samantha.

"Right," agreed Professor Dowers. "And the good news is when the economy picks up again, the person who is out of work because of cyclical unemployment is usually hired back. That is not the case with the second type of unemployment, which is called structural unemployment. This is the kind of unemployment that happens because of a change in technology. Unlike cyclical unemployment, where the job comes back when the economy picks up, these jobs are permanently lost."

"But I can't get a job in teaching. Couldn't that be an example of structural unemployment?" asked Samantha.

"No," said Professor Dowers, "structural unemployment means that you no longer have the skills to do the job. Say, for example, you are a bookkeeper. Your whole life you have used a ledger book and pencil. One day your boss brings you a calculator. With a little practice, you figure out how to use the calculator and you continue doing your job, probably even better than before you got the calculator. Then your boss decides to put in a new computer system. This time, you just don't have the skills to change to the new technology. Someone who has computer skills replaces you. You are never going to get your job back because you don't have the necessary skills. This is a classic example of structural unemployment. Another classic example is a car assembly worker who is replaced by a robot.

"Sometimes people will come up with rules to limit the effect of structural unemployment. A union, for example, may place limits on how many workers can be replaced by robots. This can help the workers in the short-term, but it hurts the competitiveness of companies.

"Companies or the government can also help to lessen the effect of structural unemployment by offering training programs. If workers can be trained to do new jobs, it will lessen the effect of structural unemployment.

"In your case," the professor continued, "you might not get a job in education. But you are perfectly trained for many other positions. Many people get jobs in fields outside of their specific field of formal education."

"Okay," said Samantha, "so that's structural unemployment. What is the third category that isn't going to fit me?"

"Well, come to think of it, you may fit this one," teased Professor Dowers. "Besides cyclical unemployment and structural unemployment, which are related to the overall economy, the next three reasons for unemployment are more related to personal reasons. Maybe I'll start with the two that definitely don't fit you, and then we can decide if the last category might fit after all."

"You are a lot meaner than I remember," laughed Samantha.

"Well, I try to be nice until students fill out my teaching evaluation. After a student is done with the evaluation, I can be my natural self."

"So that explains it," said Samantha. "Please continue with the personal reasons for unemployment."

"The first personal reason for unemployment is called frictional unemployment. Frictional unemployment basically means that someone chooses to change jobs, so when they are between jobs, they are considered unemployed. Let's say you are married . . ."

"Fat chance," interrupted Samantha.

"Aha, confirming that you are a candidate for the last reason for unemployment. But to continue my very hypothetical example, say that you are both working in Indianapolis. You get a great new job offer in St. Louis, so you decide that you will both move. Your husband will look for a new job in St. Louis once you both get there. For the time between the day your husband quits his old job and the day he starts a new job, he is unemployed. This is called frictional unemployment, because there is natural friction in the economy as people leave one job and spend time looking for a new job."

"It would have been better for my husband to have found a new job before leaving his old job," observed Samantha.

"That's true," agreed Professor Dowers, "but that may have meant living apart for a while, and I'm sure your husband would not want to spend a single day away from you."

"How romantic," said Samantha. "But I know you are going to make fun of me soon, and you are already feeling guilty for it and trying to make up."

"Maybe so. The next personal reason for unemployment is called voluntary unemployment, and this doesn't apply to you either. Let's say there is a mother who has small children. She wants a job where she can work from 10 to 3 so she can get the kids off to school in the morning and be with them when they get home. She gets offers for 9 to 5 jobs, but she doesn't want to take them because of her children. She continues to be unemployed, but it is her choice. It is voluntary unemployment."

"Okay, I'm ready. What's the last personal reason for unemployment?" asked Samantha.

"I called this one the unattractive employee reason for unemployment," said Professor Dowers.

"Thanks a lot," objected Samantha.

"By unattractive, I mean the person cannot get or keep a job," explained Professor Dowers.

"And that's supposed to make me feel better?" asked Samantha.

"At least I wasn't calling you ugly. But maybe I should keep going before I get into real trouble."

"Yes, maybe you should," Samantha kidded.

"The unattractive employee may have inadequate education or perhaps a poor attitude or bad character. Now that I think about it, you definitely don't fit this category either."

"Okay, you are slowly winning back some points."

"It could be the person doesn't have any personal problems," Professor Dowers continued. "Maybe the person is discriminated against or might always be in the wrong place at the wrong time. In any case, this person doesn't find a job because there are no employers that want to hire him or her."

"But seriously, how can you know if this applies to me?" Samantha asked.

"By looking at your success in class, you don't strike me as an unattractive employee. There are obviously many jobs that you could do very well and companies would be happy to have you working for them. It is more likely that you could be a victim of cyclical unemployment if the economy wasn't so good now. Or maybe later in life you may choose voluntary unemployment if you turn down some job offers to wait for a great position to come along. Or you could go through a period of frictional unemployment when changing jobs. You might even go through structural employment if technology eliminates your job. I don't really see you as a very good candidate for being an unattractive employee, however."

"What happens to the unattractive employee?" asked Samantha.

"This can be a sad situation," said Professor Dowers. "The person may apply for fifty jobs and get fifty rejections. At some point, the person becomes discouraged and stops looking for work. At that point the person is no longer considered unemployed. This person is called a discouraged worker. This is especially unfair if the person is not employed because of discrimination, because he or she may be very well qualified for one of the jobs. But things are much better on this front then they were 20, 30, or 40 years ago.

"But going back to your original question, if you take the really long view, this is an especially good time to be looking for a job. The last 150 years has been a tremendous growth period for society. From the fall of the Roman empire in 300 A.D. to 1830 there was essentially zero growth in GNP per capita," said Professor Dowers. "In today's dollars, GDP per person stayed at about $600 per person."

"You really are taking the long-term perspective, aren't you?" said Samantha.

"It helps to give a little historical perspective to your job search," said Professor Dowers. "So for almost 1,500 years, there was no growth in economic output per person. Starting in 1830, however, the economy has soared! Real GDP in the United States increased from $600 per person in 1830 to $23,000 per person in 1970. The economy has continued to grow since then, and now GDP per capita is over $30,000."

"Wow, that is incredible. What caused the big change?" asked Samantha.

"Most of the growth came from improvements in technology. You have to remember than in 1830, over 90% of the people in the United States worked in agriculture. Just growing enough food to eat was a big challenge for people. It may be tough for your generation to believe this," continued Professor Dowers, "but the major staple for most people was bread.

"Starting in 1830, people started to replace human labor with animal labor, which gave a big boost to economic growth, the annual percent increase in the amount of goods and services available per person. Then people started to replace human and animal labor with mechanical power. Since 1830, we went from plowing by hand, to plowing with a team of oxen or horses, to plowing with a *John Deere* tractor. As you might imagine, these changes increased productivity tremendously."

"Why did all this start in 1830?" Samantha asked.

"The key to all this was investment," said Professor Dowers. "If you recall from my class, investment is an increase in the stock of durable manmade goods and services used for production. Starting in 1830, there was a huge increase in investment, which led to a huge increase in growth. People invested in machinery and factories. People invested in increased research to find better ways of doing things. They invested in education. And they invested in infrastructure, things like roads and weather forecasting services. All of this investment led to economic growth, which in turn has led to a higher living standard."

"What about the Great Depression? How does that fit in?" asked Samantha.

"There are a lot of fancy explanations for the Great Depression," said Professor Dowers, "but a lot of it comes down to optimism and pessimism. As long as people are optimistic about the economy, they will buy things. When they buy things, factories have orders to produce. The factories continue to hire people to increase production. Everything runs well.

"In the 1930s, people started to get pessimistic. They were scared to buy things. When spending went down, factory orders slowed. The factories laid off workers, further decreasing spending and making people even more pessimistic. All of this led to the Great Depression. Overall, optimism leads to economic growth, and pessimism leads to recessions and depressions."

"Could a depression happen again?" Samantha asked.

"Probably not," said Professor Dowers. "Since the Great Depression, we have government programs like unemployment insurance and welfare programs. These tend to keep spending up even in bad times. We will have some slowdowns and recessions along the way, but as long as people keep investing, we should have economic growth, leading to a higher standard of living and good job opportunities for people like you."

"I was wondering when we were going to get back to that," Samantha said. "We took quite a detour at the fall of the Roman Empire."

"Sorry about that," Professor Dowers laughed.

"So, bottom line, you tell me I'm going to get a job," Samantha concluded.

"Yes," Professor Dowers agreed confidently. "By the way, what are starting salaries for graduating students now?"

"The average for my major is about $25,000," said Samantha.

"In my first job out of school, I only made $5,000," reminisced Professor Dowers. "Do you think students are worth five times more than I was?"

"You're trying to trick me," said Samantha. "I remember you asking the same question in class. The difference in salaries is due to inflation. It's not that today's students are worth more, the dollar just has less purchasing power."

"Very good," said Professor Dowers. "If you don't get a job, you can always go to graduate school and become an economics professor."

"I'm not sure I want to be a professor of a subject that is called the 'dismal science'," said Samantha, trying to get the good professor back a little for the unattractive employee conversation. "Plus, you have almost guaranteed me that I will get a job, so I don't have to worry."

"You are right there," said Professor Dowers, getting up from the bench. "If people like you can't get a job, I don't know who will. Anyway, I need to get going. It's getting late."

"Me too, Professor Dowers. Thanks for the talk. I felt like I was a freshman back in your economics class."

"You might be a little young to be getting nostalgic. Good luck to you."

"Bye, Professor Dowers." Samantha got something to eat and headed back to her apartment, hoping that Susie had left. No such luck. She was greeted by nail polish fumes. Christina and Susie were painting their nails.

"Hiiiiiiii Sammy!" Susie said, knocking over a bottle of nail polish.

"What a ditz," Samantha thought.

"Oops! It got all over this paper!" Susie said, jumping up.

"Susie!" Christina exclaimed. "That's Samantha's homework!"

"Oh, I'm so sorry, Sam!" Susie said.

"It's fine," Samantha said, gritting her teeth. She could have killed Susie.

"Well, we've got to run!" Susie said, wiggling out the door.

"Bye, Sam. Sorry." Christina said, going out after Susie.

"Yeah, no problem." Samantha said to them. The door slammed. Samantha opened a window, trying to let out the nail polish fumes. Then she sat down to redo her homework.

Key Economic Terms – Chapter 3

Unemployment
Five types of unemployment
- Cyclical unemployment
- Structural unemployment
- Frictional unemployment
- Voluntary unemployment
- Unattractive employee unemployment

General economy reasons for unemployment: cyclical and structural unemployment

Personal reasons for unemployment: frictional, voluntary, and the unattractive employee
Discouraged worker
GNP per capita
Investment
The Great Depression
Infrastructure
Recession
Unemployment insurance
Welfare

Chapter 4
Jason and Samantha Meet: The Car Buying Chapter

Samantha felt great. She had received a job offer letter from *Switches.com*, a computer company in Indianapolis the previous week, and she had written back her acceptance letter. Her job worries were over. Even better, she only had one final to take next week, on Monday. She decided to spend Saturday in Indianapolis, shopping for a car. She would need one once she started her new job. She could study for her final on Sunday.

Samantha had already spent several hours on the Internet, researching different models, options, performance, safety features, and pricing. She concluded that a *Saturn* or *Chevrolet Cavalier* would work. There was an outside chance she could find her way to a *Honda Civic* as well. There was also still the issue of fixing up the used car she was driving and foregoing the new car. She decided she would visit *Lancaster Chevrolet-Saturn* since that one dealership offered two of her three choices. It was also close to her new job location, which she thought might be convenient when it came time to service the car.

On Saturday morning she made the one-hour drive to Indianapolis. As she walked up to the dealership showroom, a young man who appeared to be a salesperson greeted her.

"Hi, my name is Jim Chester, welcome to *Lancaster*. What's your name?"

"Samantha, Samantha Fletcher," she responded with some trepidation. Salespeople always seem to be overly aggressive and Samantha promised herself that she would remain guarded. Today is only a scouting mission; no buying decisions are in the cards.

"Well, Sam. I can call you Sam, can't I? What kind of car can I sell you today?"

"This guy is too friendly already; maybe I should just leave," Samantha thought. She then responded forcefully to his question, "No, you may not, Samantha is just fine and I'm interested in looking at a *Saturn* and a *Cavalier* coupe."

Jim was a good salesperson, although sometimes somewhat impatient. "I got me a liberated one here," he thought, "I guess I had better cool it."

"Good, good, those are great choices," Jim said to Samantha. "What do you say we see the *Saturn* first? We have the best selection in the area and no one beats our great deals. Hey, you got anything to trade in?"

"Yes," replied Samantha, "that gray *Honda* over there."

"You had that ride very long?" asked Jim.

"Ride?" asked Samantha.

"Yeah. Ride, car . . . you know what I mean," Jim continued with the lingo.

"Yes, the car was my parents," Samantha replied. "They bought it new. It was a great college car."

Jim considered how many stories that car could tell but dismissed that thought before he got himself into more trouble. "Boy, it doesn't owe you anything does it?" Jim said.

Samantha wondered where this guy was going with the conversation. "What do you mean?" Samantha asked him.

"Well," explained Jim, "I just meant that it looks like you got your money's worth out of that car."

Samantha was clearly offended. "My *Honda* is a very good car."

"Sorry," Jim said, "I did not mean to imply otherwise. Tell you what, give me the keys and I will have our chief appraiser look at it, okay?"

"Yeah, I guess that's all right," Samantha conceded.

Samantha had a moment to reflect while Jim was doing the appraisal. "This car buying business is going to be a chore," she thought. "I just hope they don't try to snow me with a bunch of statistics and unfamiliar jargon."

"Hey Sam, I mean Samantha. I'm back." Jim was back with a fake smile. Samantha thought that was quick; it must not take long to assess the value of cars nowadays. "You know what the appraiser told me," Jim said. "You are in luck. It seems that he knows of three or four people right now that would be potential buyers for your trade-in. All I need to do is make a deal with you. Man, I can't lose," Jim continued. "You get a new car and my used car guy gets a great unit for resale."

"Jim sure likes to talk," Samantha thought.

"Let's get this nailed down Samantha. Give me a color choice, do you want a hand shaker, I mean a manual transmission, or do you want an automatic? Will you want a CD player or cassette or both, are you thinking about leasing or financing the new car?"

"Stop, stop," said Samantha. "You're going too fast for me. Can't we just look at some *Saturns* and see what you have?"

"No problem," said Jim, "they're over here." He pointed to one corner of the lot.

As they were walking through the rows and rows of vehicles, Samantha stopped and said, "I like the looks of this green one."

"Wow," replied Jim. "That's you. What an eye you have."

Still uncomfortable with the whole process, Samantha asked if she could test drive the green one. "You're on," said Jim, "Why don't I drive first and kind of show you the ropes." That sounded fair to Samantha. After a few miles Jim pulled into the Mall parking lot and offered Samantha her opportunity to drive HER new car.

Back at the dealership, Samantha handed the keys to Jim. "It drove nice, I like it. So tell me, how much my car is worth?"

"Not to worry," Jim explained, "I will get you the top dollar for the retiring *Honda*. We will just work it into the deal."

Samantha's antenna was fully up at this point. This guy is scary, she thought. Kind of like an unsuccessful blind date. "No, no," she said. "I want to know what you think my *Honda* is worth."

"Well," said Jim, "that depends on what you want to buy. The higher the value of the new *Saturn*, the more I can get you for your *Honda*."

That makes absolutely no sense, Samantha thought to herself. My car is worth what it is worth; it sounds like I am about to be ripped off. She was only paying half attention when Jim suggested they go into his office and talk about the numbers, whatever that means. With some reluctance Samantha followed Jim to his office.

Jim's desk was covered with papers, pens, pencils, phone messages and a half-full cup of what appeared to be three-day-old coffee. "Now Samantha, I need to get some pertinent information from you for the finance guys. You know what I mean."

"No, I don't know what you mean. I just want to know what my car is worth," pleaded Samantha. "Why don't you answer my question and then tell me how much that green *Saturn* will cost me?"

"What do you think Samantha, will you be leasing or financing your purchase? Residuals are pretty good right now if you want to lease. How much money are you going to put down? Where do you work? All that stuff is important to our deal."

"I told you Jim, that I was also interested in a *Cavalier*. Maybe I should look at them before we get much further along?"

"Yeah, I know," Jim said, "but I could tell that the green *Saturn* was just right for you."

"I don't know," said Samantha. "Lease or finance, money down, work the value of my *Honda* into the deal; the only thing I know right now is that I am confused. Why don't you give me a brochure on the *Saturn* and one for the *Cavalier* and let me try to sort things out by myself? I sure would like you to give me a price before I leave, however."

"Hey, don't leave. Let's not waste this hour we've spent together," said Jim. "I'll bet we can make a deal right now and you can drive home in that new green *Saturn*. For peace of mind we can include a great service contract that will take care of all your future driving worries. I tell you what; I will throw in three car washes and a no cost oil change with the new *Saturn*."

By now, Samantha was really confused and she even felt a little sick to her stomach. "No, just give me the brochures. I need to sleep on it."

"Well, okay," said Jim. "Here's my card too. When you come back ask for me and I will take care of you."

Samantha grabbed her *Honda* keys from Jim's cluttered desk and made tracks for the front door. She got to her car, got in, locked the doors and felt somewhat relieved. As she drove away, she began to wonder if the old *Honda* might just run a little bit longer. Maybe I'll sink a few bucks into repairs and buy some new tires. But then again, I sure would like to have a new car.

She was uncomfortable that she was so unprepared. Lease, finance, service contract, trade-in value, interest rates, lease rates, residuals, keep the old car or buy new. What's the answer? She decided to stop for something to eat, and maybe try the *Honda* dealer before heading back to school.

Samantha stopped at an outside frozen custard store. She was standing in line when she heard an awful noise.

She looked across the parking lot to see the ugliest car she had ever seen drive up. It was really rusty, the muffler was dragging, and the front right tire was flat. To add to the ugly appearance, there were boxes and suitcases filling every spare inch of the car.

A boy jumped out of it, about the same age as her, wearing a Bloomington University sweater. An older man got out of the passenger side.

"Oh, great. A flat tire." Samantha heard the boy say.

"Well, that's okay, Jason. I can walk over to a gas station and buy a new one." The older man said. "Why don't you stop and get something to eat?"

"I guess so. Thanks Uncle Mitchell," the boy said. He sighed and walked up to the frozen custard store. He stood in line right behind Samantha.

"Excuse me." she said to him, being a little more forward than usual.

"Oh, uh, yeah?" Jason said, looking at her.

"I was just wondering, are you moving or something? I mean your car has all that stuff in it . . ."

"Yeah, I just graduated from Bloomington University, and I am moving here to start my new job."

"Me too. I mean, I'm going to be starting a new job too, except that I graduated from West Lafayette University. Maybe I shouldn't even be talking to someone from BU," Samantha teased.

"Where are you going to work?" Jason asked.

"A small computer company called *Switches.com.*" Samantha replied. "You've probably never heard of it."

"I sure have," Jason continued. "That's where I am going to be working. This is really weird. Are you moving today?"

"No, I'm not moving until next weekend. I have one more final to take on Monday. Today I am out looking for a car. I was hoping to buy at a dealership near work. I just went to the *Chevrolet-Saturn* dealer, and I'm trying to figure out what the salesman said to me," Samantha said.

"This isn't the time to be talking to me about cars, but my uncle knows everything about buying cars. He owns a car dealership. Maybe he could help you. He'll be back in a minute."

"Hey, that would be great!" Samantha said, relieved. "What's your name?" she asked.

"Jason. What's yours?"

"I'm Samantha."

"Hey, here comes my uncle right now!" Jason said. Sure enough, the older man was heading up to them. "That was really fast," Jason said to Uncle Mitchell as he walked up.

"Well, they had a nice *Goodyear* tire that almost matches your other tires, not that it matters much on your car," Uncle Mitchell smiled as he looked at Samantha. "The tire will cost you $40, and I talked them into coming over and putting it on for us. I wouldn't want to see a new college graduate changing a tire."

"Uh, okay. Hey, Uncle Mitchell, I want you to meet Samantha." Jason said, gesturing to his new friend.

"Hello," the uncle said. They shook hands.

"Jason tells me you know a lot about buying a car." Samantha said.

"Yes, do you need help?"

"Yes, please. I was just shopping for a new *Saturn* and the stuff the salesman said made no sense to me."

"Well, what is your first question?" asked Uncle Mitchell.

"Well," Samantha began, "he asked me if I wanted to buy, finance, or lease. I don't have enough money to buy a new car outright, and I don't think I want to lease, because I believe that is what you do if the car will be used for business. I guess that means I will be financing. Does that sound right to you?"

"Maybe not," said Uncle Mitchell. "If you don't have the money to buy the car outright, that takes care of that option."

"Maybe I should go with a used car. I've heard you can get a better deal if you pay cash," said Samantha.

"Well, lots of people think a cash buyer gets a better deal, but that's pretty much a myth nowadays. Car dealers, including me, don't care if a customer buys cash or finances. We get our money either way," Uncle Mitchell joked.

"Well, I would rather get a new car," said Samantha. "I don't want to worry about maintenance and I want the car to be dependable."

"That sounds fine," agreed Uncle Mitchell. "You might be able to get less expensive transportation by buying used, but you need to know about cars and accept the fact that maintenance is going to be a bigger problem."

"So that means I buy a new car and finance, right?" said Samantha.

"Well, not so fast," said Uncle Mitchell. "Let's go through all the options carefully. We've eliminated buying outright because you don't have the money right now. What about leasing?"

"Like I said before, this car is for personal purposes. It's not a company car or anything," explained Samantha.

"Well, that may have been true in the past, but now many people are choosing to lease cars instead of buying them," said Uncle Mitchell.

"Why is that," Jason said, joining back into the conversation.

"Lots of reasons," said Uncle Mitchell. "First of all, let me explain how a lease works. With a lease, you drive off with a new car and make monthly payments for 2, 3, or maybe 4 years. The amount of the payment depends on the initial cost of the car and what is called the 'residual' value, the value of the car at the end of the lease. If you lease a $20,000 car for 3 years and the residual value of the car is $8,000 at the end of the three years, you make monthly payments on the equivalent of the $12,000 difference between the original cost of the car and the residual value."

"I see," said Samantha. "That's why a monthly lease payment is lower than financing a car for three years."

"Right," said Uncle Mitchell.

"Wait a minute," said Jason. "I don't get it. Why is it lower than buying the car and financing for 3 years."

"If you buy the car and finance it for 3 years," Samantha explained, "your monthly payment needs to cover the entire $20,000 cost. With a lease, the monthly payment is only based on $12,000. Of course, with a lease, you have to give the car back after 3 years because you don't own it."

"Or buy it," said Uncle Mitchell.

"For $8,000?" asked Jason.

"Right," said Uncle Mitchell. "Most leases are closed-end, which means the residual value is established at the time the new car is leased. You can also get an open-end lease, which means the residual value is established when you bring the car back at the end of the lease, but this type of lease is not very common anymore."

"But why would I want to lease? I don't own the car, and I have to give it back, or buy it, at the end of the lease," Samantha asked.

"Why do you want to buy a new car?" Uncle Mitchell asked Samantha.

"Well, like I said, I want a reliable car and I don't want to deal with repairs," Samantha answered.

"So you don't want to buy a three-year-old used car?" asked Uncle Mitchell.

"Not really," said Samantha.

"So why do you want to keep your new car after it gets to be three years old? You will start to run into all the maintenance issues that you would have if you bought a 3-year-old car now," Uncle Mitchell responded.

"I see what you mean," said Samantha. "So a lease is good if you want to always drive a relatively new car."

"Right," said Uncle Mitchell.

"Doesn't that get expensive?" asked Jason.

"How much do you spend on your clunker," Uncle Mitchell asked Jason.

"My car has a few problems, but I don't spend that much on it," Jason said defensively.

"How much," said Uncle Mitchell, trying to get to the point.

"Maybe a couple of hundred every so often," Jason answered.

"How long is 'so often'?" Uncle Mitchell probed.

"Every few months," Jason replied.

"Well, let's see," said Uncle Mitchell. "I'll just go through the ones I know about. Today we've spent $40 . . . so far. Last week you paid $150 to get the car ready for the trip. Last month you paid $250 for a new fuel pump. The month before that you paid $100 for a new brake job."

"Okay, maybe $200 every month or two," Jason gave in.

"Do you know how much a lease on a new car costs?" Uncle Mitchell said. "There are many new cars that you can lease for $179, no down payment, 36 month term. I'd say your inexpensive old car may start costing you more than a new car soon."

"But I can't give up my old car. Look how much I have invested in it," Jason said.

"That's called sunk cost," Uncle Mitchell replied. "Any money you spent in the past has nothing to do with a future decision. You should make your best decision based on where you are right now and how much you will have to pay in the future."

"So, bottom line, if you want to drive pretty new cars, leasing may be better than financing," Samantha said, getting back to the subject.

"That is a pretty good rule of thumb," Uncle Mitchell agreed. "Financing would only be better if you plan to keep the car for a long time and you don't mind dealing with all the maintenance and dependability issues."

"Can you tell me more about leases?" Samantha asked. "What else do I need to know?"

"The term of any lease is of critical importance. The best lease term is 24 or 36 months. In some cases 48 months may work, but generally shorter terms are better. Most new vehicles have warranties that fully cover all failures for up to 36 months or 36,000 miles, whichever occurs first. Therefore, any lease up to 36 months or less usually means the vehicle is covered by warranty in the event or a failure.

"A popular leasing myth is that excess miles unfavorably affect a lease. That is true, but that is also true of any scenario. If you pay cash or finance, excessive mileage accelerates depreciation. With leasing you can tailor the number of miles you expect to drive as part of the contract and avoid the high mile pain."

"So I need to know how many miles I plan to drive?" asked Samantha.

"Exactly," said Uncle Mitchell. "That will help you customize the lease contract for your needs.

"Most new vehicle leases also include what is called Gap insurance," Uncle Mitchell continued. That means if anything were to happen to the vehicle that would result in a total loss, you, the customer, are not responsible for making up any difference between actual value and the value of unmade lease payments. This is not usually the case in a finance arrangement. I have seen that provision save many families extraordinary agony."

"What about the down payment?" asked Jason. "You just talked about the Escort lease with no money down. Is that the best kind of lease?"

"It usually is a good practice to avoid any down payment on a lease. The only impact of a down payment is a reduction in the monthly payment. Your money will probably be better invested in a securities program than used for a down payment."

"Why do car companies offer such good deals on leases?" Samantha asked.

"Leasing has become a crucial part of most vehicle manufacturer's economic strategy and stability," answered Uncle Mitchell. "Ford Motor Company, for example, provides significant incentives to customers who choose to lease for 24 or 36 months. The incentives are so good sometimes that we might question their sanity. As an example, in the spring of 1999, Ford focused on selling new Ford Ranger supercab pickups with four doors, four-wheel drive and generously equipped with options. The selling price for the Ranger was in excess of $24,000, however, with incentives the lease payment was as low as $220 per month for 36 months, including all taxes. There was not even a down payment required. That means a customer can drive the Ranger for three years, enjoy warranty protection, and all at an investment of less than 33% of the selling price. This is not necessarily an isolated case."

"You are starting to sound like my economics professor at West Lafayette University," said Samantha. "What is the reason?"

"It's simple," said Uncle Mitchell. "Leasing encourages vehicle replacement at short intervals, say 24 or 36 months. This works for the customer because they can drive a new vehicle that will always be under warranty, and the cost will be a fraction of the full cost. Think about my Ranger example. Drive a new vehicle, under warranty, for three years for 33% of its cost. Let's say I do that three consecutive times and then compare my total cash outlay with that of another person who buys once and keeps the vehicle for nine years. And remember to include the increased maintenance and repair costs as the car gets older.

"And what's in it for the manufacturer?" Uncle Mitchell continued. "The car company delivers three new vehicles in nine years. There is an enormous investment in plant and equipment by any car manufacturer. The more new cars they produce, the better they spread out their fixed costs."

"What does 'spreading out fixed costs mean'?" asked Jason.

"In other words," said Uncle Mitchell, "if they make a lot of cars, they make good use of their equipment and people. Manufacturing facilities operate at their very best at near capacity."

"Okay, I see now why car companies want to offer aggressive lease programs. So we have decided that I should lease a new car. What kind of car do you think I should get?"

"Well, you probably have a personal preference after looking over a few cars," said Uncle Mitchell.

"Actually, I spent a few hours on the web comparing cars," offered Samantha.

"That's a very good way to do it. There are also some good magazines that review all the new cars. Beyond personal preference, supply and demand plays a major role in the cost of a vehicle. I know a person who in 1990, the first year for the Mazda Miata, told a dealer he wanted a Miata regardless of the price. Production was limited and dealers were charging full price and sometimes even charging a premium for the new Miatas. A newly introduced vehicle is generally expensive because lots of people want to buy one and there are not many available. It happened in 1990 with the Miata, in 1993 with the Mustang Cobra, and in 1997 with the Ford Expedition.

"On the other hand, Dodge Neons, Ford Mustangs, and Cadillac Sedan DeVilles are widely available right now. For these cars, deep discounts off the manufacturer's suggested retail price and rebates are common. Additionally, at the end of a model year, the passing year carryover vehicles are sold with deep discounts and significant rebates. Year-end buyers will shop in October, as that is when dealers have the new models in stock and they are anxious to sell the prior year inventory.

"Of course," said Uncle Mitchell, "if you need a car right now to start a new job, that doesn't really apply to you."

"That's true," said Samantha, "but that will be a good thing to remember for next time."

"So in summary," Uncle Mitchell wrapped up, "the objective is to minimize any investment in a vehicle. Once the money is spent, it may not be recovered. Strive to line up any monthly payment term with the vehicle warranty term: a 36-month lease with a 36-month warranty, for example. Unless we experience an explosion in inflation followed by unreasonable interest rates, minimize any investment in a vehicle. A vehicle is like an insurance policy; it is necessary, but it makes a lousy investment."

"Well, I feel much more equipped to handle my decision thanks to your advice," Samantha said happily. "In fact, I think I will go back now and try to get things wrapped up. I was sure lucky I stopped for something to eat and met you two."

"And I guess I will see you around *Switches.com*," said Jason.

"What's this?" asked Uncle Mitchell.

"Oh, sorry," said Jason. "Before you came, I found out that Samantha is starting at *Switches.com* in a week."

"That is quite a coincidence," said Uncle Mitchell. "That means I'll be able to check in on your car decision when I come to visit Jason some time."

"Absolutely," said Samantha. "And thanks again for the help!"

Key Economic Terms – Chapter 4

Trade-in value	Lease term
Leasing	Excess miles
Financing	Gap insurance
Residuals	Spreading out fixed costs
Closed-end lease	Supply
Open-end lease	Demand
Sunk cost	Premium

Chapter 5
Jason Wants a Honda: The International Economics Chapter

"Hey, Samantha."

Samantha looked for the sound of the voice. "Jason! How are you?" It was Samantha's first day at work, and she was in the company lunchroom.

"Great," said Jason. "Why don't you join us?"

"Okay," said Samantha. "Thanks. We have staggered lunch hours in my department, so only one of us is off for lunch at the same time. It's nice to find someone I know to eat with."

"Samantha, this is Tim." Jason introduced the other person at the table. "Tim graduated from BU with me, and now we are both in the marketing department."

"What department are you in?" Tim asked Samantha.

"I am in customer service," said Samantha. "That's why we have the staggered lunch hours, so we are well staffed at all times. We have staggered starting and quitting times also."

"Did you go to BU?" Tim continued his questioning.

"Actually, I went to West Lafayette University. I met Jason and his Uncle Mitchell when I was shopping for a car the weekend before last."

"How did that work out?" asked Jason.

"Great," said Samantha. "Thanks to your Uncle Mitchell, I went right back and leased a green *Saturn*. I'm driving it now."

"Actually, after the conversation, Uncle Mitchell convinced me to get a new car too. I went to look at *Hondas* on Saturday."

"*Hondas*?" Tim interjected. "You should buy an American car."

"Why's that?" asked Jason. "What's wrong with *Hondas*?"

"Nothing," said Tim, "except you will put Americans out of work."

"What about the computer equipment that we sell?" Samantha asked Tim. "Most of that comes from the Far East. Should we switch to only American products?"

"I wish we could," said Tim, "but Americans don't make this computer stuff as cheap as the people in the Far East do. We don't really have a choice there."

"So you think we should import computer equipment, but we shouldn't import cars?" Samantha asked.

"Exactly," said Tim.

"I once had a fat economics professor," said Samantha.

"What does that have to do with anything?" asked Jason, trying to get back into the conversation.

"He told us there are four possible diet plans. You could

- eat more and lose weight,
- eat less and gain weight
- eat more and gain weight,
- or eat less and lose weight.

"It would be nice to eat more and lose weight, but that doesn't happen. Eating less

39

and gaining weight doesn't make sense either. The only real choices are to eat more and gain weight, or eat less and lose weight." Samantha had Tim and Jason totally confused. She took a bite of her sandwich while they thought about it.

"Okay," Tim finally answered. "I get that, but what does that have to do with importing cars or computer equipment?"

"Well, you said you want to import the computer equipment but not the cars. It doesn't work that way. The only real choice is to trade more with other countries or trade less."

"That's not true," interjected Tim. "I could put a big tariff on Japanese cars, and then people wouldn't want to buy them."

"What's a tariff?" asked Jason.

"A tariff is a tax on an imported product," Samantha answered. If you decide to buy a *Honda*, you would have to pay an extra $1,000 as a tariff, for example. Or the U.S. government could put a quota on Japanese cars, which means the number of Japanese cars that can come into the U.S. would be limited."

"A quota sounds better to me," said Jason. "I wouldn't want to pay a tax just to buy a Japanese car."

"Except you would pay more with a quota too," said Samantha. "If the Japanese can only bring in 10,000 cars, for example, they will be able to raise prices because these cars will be more scarce. The consumer still ends up paying more, but with a quota the Japanese manufacturer gets the extra money. With a tariff, the U.S. government would collect the extra tax. Either way, the consumer pays more. Also, the Japanese will probably retaliate with import tariffs or quotas of their own, and we will have a trade war on our hands."

"How come every conversation I have with you turns into an economics lesson?" Jason asked Samantha.

"Funny how that seems to happen," Samantha agreed.

"I guess I want to trade less," Tim decided. "I don't want to put Americans out of work just because Jason wants a *Honda*."

"Okay," said Samantha. "That's a valid choice, but let's look at what you give up. Your Nike shoes have to go, because they are probably made in Thailand. Your nice expensive watch is gone, because it was probably made in Switzerland. That banana on your lunch tray probably came from Central or South America, so that is gone."

"Enough," said Tim. "I get your point. But most of those things could be made in the U.S., or I could get something else, like a Florida orange instead of the banana."

"True, but you will end up paying more for the things you want and you will have fewer choices. The result will be that your standard of living will go down if you decide to trade less," Samantha stated.

"But what about the American workers?" said Tim. "Shouldn't we be trying to help them?"

"That is the big trade-off," Samantha answered. "If you allow trade, consumers are always better off. Other groups get hurt by trade, however. If people decide they like Japanese cars better than American cars, then American automotive companies will go out of business and people will lose their jobs. The Japanese automotive companies will grow and they will hire more workers."

"So we've exported American jobs," said Tim. "That is exactly my point."

"That's true. But if you don't allow trade, you are really protecting the inefficient producers. Back when the American car companies didn't have much competition, they became bloated and inefficient. Once challenged by foreign competition, they became more efficient. There were some inefficient American car factories that were shut down, and that was a big short-term problem. But eventually most of the people that used to work in these factories found new jobs."

"Probably not jobs that paid as much as the automotive jobs," Jason offered.

"That's true. And that is the cold reality of international trade. Some groups gain and other groups lose . . . consumers gain, efficient producers gain, and inefficient producers lose," summarized Samantha.

"You sure know a lot about this," said Tim. "I've never heard it explained in such precise terms."

"I had a great Econ 101 professor," said Samantha modestly.

"You mean the fat guy?" asked Jason.

"That's the one. But he was also pretty cute, in a teddy bear sort of way," Samantha smiled.

"So are there any cases where you might want to restrict trade," asked Jason. "They probably told me this in Econ 101, but I didn't have a cute teddy bear to keep my attention."

"There are a few cases where domestic industries should be protected. For example, you usually want to make sure there is a domestic supply of critical items, especially things that might be needed in a war. That's why the government usually takes action to protect our defense industry. Sometimes people take this 'essential industry' argument a bit too far. People use the essential industry argument to protect our domestic sugar industry, which means domestic prices for sugar are four times the world price, which is also why corn syrup has replaced sugar in soft drinks in the U.S. In fact, you have to go to Mexico to get a Coke made with real sugar. Some also think you should protect infant industries to give them a chance to develop before they have to face international competition."

"Whatever," said Jason, losing interest in the infant industry argument. "So bottom line, you are telling me it's okay if I buy a *Honda*."

"Yes, except they are pretty expensive right now," said Samantha.

"Because of tariffs or quotas," said Jason, proving that he had paid attention.

"No, more because of exchange rates," said Samantha.

"Uh oh, here comes another economics lesson," warned Tim.

"Can you give me a chance to eat for a second?" asked Samantha. "Why don't you tell me what you learned in Econ 101?"

"Obviously not much," admitted Jason. "We had a bunch of supply and demand curves, and when they intersected that meant something."

"In my class we talked about the gold standard," offered Tim, "but I'm not sure what that had to do with anything."

"Actually, the gold standard is related to exchange rates," said Samantha, quickly finishing her salad. "Before 1971, all the major currencies of the world were on a gold standard, meaning the currency had a value based on gold. One ounce of gold was worth $35. If you wanted to trade with Japan, you figured out the values of the currencies based on how much the currency was worth in terms of gold. That essentially gave us fixed exchange rates between different countries. There are still some countries that maintain fixed exchange rates. They usually fix the value of their currencies in terms of U.S. dollars."

"But the gold standard is gone now?" asked Tim.

"Yes, now we have floating exchange rates, meaning the value of the currencies go up and down based on supply and demand," Samantha responded.

"What does that mean?" asked Tim. "I understood the part about every currency being worth so much in terms of gold. That seems to make sense. I don't understand this floating currency stuff."

"Okay, let's look at Jason's *Honda*. Is the model you want made in the U.S. or in Japan?" Samantha asked Jason.

"In Japan," Jason answered. "In fact, the salesman told me that was one reason that particular model was more expensive, but I thought he was just trying to rip me off."

"Maybe not," said Samantha. "It's actually pretty simple, but you have to follow the story. The car you want is made in Japan. If you are a Japanese company, you want to get paid in yen, right?"

"That would make sense," agreed Jason. "If I ever get a paycheck, I want to be paid in dollars."

"Right," said Samantha. "So to get paid in yen, you essentially have to convert your dollars into yen, and then the Japanese auto company gets paid in yen. This is all behind the scenes, of course, but that is essentially what you are doing. To buy a Japanese product, you convert your dollars into yen, and the Japanese company gets the payment in yen."

"Okay, we are both with you," Tim said looking at Jason.

"Let's say the Japanese car company wants 2 million yen for the car that Jason wants to buy," Samantha continued.

"That seems like a lot," said Jason.

"And one dollar is worth 100 yen," continued Samantha. "That means the Japanese auto company wants the equivalent of $20,000."

"Maybe that's not so bad after all," said Jason, "but I can't divide 2 million by 100 as fast as you do."

"But that's when the value of the U.S. dollar is strong. What if the value of the U.S. dollar goes down, and now one dollar will only buy 80 yen? The Japanese company still wants 2 million yen for the car, but now to come up with 2 million yen, you need whatever 2 million divided by 80 is," said Samantha.

"$25,000," said Tim, working it out on a napkin.

"So the same car that costs 2 million yen might cost me $20,000 one day and $25,000 another day," said Jason.

"Right, depending on the value of the U.S. dollar," said Samantha. "And right now the U.S. dollar is weaker than usual, so it will cost you more to buy your Japanese car."

"That 'buy American' idea is looking better," Jason said to Tim. "I can get a less expensive car and keep Americans working too."

"And that's how things even out," said Samantha. "If Japanese products become too expensive because of exchange rates, people will import fewer Japanese products. That means they will need fewer yen, so the demand for yen won't be as big. The yen will fall in value, and the U.S. dollar will gain in value."

"And my Japanese car will fall in price to $20,000," Jason finished. "Maybe I should wait to buy the car until the dollar gains in value."

"From the look of your car," Samantha said, "I don't think you can wait that long."

"Finally something we can agree on," said Tim. "I'm embarrassed to be seen in that old clunker."

"Of course, the flip side of *Hondas* being more expensive for Jason is that American products are currently a good deal for foreign buyers," said Samantha. "American exports increase when the dollar is weak for exactly the opposite reason that Jason doesn't want to buy a *Honda* right now."

"This discussion about foreign currencies also brings us back to why the only choice is to trade more or trade less," said Samantha, trying to get the conversation back on track. "If you always try to export more than you import, you would have an imbalance of currencies. For example, if your strategy is to export goods to Japan but never import, the Japanese would need to get dollars to pay for the products exported by the U.S to Japan. But where would the Japanese get the dollars? If the U.S. never imports anything from Japan, people in the United States would never want to trade dollars to get yen, because the people in the U.S. would not need any yen to buy Japanese products. Eventually, the Japanese would not be able buy the U.S. exports. The Japanese would never be able to get dollars to pay for the exports because people in the U.S. would never want to trade dollars for yen. Ultimately you need a balance between products flowing between countries and currencies flowing between countries."

"That can't be true," said Tim. "I always read that the U.S. has a trade deficit. How can we always have a trade deficit if ultimately we need to have balance."

"That's a good point," said Samantha. "We have been running a trade deficit in the U.S. for a number of years. We import much more than we export. The reason this works out is because foreigners want to buy dollars in order to buy U.S. investments. People in the U.S. need more foreign currency to buy foreign products than we bring in from exports, but we can trade dollars for foreign currency because foreigners want the dollars to make investments in the U.S. The large foreign ownership of U.S. investments has it's own problems, but that's how things have been staying in balance. Normally a country's currency will fall in value against other currencies if a country continues to import more than it exports, but since the demand for U.S. dollars is strong because of foreign investment in the U.S., the dollar has remained strong."

"So what are you going to do about the car?" Tim asked Jason.

"Given the state of international exchange rates," Jason said in a scholarly voice, "I think I will confine my choice of automobiles to domestic manufacturers. The current exchange rates between the yen and the dollar is making the purchase of a *Honda* less than attractive."

"Well, I need to get going," said Samantha while folding up her napkin. "I don't want to get back from lunch late on my first day."

"It was nice to meet you Samantha," said Tim.

"It was great to see you again. Maybe we will see you tomorrow at lunch," Jason said hopefully.

"I would really look forward to that," Tim said sarcastically once Samantha was out of earshot. "I would love to spend another lunch hour discussing economics."

"I don't know," said Jason. "I think Samantha is really interesting. She knows a lot."

"Uh oh," said Tim. "I know where this is going."

"What do you mean?" Jason asked.

"Never mind," Tim said. "Let's get back to work. We need to recommend some pricing for those new CD drives that are coming in."

Key Economic Terms – Chapter 5

Buy American
Trade
Tariffs
Quotas
Trade war
Exporting jobs
Inefficient producers
Essential industries

Infant industries
Exchange rate
Gold standard
Fixed exchange rates
Floating exchange rates
Trade deficit
Foreign investment

Chapter 6
Rent or Buy? The Housing Chapter

The next day, Samantha came to the lunchroom and found Jason and Tim at their regular table. Jason waved her over, but Samantha didn't think that Tim looked too happy about it.

"So how was your first day on the job?" Jason asked Samantha.

"Pretty good. I have a lot to learn, though. This morning I was studying our catalog. We sure sell a lot of different computer components. Half of this stuff I have never even heard of."

"I don't know why you say that," Tim said condescendingly. "Everything we sell is pretty standard. It all seems pretty clear to me."

Jason looked at his friend with surprise. That seemed to be an unprovoked attack. "Well, we have a one week jump on you," Jason said encouragingly. "If you find something you don't recognize, you can call me or Tim. We have been working on setting prices. The prices for this stuff change almost every day, you know."

"Where are you living, Samantha?" Tim asked. "Jason and I are roommates at Lynch Apartments down the street."

"Really, I live in the next complex down the street, Manka Manor. But I only have a three month lease."

"Why is that?" Jason asked. "Don't you like it?"

"Yes, it's fine. But I am going to buy a house."

Jason and Tim were startled. They hadn't even thought about buying a house. Renting was the only option they had considered.

"It just doesn't make sense to pay rent month after month and not have anything to show for it," Samantha continued. "Plus I really like the sense of ownership that goes with having my own house. Did you know that one of the best investments today is real estate?"

"Sure," replied Tim. "It is expensive to buy a house though. Think about it, Samantha, you have to be hassled with all maintenance and repairs, property taxes are out of sight, and don't forget about insurance," Tim said, sounding like a know-it-all.

"Oh come on, Tim, get real," Samantha said, fighting back. "If I buy a new house, there will be a built-in warranty for at least a year. And as for taxes, they are fully deductible for both state and federal tax purposes. On top of that, I can borrow against any equity I have in the property at a favorable rate of interest. If that's not enough, the interest I pay on that home equity loan is also tax deductible."

"I hear you, Samantha," replied Tim, "but don't forget the renter's deduction for tax purposes. That provision in the tax law helps to level the playing field between homeowners and renters."

Jason was lost with all this talk about taxes, but he knew he'd better say something to cool these two off. "All I know is that I love the freedom of renting," Jason interjected. "I'm not tied to one place. If I want to move or upgrade myself, I don't have to go through the pain of selling what I have before I can live somewhere else."

"That's true," Samantha said, speaking a little gentler with Jason compared to Tim. "But rental agreements also result in long lease requirements and substantial security and damage deposits. Those leases are not easily broken. There goes your freedom, Jason, and your rent money is down the drain. Plus renting really is a hassle. Where do I park when someone is in my parking place, why did 3B fill up the dumpster with moving boxes 30 minutes after the trash truck left, and so on."

"You still haven't answered the money part," said Tim. "Instead of putting my money into a down payment on a house, I can buy into a mutual fund, perhaps one that focuses on the S&P 500. Did you know that for three years ending with 1998, the S&P 500 had returns well over 20%? Now, Samantha, where are you going to find a house that appreciates 20% a year for three years?"

"Okay, okay. You made your point. But are you willing to guarantee 20% returns for the future. I don't think so. Plus, how much of that down payment money have you invested in the S&P 500 so far?" Samantha asked.

"Well, none so far. But I plan to," said Jason.

"That's another advantage of buying a house . . . forced saving. Especially for people who lack discipline," Samantha said in an accusative tone.

"Have you considered the cost of money to buy a house?" Tim continued. "I mean some interest rate quotes I've seen are not real attractive."

"Interest rates, now that is an interesting topic," Samantha agreed. "Have you ever heard of the difference between nominal and real interest rates, or did you sleep through your Economics classes?"

"Sure I know about interest costs," said Jason. "The bank says the rate is 8%, so I know that for every $100 of principal, I shell out eight bucks. What's so hard about that?"

"Well," explained Samantha, "it is not always that simple. You do know about inflation, don't you? That's where prices steadily creep up. Inflation increases interest costs."

"How's that," asked Jason.

"Well, say inflation is rising at an annual rate of 3% and the bank quoted interest rate is 8%," replied Samantha. "The 8% is the nominal interest rate, however, the real interest rate is 8% minus 3%, or 5%. That's how much it costs you to borrow the money after taking inflation into account. All other things being equal, your real cost will be $5 per $100 principal. It's beginning to sound better all the time, huh?"

"What's all this noise I hear about indexed mortgages," Jason asked. "I have heard it said that these variable rate mortgages are the way to go when times are good."

"Oh, that's an easy one, Jason," Samantha said, getting the upper hand on Tim. "Some lending institutions will offer the variable rates as an alternative to traditional fixed rate mortgages. Fixed rate means just that, the rate does not change over the life of the loan. Variable rate mortgages are tied to actual money conditions in the financial markets. If banks can borrow cheaply, they may choose to pass on a cheap rate to a customer as a way of generating more business. If the banks borrowing costs go up, however, so does the rate of interest you pay on your loan. These indexed mortgages are tied to some index of interest rates, like the average rate on 30-year bonds."

"Sounds like Las Vegas to me, Samantha," Tim observed. "I am not sure the risk is worth it."

"Well," said Samantha, "maybe indexed mortgages are not for the weak-hearted. However, in times of low inflation and a booming economy, they can be a good alternative. There are even some lenders that will offer a variable rate and further stipulate the rate will not change for two or three years. That's dynamite for someone who moves often due to job changes or someone who merely wants to trade up to better housing.

"Jason, it's really a supply and demand deal," Samantha continued, ignoring Tim. "If the lenders have lots of money to lend then interest rates will be low. Remember, banks and finance companies do not make money by investing in certificates of deposit. They make money lending to people like you and me. Like anything else, if money becomes scarce, meaning a limited supply, then it will cost more."

"Well, I am sure interested in this economics lesson, but I need to get back to work," Tim said, getting up from the table. "Are you coming, Jason?"

"I'll be there in a minute," Jason answered. "I'm just going to finish my drink."

"Fine," said Tim, as he walked away.

"I'm afraid that didn't go very well," Samantha said. "I don't think Tim likes me very much."

"Don't worry about it," Jason consoled her. "He was asking for it from the very beginning. I don't know what's wrong with him sometime."

"There's another guy in my group who treats me just like Tim," Samantha said. "They don't think women know anything about computers. Of course, in my case, it's true. I was an education major, and I really don't know about all these electronic components."

"Maybe I can help you," Jason offered. "I have been taking apart computers my whole life. Would you like to go through the catalog with me tonight?"

"Are you asking me on a date?" Samantha smiled.

"Well, not really," Jason stammered, not really knowing the right answer. "I would just be glad to help you."

"I think you had better come to my place. I don't think your roommate Tim would be too happy to see me after work too. Plus you won't have long to see Manka Manor before I move into my house."

"Have you already found a place?" Jason asked.

"No, but I have the neighborhoods narrowed down. There is one area near work where houses have been appreciating 10% per year."

"Wow, your house value would double in ten years at that rate," Jason said impressed.

"Actually, the value would double in about seven years," Samantha smiled. "You may know computers, but I know money."

"I thought you said 10% per year," said Jason, confused.

"That's right, but the growth is compounded."

"What does that mean?"

"If I buy a house for $100,000, after one year, it's worth $110,000," Samantha started to explain.

"Right, $10,000 more, or 10%," Jason agreed.

"But the next year, since the house is now worth $110,000, a 10% increase would be another $11,000, so the house would be worth $121,000."

"That doesn't seem like a very big difference," Jason said.

"It doesn't for the first few years, but the difference really starts growing rapidly. That's called the magic of compound interest," Samantha smiled.

"How did you know the house value would double in 7 years? Had you already figured that out?"

"Actually, I knew that from a trick my father taught me. If you divide 72 by the interest rate, that's how long it takes to double your money."

"So 72 divided by 10 is 7.2, or about seven years?" Jason asked.

"Right," said Samantha. "If the house values were going up 5% per year, it would take 72 divided by 5, or 14 years, for the house value to double. It's called the rule of 72s."

"Good trick," said Jason. "I'll remember that. I need to get going. So what time tonight?"

"How about 6 p.m.? We can order a pizza."

"You mean you don't cook?" Jason teased. "Tim would be disappointed. He would expect that sort of thing."

"I think you will be happier with pizza. I'm in unit 44. I'll bring a copy of the most recent catalog."

"Sounds great," Jason said. "See you around 6."

Tim noticed Jason when he came back to his cubicle. "What took you so long?" Tim asked. "Did you need to hear the rest of the economics lesson from Samantha?"

"Look, I don't know what your problem is, but you weren't very nice to her," Jason responded with a mild degree of anger.

"I think she can take care of herself," Tim responded. "Plus, she was the one who was being a jerk."

"Whatever," said Jason, turning back to his computer.

* * *

"I'm glad you found the place," Samantha said, opening the door.

"No problem," Jason said. "The biggest problem was sneaking out before Tim could ask where I was going."

"So this is a secret?" Samantha said mysteriously.

"Not really," said Jason, again not knowing what he was supposed to say. "I just didn't want to get into a long conversation. Hey, what's all this?" Jason asked, looking at a table full of computer spreadsheets. "Is this work stuff?"

"Actually, it's my analysis for buying the house. Maybe I should be spending more time on work, though."

"We're going to work overtime tonight on the catalog. That's pretty good. So tell me about all these spreadsheets," Jason asked.

"These were my calculations to tell me if buying a house is a good idea. That was a no-brainer, so now I am looking at how much I should pay for different houses."

"You certainly are analytical," Jason said.

"Do you like that in a woman?" Samantha said in a flirting way.

Jason again wasn't sure what to say. He had never met a woman like Samantha–talking about economics and money one minute and flirting the next. "Why is this so difficult?" Jason asked, conveniently ignoring Samantha's question. Don't you just compare how much you pay in rent with how much the house payment would be?"

"It's much more complicated than that," said Samantha, going back into economics mode. "You have to consider the down payment, the interest rate on the mortgage, maintenance costs, tax consequences, and especially the time value of money."

"Time value of money? I don't think I've heard that one before."

"Tell you what," said Samantha. "You loan me $1,000 today towards my down payment, and I will give you back $1,000 one year from today."

"That's not a very good deal," Jason complained.

"Why?" Samantha asked.

"Because I could invest that money and earn interest, and then it would be worth more that $1,000 after a year."

"Exactly," said Samantha. "That's the time value of money."

"That's it?"

"Yep. The time value of money just says that a dollar today is worth more than a dollar in some future time."

"How do you work that into your spreadsheet?" Jason asked.

"If you invest the $1,000, how much will you make in one year?" Samantha asked.

"Maybe $100," answered Jason, "assuming I can make 10% on my money. Plus, 10% is an easy number to calculate," Jason confessed.

"Not as good as Tim's 20% gain on the S&P 500, but let's use your 10%. If I think I can make 10% per year on my money, that means $100 one year from today is only worth $91 today."

"Because if I invest $91 today at 10% interest, I will have $100 one year from today," Jason said.

"Exactly, you just take $100 divided by 1.1, which is one plus the interest rate of 10%."

"What about $100 two years from now? How does that work?" Jason asked.

"This gets into that compound interest idea," said Samantha. "You can't just say it is 20 percent less, because the money would earn compound interest. Instead you divide by 1.1, and then divide by 1.1 again."

"So $100 two years from now is worth $100 divided by 1.1, which I know is $91, and then divided by 1.1 again, which is ..."

"Here's a calculator," Samantha offered.

"Thanks. So $100 divided by 1.1 divided by 1.1 again is ... about $83."

"That sounds about right," said Samantha.

"So $100 two years from now is worth $83 in today's dollars. And $100 one year from now is worth $91."

"Right, in today's dollars. So to figure out whether you have a good deal or not, you calculate all your future payments or income in terms of today's dollars."

"Like comparing oranges and oranges," Jason said.

"Right, you put all the flows of money into the same oranges and see if you have positive or negative oranges at the end. The final number that you calculate after putting all the cash flows into today's dollars is called the net present value. If your net present value is positive, it is a good deal. If the net present value is negative, it's a bad deal. You would be better off investing your money at 10%."

"How much does your spreadsheet say you will make on your house?" Jason asked. "Or is that too personal."

"Not at all. I project I will make 45% on my investment," Samantha said with some satisfaction.

"How can that be?" Jason asked. "You said the houses were only appreciating 10% per year, plus you will have all those expenses."

"In a word, leverage," said Samantha.

"What do you mean?"

"Well, my down payment will only be $20,000 on a house that costs $100,000. Without getting into all the details, if the house appreciates 10%, the value of my investment has gone up $10,000 and I've only invested $20,000. That's a 50% return in one year. Of course, I would have some expenses that would need to be considered."

"Sure, but I see what you mean. That's amazing. Maybe I should buy a house."

"It really depends on how long you plan to live somewhere. If you are going to move in 2 or 3 years, you are probably better off renting because the closing costs on real estate can be pretty high. Otherwise, it is usually better to buy a house. Are you the type who is comfortable making a commitment?" Samantha asked.

"Uh oh," Jason thought, another uncomfortable moment. "I am okay with commitment," said Jason. "If I see something I like," he added. "Two can play this game," he thought.

"What do you want on your pizza?" Samantha asked. Now she was feeling a little uncomfortable.

"Anything but anchovies."

"Does anyone like anchovies?" Samantha asked. "I don't even know what they are, I just know I don't like them."

"Have you ever had them?" Jason asked.

"No, but I'm sure I don't like them. Don't you have any foods that you've never tried that you don't like?"

"That makes no sense," Jason laughed. "If you've never tried it, how do you know you don't like it? I think you should go back to your spreadsheets to figure out that one."

"Maybe," Samantha smiled. "How about sausage and mushrooms?

"That's my favorite" Jason replied affirmatively.

"Okay, I'll order the pizza. Can you get the catalogs out of my briefcase on the table?"

"Okay," said Jason. He looked around as he was getting the catalogs. Most everything was still in boxes. The apartment didn't give him many clues about Samantha.

"What ever happened with your car?" Samantha asked, getting off the phone. "I meant to ask at lunch, but we got off track."

"Uncle Mitchell is leasing me a car from his dealership, a Ford Mustang. In fact, he's bringing it over this weekend."

"Can I have a ride?" Samantha asked.

"Absolutely. Actually, Uncle Mitchell was asking me how you were doing. Maybe you would like to have lunch with us on Saturday."

"Another date?"

"I don't think having lunch with my Uncle counts as a date. And pizza and a catalog doesn't really count either. How would you like to go out for dinner this Friday?" Jason asked impulsively.

"Is this a date?" Samantha asked.

"Absolutely."

"Then I would love to. But do you mind if I drive? I would rather not experience your clunker. I could pick you up in my *Saturn* and see what Tim says."

"I'll never hear the end of it, but okay, it's a deal."

With that out of the way, both Samantha and Jason found it easier to concentrate on the catalog. Jason really did know a lot about computer equipment, and he taught Samantha almost everything she needed to know in just one night.

"Thanks, Jason," Samantha said, finishing the catalog. "You were a great help."

"I've felt like an idiot in all of our previous conversations. I'm just glad we've finally found something that I know more about than you," Jason said half seriously as he walked to the door.

"What time should I pick you up on Friday?" Samantha asked.

"How does seven sound?"

"That's great," Samantha agreed. There was an awkward moment as they got to the door.

"Bye," Jason finally said. "See you Friday," and he walked out to his car.

Key Economic Terms – Chapter 6

Renting

Warranties

Property taxes

Home equity loan

Renter's deduction

Security and damage deposit

Forced saving

Nominal interest rates

Real interest rates

Indexed mortgages

Variable rate mortgages

30-year bonds

Certificate of Deposit (CD)

Appreciation

Compound interest

Rule of 72s

Time value of money

Leverage

Chapter 7
The First Date: The Paycheck and Financial Planning Chapter

Fridays are always special days; however; this Friday is particularly special for Jason and Samantha. Not only were they going out on their first date, but they also received their first paycheck. *Switches.com* pays the professional staff every other Friday. Jason got his check for two weeks of work while Samantha got her check for one week.

The checks were delivered to Jason's department at 11:30 a.m. Jason eagerly opened his envelope in the privacy of his cubical. "This can't be right," he thought. "They must have only paid me for one week instead of two." He pulled out his calculator. His salary was $42,000 per year. He punched in $42,000 divided by 26 pay periods per year. $1,615 plus some change. But his check was only for $1,112. He thought about asking Tim, but he reconsidered because it might look like he was trying to compare salaries. He spent about 20 minutes trying to understand all the details on the detailed statement that came with the paycheck, but it made no sense. There was a big deduction for "Fed Tax", which he figured out was federal taxes; another large deduction for "IN Tax", which was Indiana tax; and then many other items with abbreviations and initials that he was not familiar with: "FICA", "401(k)", and so forth. Some of these other categories had dollar deductions; some did not.

"Hey, some of us are going out for lunch." Tim interrupted Jason deep in thought. "Do you want to come?"

"No, thanks, I have too much work," Jason replied, hoping he would see Samantha for lunch. Her lunch schedule varied depending on the staffing in customer service, and they had only been able to have lunch one day together since having pizza Monday night.

"Yeah, right," Tim said, "too much work." Tim said something to the other guys as they walked down the hallway. The whole group laughed. Jason couldn't hear what Tim had said, but he suspected it was something about his relationship with Samantha. He walked down to the lunchroom, still thinking about the paycheck and hoping he would see Samantha.

He was in luck because Samantha was already in the lunchroom and sitting by herself. Jason went up to her table and sat down. "Hey, Samantha, get your paycheck yet?" inquired Jason. "Mine came in the morning mail."

"It's sometimes polite to say 'Hello' first," Samantha chastised him jokingly. "And no, I will never get a paycheck, Jason."

"You do this just to bother me," Jason thought. "You say stuff that makes no sense just so I will ask you about it."

"True," Samantha agreed, "but you like it."

"Okay, I'll play along. Why won't you ever get a paycheck?" Jason asked deliberately.

"Because I get direct deposit," said Samantha matter-of-factly. "My money is already safely in the bank, while you are probably carrying around a check, or even worse, maybe you left your check on your desk."

Jason had left his check on his desk. "You know me pretty well," Jason admitted, feeling somewhat embarrassed. "My check is on my desk. Do you think it is safe?"

"That depends. Is that Neanderthal Tim or any of his friends still around?" Samantha asked.

"No, they all went out for lunch just before I did," Jason replied.

Samantha thought about asking why Jason didn't go along with them, but she stopped herself. She hoped she knew the answer.

"How do you get direct deposit?" Jason asked Samantha.

"You just sign up with Human Resources. They have a form that they will send to your bank for you. You just need to give them a voided check."

"Oh, I remember. Human Resources asked me that the first day, but I didn't have a check with me. I wasn't sure what they wanted it for."

"The voided check just gives the payroll department your account number and the bank number, and then your paychecks are automatically deposited electronically instead of printing you a check."

"How do you know how much you got paid?" Jason asked.

"You still get a statement telling your gross pay, the deductions, and the net amount that was deposited in your account," Samantha answered. "I received my statement this morning."

"I was just trying to figure out my statement before lunch," Jason confessed. He realized he always looked stupid, but Samantha didn't seem to mind. In fact, she seemed to enjoy explaining this stuff. "Federal tax, state tax, FICA—whatever that means—and then there was county tax, Medicare, medical insurance, and a bunch of other stuff."

"FICA is the term for Social Security tax. It stands for . . . well, I guess I don't know what it stands for" Samantha confessed.

"There's a first," Jason laughed. "I thought you knew everything about money."

"I'll have to look that one up. I have my statement with me; maybe it tells on that." Samantha pulled out the statement from her purse. Jason looked away so not to appear nosy. "No, it doesn't say. Do you want to go through the other deductions?"

"Sure," said Jason.

"Okay, we have federal tax, state tax, county tax, and city tax," listed Samantha.

"Boy, everyone wants a piece of my money," Jason complained.

"Your government at work," Samantha responded. "Together, these taxes are about 30% of your gross pay. And then FICA takes another 8%, which is really just like another tax."

"You know Samantha, I hear a lot about Social Security in the news. If they're taking 8% of everyone's salary, you would think we have enough money for all the retirees," Jason stated.

"Actually, they only take 8% up to a certain salary amount, so it doesn't work out to be 8% of total earnings. On the other hand, employers match the 8% contribution, so the government ends up getting well over 10-15% of peoples' total earnings for the program," Samantha gave the rough calculation.

"I wonder if Social Security will be there when we reach the magic age?" Jason asked. "It will be just our luck that they will change the program and we will be out in the cold."

"Jason, things may change but I seriously doubt they will get rid of the program," said Samantha. "There are definitely some problems, however. In the past, there was something like 30 people working to support one retiree. Now it's more like 10 to 1, and when we retire it might only be 5 to 1, or maybe even less. Taking 10-15% or so of people's earnings might not be enough."

"Well, I don't want to pay more in taxes. After seeing my first paycheck shrink to practically nothing, I don't think I can afford more taxes. Maybe the company contribution should be increased," Jason suggested.

"Some people want to do that. That makes it more expensive for companies to hire workers, however, so they will either have to hire fewer workers or pay them less. It's more likely they will raise the retirement age, which they have been gradually doing, or they will means test Social Security."

"What does 'means test' mean?" Jason asked quizzically.

"That means only the lower income people will get Social Security. If you have means, or a lot of money, you will get less or maybe even no Social Security payments. Since we have good jobs, we will probably end up in the wealthier category when we retire, so we might not get much, if any, in Social Security.

"I truly hope you are not seriously planning your retirement around Social Security, Jason," said Samantha. "Even if it is in place, as we know it today, it will likely not keep us much above the poverty level. We need to begin now with our own managed retirement program," Samantha explained. "In addition to Social Security, we should be allocating part of our pay to savings programs. These programs may include IRAs–Investment Retirement Accounts–an employee-sponsored 401(k) program, or maybe independent savings in the form of money market accounts or securities investments."

"You know, I saw 401(k) on my pay statement, but it didn't have any deductions by it," Jason said.

"We did get sidetracked on this Social Security. Let's finish going through the pay statement, and then we can talk about 401(k)s. Besides taxes and FICA, there is Medicare and unemployment insurance. Medicare pays into a fund for health insurance for senior citizens similar to how Social Security provides retirement benefits. Unemployment insurance pays into a fund to pay unemployment benefits for people who lose their jobs."

"Do I have a choice in paying into any of these things?" Jason asked.

"I'm afraid not. But next we will get into some of the deductions where you have a choice," Samantha answered. "But I think we will need to finish this discussion tonight. I need to get back to work."

"That's right. You need to pay your federal taxes, state taxes, FICA, and on and on," Jason said despondently.

"You're right, Jason. Did you know the average person has to work from January to sometime in May just to pay all of the taxes? In fact, there is a group that has a tax freedom day every year on the day that you have finally paid all the taxes for the year."

"I think I saw that on the news once. What time are you picking me up tonight?" Jason asked, changing the subject abruptly.

"How about 6:30?" said Samantha.

"That's good for me. Do you like *Damon's*?" Jason asked.

"Yes, that would be great. I haven't been there for a while. See you tonight," Samantha said as she hurried back to work.

"That Samantha sure is impressive," thought Jason as he walked back to his cubicle. Even though they were seeing a lot of each other, somehow the conversation was always about business. It's like Samantha had a burning desire to cover all the topics in an introductory economics course in her conversations with him.

"Samantha is different from most of the girls at Bloomington University," Jason continued his thoughts. "She is smart, articulate and always seems to be on top of everything." Then he remembered he had better retrieve his check off his desk before one of the Neanderthals got back.

Samantha picked up Jason at 6:30 sharp. Before Jason could get out the door, Tim was on the phone broadcasting to his friends how Samantha was picking up Jason for a date. Jason knew he was going to have a rough Monday with the guys at work. Maybe he could distract them by showing off his new Mustang.

"So how bad was it?" Samantha asked as Jason got into the car.

"What do you mean?" Jason asked. "How bad was what?"

"Tim."

"Oh, that. He's on the phone already," Jason responded, understanding the question.

"I figured that. Maybe this was a bad idea, me driving," Samantha said.

"There's still time. There's my car," Jason pointed across the parking lot.

"On second thought, it's lucky that I'm driving. What time does your Uncle come with your new car?" Samantha asked.

"Sometime in the afternoon," said Jason. "Do you want me to call you when he gets here? Uncle Mitchell said he would like to see you again."

"Sure, I'll make sure I'm home." Within minutes they arrived at *Damon's* and went inside.

"Do you want to sit at the Sport's Bar?" Samantha asked.

"Sure," said Jason. "She is certainly full of surprises," he thought. Jason wondered if Samantha suggested the Sport's Bar because he would like it or because she was interested in sports. With all this talk about economics, he wasn't sure about Samantha's other interests.

"Are we going to watch baseball or talk savings programs tonight?" Samantha asked.

"I am ready for my savings lesson, Samantha. You left me hanging there at lunch. Should I take notes?" Jason asked with a smile.

"You need to get serious on this one," Samantha said. "This is important and critical to your future."

"Now I know how Tim feels," Jason thought. "I'd better watch my mouth. Samantha tends to be a little sensitive about this condescending attitude-stuff."

"Sorry about that," replied Jason. "I'm ready to get serious."

"Before we get into the savings options there are a couple of other pay issues we should review," explained Samantha. "First there is the issue of insurance. Now insurance has two major pieces, one is life insurance and the other is health and accident insurance."

"I know I should be bored," Jason thought, "but Samantha sure is cute when she talks economics." He tried to focus on the lecture in case there was a test at the end.

"Our company provides each new employee at our level $20,000 worth of term life insurance at their expense. We are offered the option to double that amount to $40,000. We are responsible for the premium cost for the second $20,000. For people like us, unmarried and no children, $20,000 is probably the right option at this point," Samantha explained.

"Marriage . . . children . . . Is there a message here?" thought Jason defensively. He'd better pay really close attention. He didn't know this economics lesson was going to start getting so personal.

Samantha continued, "Notice I said the company provides 'term' life insurance. That is in contrast to 'whole life' or what some call a 'savings insurance policy'. In general, however, we should buy life insurance to provide a death benefit. Insurance is usually a poor program for investment, so term insurance is the way to go."

"Which is what we have," Jason said, just to show that he was paying attention.

"The second insurance deduction from our pay is health and accident coverage. The company provides basic coverage for all employees. They offer an option to upgrade the coverage at employee expense. Upgrades may include smaller deductibles and coverage for spouses and other family members."

"Oops, there she goes again talking about children and families," mused Jason. "It pays to be alert," he thought. The waitress came to take their order. Samantha knew exactly what she wanted without looking at the menu. Jason quickly looked over the menu and made his selection. "Great ribs here, don't you think?" Jason said, trying to break the moment.

"Sure, the food is always good here, but let's focus on the savings issues," said Samantha, looking rather serious.

"Boy, once she gets set on something, she is not easily dissuaded," Jason thought. "But that can be a good characteristic, as long as she is on your side."

"There are several pieces to savings," Samantha said. "Your savings plan should include Social Security, Money Market Accounts or Personal Savings, 401(k) Programs, and IRA Accounts."

"Do you practice this stuff, or does it just come out naturally?" Jason asked rather strongly. He immediately realized that he had made a mistake. Fortunately, Samantha continued without commenting on what he said.

"We have already discussed Social Security to some extent. The program is contributory, that is an employee and the company each makes a similar contribution to the government every payday. The theory behind the Social Security Trust Fund is that the current program receipts should be enough to subsidize those who have reached retirement age. The problem today is that people are living longer than earlier expected, thus increasing the number of people who have earned an entitlement. This could cause a serious negative drain on Social Security reserves in the future."

Jason interrupted, "That is just what I was saying earlier at lunch. The media has me convinced that when I reach retirement age, the fund will be bankrupt!"

"Well," said Samantha, "that is a problem. There are some in government that believe we should privatize Social Security to some extent. The thinking is that some fraction of the money that people contribute to the program should be invested in the securities market. The proponents argue that the Social Security Trust Fund can thereby take advantage of the good economy and the success in today's investments. The disadvantage, the opponents argue, is that current successes can't go on forever. Investing in the securities market involves too much risk some believe. Which is right depends on where you stand on the issue of continued business and investment success. For now, don't expect any changes soon."

"Hey, Samantha, I heard that Social Security provides a burial benefit," said Jason, trying to dig out of his previous comments by showing he knew something (pun intended). "I guess that means any life insurance is double coverage, right?"

"Jason, do you know what the death benefit is?" asked Samantha. "The benefit is a mere $225. Now just what will that buy in today's market?"

"Is that all?" asked Jason. Obviously his effort to add to the conversation was not too successful.

"That's it and it doesn't look like that will change any time soon," said Samantha.

"Hmm," said Jason, "I wonder how many people realize the benefit is so small."

"Okay, Jason, now let's move on to personal savings or money market accounts," Samantha suggested. "I recommend money market accounts rather than a passbook savings account because interest rates are generally better with the money market account and you have no loss of liquidity. You do understand liquidity, don't you, Jason?"

Jason wasn't sure that he was enjoying this date. It was helpful information, but Samantha sure seemed to be in a bad mood. "Sure," said Jason. "Liquidity means that the money is available whenever you want it."

"Great answer," said Samantha. "I personally believe anyone who wishes to save should start with a money market account," said Samantha. "Conventional thinking suggests that we should always maintain the equivalent of six- to nine-months take home pay in a very liquid asset such as a money market account. If, for some reason, we should leave *Switches.com* the money market cushion helps finance living expenses while we search for a new position."

"Yeah, and it would be great for those little things not in the budget!" exclaimed Jason.

"Wrong!" counseled Samantha. "First you must learn the discipline to put the money away and then practice the discipline to leave it alone."

"This date is going downhill quickly," Jason thought.

"Now how am I going to establish such a nest egg quickly?" asked Jason. "With what I have left over after expenses, it will take years to do."

"It's really easy," said Samantha. "What you do is pay yourself first *every* payday."

"Samantha, sometimes you speak in riddles just to pull my chain. Pay myself first?" questioned Jason.

"There is no riddle here and in fact, it is very easy," said Samantha. "It does take discipline and maybe a little sacrifice, but you must do it. Have you deposited your paycheck yet?"

"Nope, got it right here," said Jason, patting his wallet.

"Good," said Samantha. "At least it's not sitting on your desk," she said a little friendlier. "I suggest you do the following when the banks open tomorrow morning. Go to your bank and see the customer service representative. Tell whoever helps you that you want to open a money market account. Endorse your check and tell the representative to put 25% in the money market account and 75% in your checking account."

"Now I know you've flipped out!" Jason exclaimed. "How can I survive on 75% of my paycheck?"

"Relax," said Samantha. "How much money did it cost you to live before you signed on with *Switches.com*? A good bit less than 75% of that check in your pocket, I'll wager."

"Well, you're right about that," said Jason, "But I wanted to live better than a starving college student does now that I've got a real job."

"Look at the numbers, Jason. You can make it work, I just know it," said Samantha. To Samantha this was a crucial conversation. She was developing more than a passing interest in Jason, and it was important to her that he demonstrated some financial discipline.

"Now," continued Samantha, "I'm not finished. Next payday your check will be direct deposited, right?"

"Sure, you've convinced me of that," said Jason. "I'll set it up with Human Resources."

"Now then, tell your bank representative that in two weeks your check will be direct deposited," said Samantha. "Further tell the representative to automatically transfer 25% of whatever is received to the money market account every payday. This way you will never see the 25% share show up in your checking account. It's called 'pay yourself first' and it works. You will be surprised how quickly the rainy day fund grows."

"So my money is gone into some black hole," said Jason.

"No, of course not," said Samantha. "Now who is pulling whose chain? You will be offered checks for the money market account and you can draw on it just like a regular checking account. But you won't do that, will you? You will let it grow, right?"

"Sure, sure," said Jason. "I do see the wisdom of the rainy day fund. I just don't like putting aside so much of my meager paycheck. But don't worry, I will do it." It wasn't a pleasant conversation, but deep down Jason knew that Samantha was right. It's lucky he had her to do the planning for him.

Just then, the waiter brought their food to the table. Jason had ordered the full rack of ribs and Samantha got the smaller portion. "Samantha really does have it together," Jason thought. He hoped he did not appear too spacey or ignorant about what must be simple economic concepts.

"Jason, aren't you going to eat?" Samantha said in a loud voice.

"Sorry," said Jason. "I was just thinking about what you said. Let's eat." She has it together, but she also is a bit pushy. "Tim isn't totally wrong," Jason thought.

"Are you ready for the 401(k) pitch," asked Samantha?

"Sure," said Jason, "but I read in the company new employee handout that it is necessary to work for *Switches.com* for a full year before we are eligible for the 401(k)."

"There is hope," thought Samantha. "You are right about that, Jason," said Samantha. That happens to be the case with many companies. It does make sense to talk about it so we are prepared, however. *Switches.com* will ask us to buy into their program as the 12-month waiting period winds down. We can authorize the company to take up to 15% of our pay and invest it in a 401(k) program for us."

"I am not sure I want anyone to take 15% more of my money. I already have given up 25% to the money market account," lamented Jason.

"I said up to 15%," Samantha responded. "You can declare less but I plan to invest the full 15%. The reason I will is that the company will make a companion investment in my 401(k) based on company earnings. Things are going good right now so I expect the maximum, which is 6%. But you are required to contribute the maximum level, 15%, to get the maximum company match of 6%. A smaller investment reduces the company share proportionately."

"Hey," said Jason. "If I put 15% in a 401(k) and the company makes a matching contribution, I can stop the 25% investment in the money market account."

"Whoa," said Samantha. "Nice try, but we are talking about two different programs. The money market account is the six to nine-month safety net or rainy day fund; the 401(k) is an investment, an investment towards your retirement. There is also another very important difference. Your 401(k) contribution is taken out before taxes and deduction. There are no taxes on this contribution when you take it. A 401(k) account has very specific and restrictive withdrawal rules also. Withdrawals are usually reserved for medical emergencies, children's education, and buying a home. Remember also, any withdrawal is subject to immediate tax and possibly withdrawal penalties."

"Not so good," said Jason. "I guess most people leave it alone. But what happens if I leave *Switches.com*? Do they keep my money or do they give it to me?"

"Well, let's assume you are vested," said Samantha. "Vesting, by the way, means that you have been in the 401(k) program for a specific term, usually five years. Once vested, then all your contributions and the company match are yours to take with you. If you are not fully vested, then you are entitled to only a fraction of the company match. Your contributions and any earnings from your contributions are yours, of course."

"Boy, that will really generate a tax bite if I switch jobs and have to take the money out of the account," said Jason.

"Not really," explained Samantha. "If you switch jobs, you take your 401(k) and 'roll it over' to an IRA at a bank or another financial institution. You can make a rollover with no tax liability. There will be no more contributions as a result of employment at *Switches.com*, however, the money will continue to grow from the investment earnings."

"And, after a waiting period, I can start a new 401(k) at my new employer," said Jason.

"Absolutely, provided the new employer offers such a program," replied Samantha. "Are the ribs making you smarter?" Jason started to understand why a condescending attitude was a little irritating now that he was on the receiving end.

"Lighten up," said Jason, mildly irritated. "Is my 401(k) at *Switches.com* the same as an IRA?"

"Yes and no," said Samantha. "While you might say that a 401(k) investment is a contribution toward retirement, it is really not an IRA by definition. The tax law created IRAs to encourage consumer saving. In some respects it can be a hedge against a failure of the Social Security system. But let's leave that alone. Now there are two IRA tools, the traditional IRA and what is called a Roth IRA, named after the Senator who sponsored its creation in 1998. The difference between the two is tax treatment. For a traditional IRA you contribute 'before-tax' dollars and with the Roth IRA you contribute 'after-tax' dollars. With the traditional variety, you pay the tax on the contribution and any earnings at withdrawal, which, by law, is sometime after age 59 ½. With Roth, since you used "after-tax" dollars, all withdrawals are tax-free. Such a withdrawal must come after age 59 ½ just like the traditional IRA."

"Sounds like we are back to the 401(k) to me," said Jason.

"Stay with me on this," said Samantha. "What we are talking about is different from a 401(k). You may contribute up to $2,000 per year to an IRA. Most people select the full $2,000 level, by the way."

"Yeah, that's because they are rich," said Jason.

"No, it's not," said Samantha. "Let's go back to your paycheck again. Remember, 25% to a money market account, 75% to checking. Now, the day before every payday, look at your checkbook balance. No matter how much is there; transfer the entire balance to an IRA account. Essentially, you take yourself to zero because tomorrow you start all over again with a new paycheck. You know, it only takes less than $40 per week to fully fund a $2,000 annual IRA."

"What IRA account? I don't have one. And, if I transfer my checking account balance, I am automatically in a Roth IRA because my checking account is "after-tax" dollars," sighed Jason.

"You catch on fast, Jason. I'm impressed," said Samantha, paying Jason a genuine compliment. "Most investment companies will be happy to set up an IRA for you. They can also advise you on the pluses and minuses of the traditional IRA and the Roth IRA. If you select the traditional IRA, then you will claim a tax credit on your income tax return at the end of the year. That moves the contribution back to 'before-tax' dollars. If you select the Roth, no further action is necessary. It may sound confusing, but it is really simple when you think about it.

"There is a further benefit with an IRA. That is, you can direct how you want your annual contribution invested each year," said Samantha. "Remember way back when we were talking housing?"

"Yeah," said Jason. "You're buying a house and I rent an apartment."

"Remember when Tim was talking about the S&P 500 and what a great return the S&P 500 index mutual funds have provided in the recent years," Samantha said. "Well, he was right about that. An index fund might be a good place to invest your IRA today. There is the story told of an investor that put $2,000 in an S&P 500 index fund every year for 10 years beginning with 1963. After 10 years, he just left it alone. In 1999, that investment, $20,000, had grown to a whopping $876,000. Now, it doesn't take rocket science to realize how easy that was. We know that there are no guarantees but history has shown that the U.S. economy will grow over time."

"Wow, this is a bunch of information you have given me on savings plans. Let me see if I have the whole picture," said Jason. "*Switches.com* will automatically transmit my paycheck to my bank every payday. From that check, I will make a contribution, whether I like it or not, to the Social Security Trust Fund, a contribution that is matched by the company. That's savings program number one. Number two; I ask my bank to make a 25% contribution from my paycheck to a money market account in my name. The intent is to create a six- to nine-month rainy day fund."

"You are on track," said Samantha.

"Hey, I'm on a roll here," said Jason. "Now, number three, I check my bank balance the day before every payday and whatever the balance is, I transfer all of it to an IRA hoping to hit the $2,000 cap each year. Finally, as soon as *Switches.com* will permit, I enroll in a company-sponsored 401(k) program where I choose a 15% contribution with 'before-tax' dollars. The company, based on profitability and performance, may add as much as 6% to that account in matching funds. And, if I leave *Switches.com* at some point, I can 'rollover' my 401(k) to a bank-sponsored program and not suffer a tax liability. It sure looks like I will be invested to the hilt. I hope there is enough left to pay for tonight's ribs."

"Jason, you've got it," said Samantha, again genuinely impressed that he had retained all this information in such a short time. "Now, the question is: Do you have the discipline to do it?"

"Well," Jason said, "with you as my counselor and advisor, how can I go wrong?" The mood was definitely warming up a bit. There was a short argument over paying for dinner, but Jason pointed out that Samantha had driven and given him a lot of free advice, so Jason picked up the check.

As they got up from the table and made their way to the parking lot Jason began to work up the courage to ask Samantha about what to do next. He was debating asking whether she would like to see an outdoor concert downtown, or maybe the new Star Wars movie or even Mr. and Mrs. Cruise in *Eyes Wide Shut*. The concert is outside and it might rain. Maybe she will think I'm childish if I suggest *The Phantom Menace* and I might blow it all on *Eyes Wide Shut*!

"Do you want to come back to my place?" Samantha asked.

"Sure," said Jason, relieved that his dilemma was resolved.

"Good," said Samantha, "I have some investment books I would like to give you."

"So much for a romantic evening," Jason thought. "It's going to be difficult to get her to talk about anything other than economics."

Key Economic Terms – Chapter 7

Payroll deductions
Federal tax
State tax
County tax
Local tax
FICA
401(k)
Medicare
Medical insurance
Gross pay
Net pay
Social Security
Means testing
Individual Retirement Accounts (IRAs)
Money market accounts
Security investments

Unemployment insurance
Tax Freedom Day
Term life insurance
Whole life insurance
Health and accident coverage
Social Security Trust Fund
Burial benefits
Liquidity
Pay yourself first
Matching contributions
Vesting
Withdrawal penalties
Before-tax savings
After-tax savings
Traditional IRA
Roth IRA

Chapter 8
Politics: The Conservatives versus Liberals Chapter

"You've got to be kidding!" Tim laughed as Jason came in the door. Jason had walked in carrying five investment books. "Pretty hot date you had there."

"Give me a break," Jason responded. "At least I wasn't sitting home watching 'Dinner and a Movie' by myself."

"Hey, this movie is a lot more interesting than those books that you have," Tim defended himself. "What are all those books, anyway?"

"Investment books. Samantha was telling me about savings plans during dinner," Jason said sheepishly.

"She never lets up, does she?" Tim laughed. "So what did she tell you?"

"Actually, it was pretty good advice. What kind of savings plan do you have?" Jason asked.

"Oh, you know, the standard: money market account, IRA, that sort of thing," Tim answered. "I'm going to sign up for a 401(k) plan as soon as I can."

"Am I the only one who's out of it?" Jason asked. "I hadn't even started to think about any of those things yet."

"Me neither. Actually, Samantha called me while you were looking over her books at her apartment and told me to tell you that. Pretty good trick, huh? You should have seen your face just now."

"I never imagined that you and Samantha would be conspiring against me," Jason said with surprise.

"Hey, her idea, not mine," Tim said. "But it was a pretty good one. Did she tell you about what happened this afternoon at work?"

"No, we spent the whole night talking economics. What happened?" Jason asked.

"They announced they were restructuring the customer service department. I thought Samantha might have mentioned it to you, because a lot of people are worried about what is going to happen. Especially since she has only been there one week," Tim explained.

"Gee, I feel like a jerk. I never even thought to ask her how she was doing. She always seems to be in total control, I never think to ask. Come to think of it, she was a little edgy tonight."

"That might be why," Tim said with surprising compassion. "I'm sure it will turn out okay. The company is growing so fast, there are always plenty of good opportunities."

"I guess that's right," Jason said. He got a quick snack in the kitchen and went to bed, leaving Tim watching *Fast Times at Ridgemont High* and learning how to make some chicken dish.

The phone woke Jason the next morning. It was 6:30 a.m. Jason had a pretty good idea who it was.

"Jason, my boy. Up and at 'em'!"

"Hi, Uncle Mitchell," Jason said sleepily.

"Hot date last night?" Uncle Mitchell asked.

"Kind of. Well, not really. Heck, I don't know."

"You were out with Samantha, weren't you?" Uncle Mitchell guessed.

"Yes. How did you know?" Jason asked.

"That just sounded like the description of a Samantha date," Uncle Mitchell explained.

Jason wasn't sure how to take that. His brain wasn't quite working yet. "What time are you coming today?"

"I'll be there with a black Mustang at 2 p.m. I just wanted to tell you that I will need a ride back home," Uncle Mitchell added.

"No problem. That will give me a chance to test the Mustang on the country roads. How long does it usually take you to get to Indianapolis? One hour? I bet I can get you back in 40 minutes," Jason said, trying to get a reaction.

"Don't even think about it! This car has my dealership name on the back. I don't want any bad publicity," Uncle Mitchell said.

"I didn't know I was advertising for you too." Jason was waking up enough to be a smart aleck.

"With the deal I'm giving you, you should be grateful," Uncle Mitchell responded.

"That reminds me. How much will this car cost? Samantha has already put most of my money away into savings plans. I don't know if I can afford this car anymore," Jason said.

"I can't wait to hear about this. Samantha is teaching you a little responsibility, huh? She is more of a woman than I thought if she can do that. Am I going to see her this afternoon?" Uncle Mitchell asked.

"Yes, she is waiting for me to call to tell her what time you will arrive," Jason said.

"Well you can call her and tell her 2 p.m. I'm always right on time," Uncle Mitchell said proudly.

"I don't think I'll call her now. It's 6:30 in the morning," Jason said.

"I'm sure she's up. She's not lazy like you. I'll see you at 2." Uncle Mitchell hung up.

"Maybe I should call," Jason thought. "I'm awake now anyway, and she'll be impressed that I am awake. Plus I can ask her about her job." He dialed her number.

"Hello." The phone was answered immediately with a cheerful voice.

"Hi, Samantha. It's Jason."

"Hi, Jason. You're up early today."

"I usually get up early," Jason lied. "I just wanted to let you know that Uncle Mitchell is coming at 2 p.m. today."

"And he just called you and woke you up?" Samantha said with a laugh.

"Man, I can't get anything by on you," Jason confessed.

"You shouldn't even try," Samantha said confidently.

"Pretty good trick you played on me with Tim," Jason said. "When did you two become friends?"

"I wouldn't call it friends . . . maybe partners in crime. I'm sorry, but I couldn't resist," Samantha apologized.

"Well, you are always full of surprises. Tim told me about the situation with the Customer Service department. I'm sorry I didn't ask you about it," Jason said.

"Yes, and I'm sorry if I was a little cranky last night. My manager told me late yesterday afternoon. When I took the job, they told me a reorganization of my department was possible. I just didn't think it would come so soon.

"I want to apologize," she said, changing the subject. "I don't think I was that nice last night," Samantha said.

"No problem," Jason said. "That's certainly understandable. And you did tell me lots of good things to do. What happens with your job now?"

"My manager said we would talk about it next week. I definitely will have a job, but I'm just not sure what department I will go to," Samantha answered.

"That's good to hear. By the way, Uncle Mitchell is anxious to see you. Why don't we pick you up in my new car around 2?"

"Sounds good. What is happening with your old car?" Samantha asked.

"I am donating it to a charity," Jason answered.

"That's nice of you," Samantha said. "Plus you get a good tax deduction."

"That's what Uncle Mitchell said. You caught me again."

"Don't forget the bank this morning, Jason."

"Right, don't worry. I'll put 25% in the money market account," Jason said.

"Great. I'll see you at 2. Bye."

"Good-bye," said Jason. And he drifted back to sleep for a few hours.

* * *

The black Mustang drove up to Samantha's apartment. Samantha was waiting outside. "Pretty nice," she said. "I didn't know it was going to be black."

"Good to see you again," Uncle Mitchell said. "I don't think you'll be ashamed to be seen in this car. Not like that last car that Jason had."

"That's for sure," Samantha agreed.

"First you and Tim gang up on me, now you and my own uncle are ganging up on me," Jason complained.

"I think you can take it," Samantha said.

"Jason tells me you are planning his financial future," Uncle Mitchell said, turning to Samantha.

"I just gave him some basic advice. I'm better at financial planning than I am at buying cars. There's the vehicle that you helped me lease," Samantha said, pointing to her green *Saturn*.

"Very nice," said Uncle Mitchell, walking over to look at the car. "I don't have *Saturns* at my dealership, but they are really nice cars. Have you tried hitting the body panels with a hammer yet? It doesn't hurt them."

"That's what the salesman told me, but I haven't gotten around to that yet!" Samantha laughed.

"I thought you were going to look at my new car," Jason said to Samantha, trying to get her attention.

"Oh, right. Sorry," Samantha apologized.

"Why don't I take you two out for something to eat and Samantha can see how it runs," Uncle Mitchell offered.

"Free food. That's just what I need for my new financial plan," Jason said enthusiastically.

"Right, and I want to hear about that financial plan too," said Uncle Mitchell.

They climbed into the Mustang and drove to the local *TCBY*. Over some frozen yogurt, Jason explained the financial plan to Uncle Mitchell, making sure he didn't omit any of the facts in front of Samantha.

"Wow, 25% of your take home pay in a money market, $2,000 a year in an IRA, and then eventually 15% of your salary in a 401(k) plan," Uncle Mitchell said, impressed with the plan. "That is a pretty responsible plan. Are you really going to do it?"

"You sound like Samantha. Of course I'm going to do it, Uncle Mitchell," Jason promised. "Otherwise, I will never hear the end of it from Samantha."

"Well, as a little added incentive, I will make your lease payments on the Mustang as long as you stick with your plan," Uncle Mitchell stated.

"You don't need to do that, Uncle Mitchell," Jason said. "I planned to pay for the car myself."

"I know, and I was going to make you pay for it. But thanks to Samantha, I'm so impressed with the new Jason that I am glad to help," Uncle Mitchell said happily. Turning to Samantha, Uncle Mitchell said, "I have spent years trying to get Jason to be responsible with his money, not to mention getting him to get rid of that clunker, with no success. And here you have done it all in just one week. You are an exceptional woman."

Samantha was embarrassed, but stammered out a thank-you.

"I'm afraid I need to ask you to drive me back now, Jason. Your aunt is waiting for me to go to some event that I don't want to go to. Why don't you come, Samantha?" Uncle Mitchell asked. "It's a nice drive, especially in a new Mustang."

"Sure," said Samantha. She wondered if Jason had set this up, or whether Uncle Mitchell was playing matchmaker. Either way, she was glad to come.

Along the way, Uncle Mitchell asked Samantha about her background. Jason listened attentively, finally glad to learn something about Samantha other than her knowledge of economics. It turned out that Samantha's parents live in a suburb of Chicago, and her dad was a commodities trader. She is an only child.

"You and Samantha have a lot in common," Uncle Mitchell said after Samantha had finished.

"What do you mean?" Samantha asked, realizing that she knew very little about Jason other than he didn't know much about economics but he did know computers.

"Didn't Jason tell you his father is an investment banker in New York?" Uncle Mitchell said.

"You're kidding!" Samantha said.

"Be careful now," Jason said. "I know what you are thinking."

"What is she thinking?" Uncle Mitchell asked Jason.

"She's thinking that if my dad is an investment banker, why don't I know more about money," Jason said.

"Pretty close," Samantha agreed, "but I would have put it a little nicer."

"I doubt it," said Jason. "My father didn't talk much about work at home, although he and Mom had lots of arguments about politics. He was very conservative, and she was, as he put it, a bleeding heart liberal."

"That must have been interesting," said Samantha. "How did you turn out?"

"Probably more like my dad," Jason said.

"I like to think I had something to do with that," Uncle Mitchell said. "Jason's dad is my brother, and the whole family is pretty conservative. Jason has lived with me and my wife since high school."

"My parents moved to New York City during my sophomore year," Jason explained. "I didn't want to change schools, so I lived with Uncle Mitchell my last two-and-a-half years of high school."

"It was worth it to get him away from that bad liberal influence of my sister-in-law," Uncle Mitchell said with a smile.

"I think I had better be careful in this car," said Samantha. "You might find me a bit too liberal and throw me out."

"With that savings plan you put together for Jason, I find that hard to believe," said Uncle Mitchell. "That plan had self-reliance written all over it."

"Well, I believe in being self-reliant, but I also feel like we need to help people who are less fortunate."

"The best way to help less fortunate people is for them to get a job," said Uncle Mitchell. "If you give people handouts, they never learn to have initiative."

"Didn't your economics professor give you something to solve this problem?" Uncle Mitchell asked.

"Actually, just the opposite," Samantha said. "He taught us that economics can't tell you the best way to distribute goods or services to people. That is more of a political or moral decision. Take the minimum wage, for example. Economic theory tells us that raising the minimum wage will put some people out of a job. Employers will find it too expensive to hire some of the marginal workers. On the other hand, the people working for minimum wage who keep their jobs will make more money. Which is best? Economics can't really answer that question. Economics can just predict that fewer people will have jobs, but the people that have jobs will make more money."

"Sort of like the situation of free trade," Jason said, remembering the conversation about the *Honda*. "Under free trade, consumers will be better off, but some producers win and others lose."

"Samantha, you may be a liberal, but your results with Jason continue to amaze me," Uncle Mitchell said. "I never would have expected a sentence like that to come out of his mouth."

"Give me a break," Jason said, "I'm not that bad."

"Yes you are," Samantha and Uncle Mitchell said almost in unison.

"Well, I am certainly getting better quickly," Jason defended himself.

"Thanks to Samantha," Uncle Mitchell said quickly. "Although I think I need to probe these political views a bit more closely to see if I will permit you to hang around my nephew. Drive slower," Uncle Mitchell commanded Jason, "I might need more time."

"So on the minimum wage," Uncle Mitchell continued, "why does the government need to set a minimum wage? Why don't we just let the wage rate be established by the market?"

"In most jobs it is," Samantha said, knowing that Uncle Mitchell already knew this. "But what about for the jobs that don't require many skills? It would be very easy for an employer to exploit people. If people are desperate for a job, they will work for almost anything. A minimum wage just makes sure they can afford to live."

"That may have been true in the past, but it's hard to get people to work for wages even well above minimum wage now. I should know. I can't get anyone to wash cars for less than $7 an hour at my dealership. Except Jason, of course," Uncle Mitchell added.

"Those days are gone," Jason said. "I am a high-tech employee now with my own money market account and IRA."

"That's because the minimum wage has not been raised in so long," continuing the conversation with Uncle Mitchell. "It is hardly a useful number anymore, because even low-skill people are paid well above minimum wage," Samantha said.

"And that's the way it should be," Uncle Mitchell responded. "We need to keep that minimum wage so low it cannot distort the workings of a free market.

"Okay, what about tax cuts?" Uncle Mitchell continued. "How did you like your first paycheck? A little less than you expected?"

"It was sure a lot less than I expected," Jason answered. "And even you were talking about how tax freedom day is not until May, Samantha."

"What do you kids talk about all the time?" Uncle Mitchell asked. "I have never heard Jason talk about these things."

"Actually, we have been talking a lot about economics," Samantha admitted. "My fault. But to answer your question, I don't think I am overtaxed. I make a good living, and I don't mind giving some of my money in taxes to help other people."

"First of all," Uncle Mitchell responded, "the reason you make a good living is because you worked for it. You went to college, worked hard, and got a good job. Second, you are not 'giving some of your money to help others.' That would be called charity, which is fine. Taxes is where they take your money whether you like it or not, and then spend the money on things that you might not agree with." Uncle Mitchell was getting a little worked up.

"That is true," Samantha skillfully defused the situation. "But our society has some common interests that we need to fund–education, for example. Some people don't have any kids and would never want to contribute to education. But having a strong educational system helps keep our society well educated, productive, and strong."

"That's a nice theory, but it usually doesn't work that way," Uncle Mitchell continued, a little calmer. "Unfortunately, we've taken away any incentives to reward good public schools or good teachers. If the students are not learning, we just throw more money at the problem. We need to have some competition in the public schools, like allowing people to have vouchers so they can decide where their kids should go to school. The best schools will attract more students and thrive, and the bad schools will lose students and go out of business."

"You know, as I listen to you two bicker like little children," Jason said, "you really always start with the same objectives. Uncle Mitchell is not arguing that people should not earn a livable wage, or that we shouldn't have good public schools. It's more on your method of accomplishing that goal. Uncle Mitchell wants the free market to set the working wage for people, and based on supply and demand, it will find a proper rate. Samantha wants the government to set the wage. In education, you both want good schools. Uncle Mitchell would like to see some competitive forces to force bad schools to go out of business or maybe improve to be more competitive, but he is still willing to use tax money on public education."

"Now he has turned into a peace-maker as well," Uncle Mitchell said. "But I guess he's right. Many of the arguments between liberals and conservatives cannot be solved by economics, just like you said, Samantha. And many of the arguments are more about methods than end objectives. A liberal wants to solve problems through a more active role by the government, and a conservative wants to solve problems through a more active role by the free market."

"I think I can agree with that," said Samantha. "My economics professor once said something that made a lot of sense to me. If we have an extra dollar to give to someone, it will make a bigger difference to a poor person than to a rich person. The rich person wouldn't even notice the extra dollar, but it could buy food for the poor person. On the other hand, if we keep giving people extra dollars all the time, they will have less incentive to work. So it's a trade-off between getting the money to people who can benefit the most and not destroying people's incentive to work."

"That's a pretty good summary," Uncle Mitchell conceded.

"And just in time," Jason said, "because here is Uncle Mitchell's house."

"Nice seeing you again, Samantha," Uncle Mitchell said as he got out of the car, "even though it was touch and go on that minimum wage question. And drive this car carefully," Uncle Mitchell said to Jason. "No showing off for Samantha."

"I promise," said Jason, a little embarrassed. "And I'll send you my bank statements to prove I am keeping up my end of the bargain for the car," Jason said to Uncle Mitchell.

"Bye," called Samantha as they drove away.

"A free Mustang," Samantha said to Jason. "You are better with money than I thought. I am paying almost $200 a month for my poor little *Saturn*."

"I owe it to you," Jason said gratefully. "What Uncle Mitchell said is right; you have made me much more responsible in only one week. But do you think we will ever talk about anything more than economics?"

"I doubt it," said Samantha seriously. "What could be more interesting than economics? By the way, I'm going to look at my three final houses tomorrow afternoon. Do you want to come look at them with me?"

"Absolutely. I'm sure I will learn something. Can I drive?" Jason asked.

"You can drive to the realtor's office. Then she drives from there. Can you pick me up at one?" Samantha asked.

"I'll see you then," Jason replied eagerly.

Key Economic Terms – Chapter 8

Charity tax deduction	Tax cuts
Liberal	Incentives
Conservative	Competition
Minimum wage	Vouchers
	Livable wage

Chapter 9
Samantha Buys a House: The Real Estate Chapter

Jason picked up Samantha at 1 p.m. in his new Mustang. Samantha directed him to the realtor's office.

"Now, remember," Samantha told Jason, "be careful what you say to the realtor. Her name is Jane Rizzo."

"Why's that? Isn't she just going to show you the houses?" Jason asked, confused.

"Actually, a realtor is usually working for the seller. If we say anything about what we are willing to pay for a house, she is obligated to use this information to get the best deal for her client," Samantha explained.

"But aren't you the client?" Jason asked.

"No, that is what it seems like, because the realtor is taking us around and generally being helpful. But in truth, most times the realtor is working for the seller, and people tend to forget that."

"So we don't mention money?" Jason asked, trying to understand the ground rules.

"Right, or even which house we like best," Samantha added.

"Okay, I can tell I am going to learn a lot on this trip. How many houses are we looking at?" Jason asked.

"The three finalists," Samantha answered. "I have already worked out the numbers on my spreadsheet including lot size, square footage of the house, number of bathrooms, and so forth."

"So now you are going to decide which house you like the best?" Jason asked, trying to understand the objective.

"Not exactly. I plan to come up with my negotiating strategy," said Samantha.

Just then they drove up to the realtor's office. The conversation was interrupted as Jason met Jane Rizzo.

"So," Jane said cheerfully, "Are we going to buy a house today?"

"Maybe," said Samantha. "At least I am going to make an offer."

"Well, just so you know, most houses are going for their full asking price now. You have chosen some very hot areas," Jane said.

"What does that mean?" Jason asked, thinking it was okay to ask some questions.

"When a person wants to sell a house, they meet with a realtor to decide on an asking price. All I was saying is that in the areas that Samantha has chosen, most of the houses are going for the asking price. In other areas, sometimes you can buy a house for less than the asking price," Jane explained.

After the initial discussion with Samantha, Jason was suspicious. It sounded like someone who was trying to get the highest price for the seller, just like Samantha had said. "How do you get paid?" Jason asked directly. He looked at Samantha, and she didn't seem to mind the question.

"I get paid on commission," Jane stated directly. "When a house is sold, the listing agent usually gets half of the commission and the selling agent gets the other half." From a quick glance at Jason, Jane could tell that he did not understand. "The listing agent is the person who filed the papers to offer the house for sale, and the selling agent is the person who brings in the person who buys the house."

"And how much is the commission?" Jason asked. "Or is that impolite to ask."

"Not at all," Jane said. "I am happy to explain this to you. There is usually a standard commission in most areas. Around here, a typical commission is 6% to 7% of the gross selling price."

"Not bad," said Jason. "On a $100,000 house, that's six or seven thousand dollars."

"That's true. But the commission is split in half unless you sell one of your own listings, and my broker gets a big share."

"Who's the broker?" Jason asked.

"The broker is the person who owns the agency. She has a number of agents like me, and she gets a share of our commissions."

"I see," said Jason. "It is interesting how all these things are set up."

"That's true. And here we are at the first house," Jane said.

They walked up to a new house in a new subdivision. There was no lawn yet, and there was mud everywhere. Once they got inside, the house had a nice, new smell to it.

"Just a few questions," Samantha said, pulling out a notebook and pen. "What will the property taxes be?"

"The house hasn't been assessed yet, but similar houses have annual property taxes of $1,100 per year," Jane answered professionally.

"And what is the builder doing with the landscaping?" Samantha asked.

"The builder is offering a $5,000 allowance," Jane answered, checking a file that she was carrying.

"And what school district is it?" Samantha asked.

"Why is she asking that?" Jason wondered, starting to get nervous again.

"Good question," said Jane. "This house is in the Tyler district. That is a good school system, and it will give the house good resale value."

"That makes sense," thought Jason. He knew that Samantha would be interested in resale value, even if she didn't have kids.

"And what is the current asking price?" Samantha asked.

"Good news there," said Jane. "The builder has lowered the price $5,000 to $112,000. Last time we were here, the listing price was $117,000, but the builder is anxious to sell this house so he can start another house."

"So much for everything going for the asking price," Jason thought.

Samantha took a cursory look around the house and then said that she was ready. They drove to the next house. The next house was in another new development just down the road. Jason thought all the houses in these subdivisions looked the same.

Samantha quickly walked through the house and then seemed to be especially interested in the backyard. Jane and Jason joined her as Samantha was gazing across an open field behind the house.

"The open field gives a nice, open feel, doesn't it?" Jane said.

"Right now it does," Samantha agreed. "What is that open field zoned?"

"Uh, light commercial," said Jane, "but I doubt if anyone would ever develop it."

"But they could?" Samantha probed.

"Yes, there is nothing in the zoning that would stop them," Jane answered.

"Okay," said Samantha. "I'm ready to go to the next house."

As they walked to the car, Jason asked Samantha, "What was that all about?"

"That could be a major externality," said Samantha.

"What does that mean?" Jason asked.

"An externality is an outside factor that can effect you," Samantha said, giving a textbook description. "For example, the open field right now is nice. It is a positive externality. I get the benefit of the field, even though I didn't pay for it. If someone decides to build a paint mixing factory on that field, then I would have a negative externality. I would have to look at a factory out of my back window and I may even be subjected to paint fumes."

"That doesn't sound too good," Jason said. "Couldn't you sue them or something if they wanted to build a factory there?"

"Probably not," said Samantha. "The property is zoned for light commercial, so people have the right to build anything that fits that zoning. Neighbors might try to fight it, but they might lose. It is always a good idea to check the zoning for any land around a property that you are thinking of buying."

"Why didn't Jane bring that up to you?" Jason asked. "She even tried to say the open field was a positive."

"Remember, Jane works for the seller, not me. She is obligated to disclose certain things about a property, but the buyer has to be smart enough to ask some other questions that she is not obligated to disclose."

They got to the car and drove to the next house, an older home in a mature neighborhood. When they were finished, they went back to the realtor's office.

"Which one did you like best?" Jane questioned Samantha.

"They were all fine," Samantha replied. "I think I will make my first offer on the first house that we looked at today."

"First offer?" Jason asked, forgetting he was supposed to be careful. "What do you mean?"

"I'll make an offer on the first house. If it's not accepted, then I'll make an offer on the next house," Samantha answered.

"Okay, let's write up the offer," Jane said, eager to get to business. She started filling out the standard forms while Samantha made some calculations in her notebook. Jason watched the process with great interest.

"Okay, I'm ready for a dollar value," said Jane.

"$100,000," Samantha said firmly, "with a $20,000 down payment. And I want the landscaping allowance increased to $7,000."

"I don't think they will accept $100,000," Jane advised.

"I think they should," said Samantha. "It's getting toward the end of the summer, and most of the people buying houses in that neighborhood have already done so. School is starting soon. I think $100,000 will give the builder a profit and let him start the new house."

"Samantha has done her homework," Jane thought. "What about the landscaping allowance?" Jane asked.

"I got some quotes, and to just seed the lawn and add some basic foundation plants will cost at least $7,000," Samantha answered with precision.

"Okay, I'll write it up that way, but I don't think the builder will go for it," Jane added, sounding somewhat annoyed. "Let me call him and see if he is in the office, and I can go and present it now," Jane said. She made a quick phone call, and it was clear that the builder was available.

"I'll need a check for $1,000 as earnest money. Why don't you two get something to eat, and I'll meet you back here in 45 minutes?" Jane suggested.

"That's fine," said Samantha, quickly writing a check. Jason didn't understand what was going on, but he got up and followed Samantha out of the office.

"I thought we were going to present the offer," Jason said once they got outside.

"The realtor does that," Samantha replied. "Then she will tell us what happened when we get back."

"And what is earnest money?" Jason asked.

"That is just a check to show that we are making a serious offer," Samantha replied.

They got in the car and drove to the frozen custard stand where they first met. "I hope I didn't mess up your negotiating back there, asking about what you meant by first offer," Jason apologized.

"Not at all," Samantha said. "You actually helped. Now Jane will tell the builder if he doesn't accept my offer, I will bid on another house. That worked out to be a perfect strategy."

Jason smiled, happy that he had done something right. They drove up to the custard stand, got their food, and sat down on a picnic table.

"Why did you have to put so much money down?" Jason asked.

"A couple reasons," Samantha answered. "First, I had to make sure my monthly payment was within my budget. My lender uses a pretty standard formula that states my monthly mortgage payment plus housing expenses like property taxes and home insurance cannot be greater than 28% of my monthly gross income. Furthermore, the lender checks to make sure my total debt payments are not greater than 36% of my monthly gross income. They pre-approved the amount for my mortgage based on these calculations."

"Actually a little more than that. But I didn't want the realtor to know that," Samantha said secretively.

"Or it might have hurt your negotiating position," Jason observed.

"Exactly," said Samantha. "The second factor I considered when deciding on my down payment was to make sure it was large enough so I didn't have to buy Private Mortgage Insurance, or PMI."

"What is PMI?" Jason asked.

"Usually if you put less than 10% down, you have to buy insurance in case you default on the mortgage. The insurance protects the lender, but the person getting the mortgage has to pay the premium."

"That doesn't seem very good," Jason said.

"It's not," agreed Samantha. "It is best to put down enough money so you don't have to purchase PMI."

"One other thing," Jason asked. "What is a landscape allowance?"

"With new homes it is typical for builders to offer an allowance for things like landscaping or light fixtures. They pay the allowance, and anything above that you pay out of your own pocket."

"So it's like real money," said Jason.

"Right," Samantha agreed. "Some people think they are getting a good deal for a house, but once they start overrunning all their allowances, they end up paying a lot more than they expected."

They talked a little more about Samantha's job dilemma and Jason's new car before heading back to the realtor's office. Jane was already waiting for them.

"It went much better than I expected," Jane said. "I thought he might throw me out of the office when I showed him the $100,000 offer. Here is his counteroffer, and it's actually very generous."

"I bet," thought Jason, now understanding how the game was played.

"He will accept $100,000 if we can close within 30 days. Instead of the $7,000 landscaping allowance, he will seed the lawn and do foundation plants similar to the house he built across the street."

"Yes, I remember that house," Samantha said, looking over the agreement. "This is fine," she finally said, and signed the bottom of the form. "Here is the information on my mortgage. I am already pre-approved."

"That will save some time," Jane said, relieved there would be no uncertainty about whether Samantha could get the loan. "I'll put the earnest money in escrow and talk to you early next week." Samantha got up to leave, and Jason followed.

"It was nice to meet you, Jason," said Jane. She was unsure about the relationship between Jason and Samantha, and thought it best not to ask.

"Yes, thank you," Jason said to Jane. "It was nice to meet you too. Maybe I can buy a house from you one day."

Jane was a little confused, but she instinctively handed Jason one of her cards before Jason and Samantha left.

"Okay, so what just happened?" Jason asked as they got out to his car.

"I just bought a house," Samantha said, finally showing some excitement.

"The first one," Samantha said, "for $100,000."

"That's what I thought," Jason said honestly. "What was that part about being pre-approved?"

"When I first started to think about buying a house, I went to a mortgage company and got pre-approved for a mortgage," Samantha explained. "That way I would know exactly how much I could qualify for, and I could close quickly. In new construction especially, sellers like it if you can close quickly."

"What is closing?" Jason asked.

"That just means buying the house. In a few weeks I will meet with the realtor, the mortgage company, the lawyers, and the seller and do the closing. That's where we sign the papers and transfer the money."

"How do you know all this?" Jason asked admiringly.

"I read a book: **How to Buy a House**," Samantha answered.

"Catchy title," Jason said. "Do you want to have dinner later? We can celebrate."

"Sounds good," said Samantha. "How about seven o'clock?"

"That's great. I'll pick you up then," Jason said as Samantha got out of the car.

* * *

Jason and Samantha went out that night, and almost every weekend for the next several months. They even had some conversations that did not involve economics, but we won't bore you with those details.

Samantha closed on her house and moved in. She got a new position with the inside sales department of *Switches.com*. Jason enjoyed his new Mustang, and he stuck with the financial plan that Samantha had laid out for him. In fact, everything was going perfectly until one Saturday afternoon.

It had been snowing all morning, and Jason realized he didn't have a snow shovel. He decided to pick up one at *Sears*. It looked like everyone else had the same idea. There was a big crowd looking over the snow shovels when he heard someone calling his name.

"Jason. Hiiiiii."

Jason looked over to see his high school girlfriend, Susie. "Susie, how are you?" Jason said, surprised to see her. "I haven't seen you for years."

"Not since high school. You went off to Bloomington University and forgot all about me," Susie said.

"I asked about you for the first couple of summers. Your parents told me you stayed at school," Jason said.

"Yes, West Lafayette University was a little harder than I thought. I should have gone to BU like you. I went to summer school every summer, but I finally graduated–only one semester late. Let's go get some coffee and I'll tell you all about it," Susie said.

"Okay, but I need to buy this snow shovel. We can drop it off at my car and then get something to drink," Jason said. He was also hoping to show Susie his Mustang.

Jason bought the shovel and they walked out to the parking lot. Susie held on to his arm, just like old times.

"Is this your car?" Susie asked. "It's really nice. You must have a great job."

"I work at a computer company called *Switches.com*," said Jason, throwing the snow shovel into the back of the car.

"Let's drive somewhere," said Susie. "I want to ride in your car."

"Of course," said Jason proudly. "Jump in." He politely closed the door for her.

Susie went on and on about the car and how good Jason looked, with a lot of giggling in between. After spending so much time with Samantha, Jason had forgotten what it was like to be with a girl like Susie where you didn't have to think.

Jason and Susie stopped at *Applebees*. They talked for a long time at the bar, and then they decided to have an early dinner. They reminisced about high school and then discussed college and their new jobs. Susie was also working in Indianapolis and had found a job in public relations with the power company.

"I'd like to stay longer," Susie finally said around 6 p.m. "But I have a date tonight. I could call and cancel if you want."

Jason thought it was a tempting idea, but he didn't want to give the wrong impression. "No, that's fine. I don't want the poor guy to be disappointed."

"Okay, but will you call me this week?" Susie asked.

"Sure," said Jason, not sure what he was getting himself into. He drove Susie back to her car at the shopping mall. Ironically, Susie had a blue *Saturn*, a car a lot like Samantha's.

When Jason got home, he had two messages from Samantha. Feeling a little guilty, but not sure for what, he called her back.

"Hi, Samantha," Jason said, trying to act normal.

"Hi, Jason. Where were you all day?" Samantha inquired.

"I had to go get a snow shovel," Jason explained.

"And that took all day?" Samantha asked.

It was an innocent enough question, but he didn't really feel like explaining everything to Samantha. "No, I had some other stuff to do."

Samantha thought Jason was acting a little funny. She decided not to pry.

"Do you want to get a video tonight?" Samantha asked. "The new James Bond movie is out."

"Sure, I'll pick it up and be over in a few minutes," Jason said. He drove to Samantha's house feeling very confused. He loved spending time with Samantha. She was smart, beautiful, and knew where she was going in life. On the other hand, it was very relaxing spending time with Susie. You didn't have to think too hard with her. Jason stopped at *Blockbuster's* and found the movie. While he was there, he watched all the other couples in the store. Some were high school kids; some were young married couples. "Which one am I?" Jason wondered to himself. "Am I still like a carefree high school student, or am I closer to being married to Samantha?" Jason thought to himself.

When Jason arrived at Samantha's house, he just walked in. He didn't ring the doorbell anymore. The house was tastefully decorated, but still pretty bare. Not much money left for furniture, Samantha had explained to him. Samantha came down with wet hair and a sweatshirt. "Not quite as attractive right now as Susie," he thought to himself.

"Sorry for my appearance," Samantha said. "But I was caulking my windows today. I was hoping you could have helped me."

"Sorry," said Jason, feeling guilty. "I'm sure you handled it by yourself without a problem."

"True, but it would have been nice caulking with you," she said and gave him a quick kiss. She went out into the kitchen and brought back some chips and salsa.

"Did they have the movie?" Samantha asked.

"They sure did," said Jason. "It was one of the 'guaranteed to be there' movies."

"That's good. I like all the James Bond movies, especially now with Pierce Brosnan," Samantha said.

They turned on the VCR, settled in the couch together, and watched the movie. The whole time Jason thought about where he was going in life. Did he have a commitment to Samantha, or was he just spending a lot of time with her? "What am I giving up by dating Samantha so much?" Jason thought to himself.

At the end of the movie, Samantha cleaned up and Jason rewound the movie. As casually as he could, Jason asked, "Do you think we should date other people?"

Samantha came back from the kitchen. "So that's what this is about. I thought you were acting funny. Did you see one of your old flames today while you were buying your snow shovel?"

Once again, Jason was amazed with Samantha's perception. "How did you know?" Jason asked.

"Men are so predictable," Samantha said. "It only takes one good-looking woman to get them all messed up."

"I don't know about that. It just got me thinking about what we might be missing. How do we know we are right for each other? Maybe we should date around a little to make sure," Jason explained.

"Opportunity cost," said Samantha.

"Huh," said Jason.

"Opportunity cost. That means the value of your next best alternative," said Samantha. "It's an economics term."

"You even work into economics terms to discuss dating. You're unbelievable," said Jason, not too complimentary.

"It's like this. Right now you are with me. You know what that is like. Now you are wondering what it would be like to be with this other bimbo you met today. If you are stuck with me, your opportunity cost is what you could be doing with her," said Samantha.

"I'm not sure I like what you are implying. And Susie is not a bimbo," Jason said, getting mad.

"Susie. I knew a Susie at WLU, and I can tell you that she was a total bimbo," Samantha fumed, not only mad but also hurt by Jason's original question.

"His Susie was from WLU," Jason thought. "No, it couldn't be the same one," he surmised. There must be hundreds of Susies at WLU."

"Well what about you?" Jason asked. "Don't you ever wonder what you are giving up?"

"Not really," said Samantha. "You are everything I want," fighting back the tears.

"You mean you can get me to do everything that you want," Jason retorted. It was a mistake, and he regretted it as soon as the words were out.

"Fine, why don't you just leave? And feel free to go out with Susie and whoever else you want as much as you want," said Samantha, starting to sob. "And don't forget your video. I wouldn't want you to have any late charges."

Jason didn't mean for things to turn out this way. He wasn't sure what to say, so he got his video and left feeling totally confused.

Key Economic Terms – Chapter 9

Realtor

Asking price

Offer

Commission

Listing agent

Selling agent

Broker

Allowance

Externalities

Property taxes

Home insurance

Private mortgage insurance (PMI)

Counteroffer

Earnest money

Pre-approved mortgage

Closing

Opportunity cost

Chapter 10
A Visit to WLU: The Monetary Policy Chapter

After the fight, Jason and Samantha did not see each other anymore. They would occasionally run into each other at work, and then would uncomfortably mumble "hello" and quickly move on.

Jason started to date Susie and several other women. None of these relationships was very serious, although he probably saw Susie the most. Jason missed Samantha; on the other hand, he also liked going on dates that did not require him to think. He took care of his job and played some basketball with Tim and the other guys from work. He even took up golf in the summer. Uncle Mitchell asked him several times about Samantha, but after a few months, he quit asking. Uncle Mitchell seemed disappointed that Samantha was out of the picture.

Samantha mainly applied herself to work and fixing up her new house. She did very well at work, getting promoted once to Midwest manager of inside sales about nine months after joining *Switches.com* and then a second promotion about six months later to National Manager of inside sales. On the night that the second promotion became effective, the whole inside sales department decided to take her to *Damon's* for a celebration dinner.

That same night, Jason had a date with Susie. "Why don't we go to *Damon's* tonight?" Susie squealed when Jason picked her up at her apartment. "We never go there."

Jason realized he had been avoiding the place, maybe subconsciously because that was the site of his first real date with Samantha. "Okay," Jason said hesitantly as he wheeled his Mustang into the traffic. Susie started talking endlessly about wanting to go to see a *Pearl Jam* concert. Jason pretended to listen.

They parked and went into the restaurant. "Let's sit at a table," Susie suggested. "I don't want you watching some baseball game on the television. I want all of your attention on me."

"Fine," said Jason, like he had a choice. "They sat down at a booth close to the entrance." Susie had finished babbling about the *Pearl Jam* concert, and now she was talking about going to the pool tomorrow. Jason was struggling to see the score of the game behind the bar.

"Samantha," Susie suddenly shrieked. "Samantha, over here. It's Susie from WLU."

Samantha looked over to see the friend of her roommate from college sitting at a booth. She couldn't see whom she was with, because his back was to her.

Jason couldn't believe it. "Could his Susie be the Susie that Samantha knew from school?" he wondered. "The bimbo, as Samantha had called her."

Jason turned his head as Samantha walked up to the booth. Their eyes met. "Samantha," Susie cried. "It's so good to see you. Who are all those people you are with?" motioning to the group at the entrance. "Are you living in Indianapolis now? Where do you work?" Susie fired out the questions, and Samantha didn't get a word in. She was trying to avoid looking at Jason.

"Oh, how rude of me. This is my boyfriend, Jason," Susie said proudly, as she reached across the table to hold his hand.

"I know Jason," Samantha said. "We work at the same company. And the people with me are from my department at work. We are celebrating my recent promotion," Samantha said, making sure that Jason knew about her success at work.

"Yes, I saw that announcement on the company web page. Congratulations," Jason said.

"Thank you," said Samantha coldly. "It was nice seeing you Susie, but I need to get back to my friends."

"Oh, sure, of course," said Susie. "Please call me sometime. I'm in the book."

"Okay," Samantha said simply, and she turned to join her group in a private room.

"That girl hasn't changed a bit," said Susie disapprovingly.

"What do you mean?" asked Jason.

"Well Samantha is so boring. You should have seen her at school: study, study, study. And now I see her here after more than two years, and she doesn't even have time to get caught up. And she treated you like you weren't alive," Susie added.

"Well, there is more to it than that," Jason started.

"What do you mean?" Susie asked.

Jason got ready to explain, and then he thought better of it. "We don't always agree at work," Jason finally said.

"That doesn't surprise me at all. I bet she is really bossy at work. And then she had to show off and talk about her new promotion. I bet you are higher than she is at work, right?" Susie asked.

"Not really," Jason admitted. "Samantha has been promoted twice since she joined *Switches.com*. I'm still waiting for my first promotion. Plus Samantha has bought a house, and she helped me set up my savings plan. In fact," Jason rambled on, "Samantha was the one who got me my new Mustang for free. We were taking Uncle Mitchell home one afternoon, and when Uncle Mitchell heard about the savings plan that I was following because of Samantha's advice, he volunteered to make the payments on my car." As Jason talked on, he realized how much he missed Samantha.

Susie, on the other hand, was listening with disbelief. "Why would you be riding in a car with Samantha and this Uncle Mitchell," she asked, starting to figure out that Jason was leaving out part of the story.

"I don't really remember," Jason said. "Maybe that was the day that I went looking at houses with Samantha. No, that couldn't be right. That didn't happen until later."

"Let me get this straight," Susie said firmly. "You went looking for houses with Samantha. Why?"

"I don't know. She asked me. She knows a lot about buying houses," Jason answered.

"I can't believe this. Did you *date* Samantha?" Susie asked in disbelief.

"Well, yes, I guess I did. In fact, I dated her pretty steady until that day I saw you again for the first time," Jason confessed.

Jason had unintentionally said the one thing that would save him. "So you dropped her once you knew I was available? That is sooo romantic," Susie said. "I guess you really do care about me. I still can't believe that you dated a girl as boring as Samantha, but I guess I look really good by comparison."

"Not really," Jason thought to himself. "How stupid have I been? When I was with Samantha, I was going somewhere. She forced me to be a better person, and I felt good about myself. Now what am I doing?"

Susie had gone back to talking about going to the pool tomorrow. She hadn't even noticed that Jason had been deep in thought.

Samantha and her group went into a private room. "Jason and Susie," she thought. "So it was the same Susie that caused their breakup. How ironic. Susie came back to torment me even after college." She tried to put Jason out of her mind and joined in the discussion with the group. Still, the thought kept coming back to her, "How could Jason date Susie? She is so shallow. Well, they deserve each other," she finally decided, but not really believing it.

Jason was tired of listening to Susie talk about the pool. The appetizers had come, but they hadn't ordered dinner yet. "Susie," Jason heard from across the room.

"Not again," he thought. "Who is it this time?"

"Amy," called Susie. "Look Jason, it's Amy." Jason didn't remember Amy. "You know, Amy from the spa."

"Oh, yeah," Jason said, pretending to remember.

"Susie, I'm so glad to see you," Amy said, coming over to the table with three of her friends. They all seemed to know each other. "We all just finished dinner in the other room. We're all going to the spa. They just got a new shipment of bikinis in!"

"I would die for a new swimsuit. Jason and I were just talking about going to the pool tomorrow. But we haven't eaten yet."

"Why don't you go ahead," Jason offered. "I'm not that hungry, and I would like to watch the game in the bar anyway."

"Are you sure you don't mind?" Susie asked.

"No problem. I'll call you tomorrow."

"Great," squealed Susie. "Let's go." Susie and her friends headed out of the restaurant.

Samantha tried to pay attention to her friends, but it was difficult. "This party is for me," she thought. "I should try to enjoy it." Just then Jason came into the room. Samantha looked, but Susie was thankfully not following him.

"Can I talk to you for a minute?" Jason asked Samantha.

"Okay," said Samantha, not sure what was coming next. They moved over to a quiet spot in the corner of the room. Some of the others in the group watched with interest. They had heard rumors of a previous relationship between Jason and Samantha.

"What happened to Susie?" Samantha asked.

"She left with some friends to buy a new swimsuit," Jason answered.

"That sounds like Susie," said Samantha.

"When I saw you today, it made me realize what I have been giving up. Opportunity cost, I guess you would call it. When we had our fight, I never realized that I wouldn't see you anymore. My opportunity cost of seeing Susie is not seeing you, and that just isn't worth it." For the second time that night, Jason had said exactly the right thing to a woman. The explanation of opportunity cost melted Samantha's heart.

"Will you take me back?" Jason asked tentatively.

"Of course," said Samantha. "I've missed you terribly." She wanted to kiss him right there, but she could sense that they had an audience.

"Maybe we could get together after your celebration?" Jason suggested.

"My place at 10 o'clock," Samantha suggested.

"I'll be there," Jason happily agreed.

* * *

Things were back to normal between Jason and Samantha. The only person happier than those two might have been Uncle Mitchell. "I don't know how you could have ever let her go," Uncle Mitchell scolded Jason at the next opportunity.

Later that fall Jason and Samantha were both invited to interview prospective candidates for *Switches.com* at West Lafayette University. The interviews were scheduled for all day Tuesday and Wednesday morning.

"Do you want to go to an economics lecture while we are at WLU?" Samantha asked Jason as they were planning their trip.

"Are you kidding?" Jason responded. "I am never taking another class in my life. Especially an economics class."

"Come on," Samantha pleaded, "you will like it. I have it all set up with Professor Dowers. I took his class when I was a freshman."

"You have a professor who remembers you from six years ago," Jason asked with disbelief. "My professors didn't even remember me when I was taking the class."

"Maybe I am just more memorable," Samantha said playfully.

"Wait a minute. Is this the fat guy? Or what was it you called him?" Jason asked.

"The teddy bear?" Samantha laughed.

"No wonder he remembers you," Jason said.

"Don't get started," Samantha warned him, "or I am going to ask you about Susie."

"Okay, you win. How many times have I admitted that I messed up with that one?"

"And showed very bad judgment," Samantha said.

"And showed very bad judgment," Jason repeated.

"And will never do it again," said Samantha.

"And will never do it again," Jason finished.

"Now that we've taken care of that, what do you say? Professor Dowers' introductory economics course is at 2:30 on Monday afternoon," Samantha said.

"Okay," said Jason. "You talked me into it. I would like to see what the teddy bear looks like."

Samantha had arranged to meet Professor Dowers before the lecture. Jason and Samantha walked into his office at 2:20.

"Samantha!" Professor Dowers greeted her. "You look great."

"Thanks, Professor Dowers. You, uh, you look the same," Samantha replied.

"At my age, that is a huge compliment, young lady. And who is this dashing young man?" asked Professor Dowers.

"Dashing?" Jason thought. "What century did this guy come from?"

"This is Jason Cooley. He works with me," Samantha said.

"Nice to meet you Mr. Cooley. Are you coming to my lecture too?" Professor Dowers asked.

"Yes," said Jason. "I am looking forward to it. On almost every date Samantha tells me about something that she learned from you."

Professor Dowers raised his eyebrow. "Date," he thought. "A little more than a work friend."

Samantha realized what was going through the professor's mind. "Okay," she confessed, "Jason is also my boyfriend."

"Well, we will take good care of him during class," Professor Dowers promised.

"What does that mean?" Jason thought. Samantha smiled after Professor Dowers said it, and he didn't like the looks of that.

They walked to the lecture room together. It was a large room with about 300 students. Jason and Samantha found a seat in the back corner. "What did he mean by, 'He would take good care of me'?" Jason asked Samantha.

"You'll find out. Professor Dowers has a bit of a reputation," Samantha smiled.

"Today we are going to talk about monetary policy," Professor Dowers started his lecture.

"What is that?" Jason whispered to Samantha.

"Ssh," said Samantha.

"I'm being quiet," Jason said. "I just want to know what monetary policy is. Why is it important?"

"DO WE HAVE A PROBLEM, Mr. Cooley?" Professor Dowers yelled out, staring directly at Jason.

"Now you've done it," Samantha whispered under her breath.

"No, uh, no problem," Jason stammered. This class was bringing back bad memories quickly.

"What were you saying to Miss Fletcher?" Professor Dowers asked.

"I was just asking what monetary policy is," Jason responded, feeling very intimidated.

"Did you attend college?" Professor Dowers asked Jason. There were snickers from the students.

"Yes," said Jason, hoping Professor Dowers would leave him alone.

"Let me guess. You went to Bloomington University," said Professor Dowers.

"That's right. How did you know?" The rest of the class was laughing out loud at this point.

"It's obvious. But to answer your question, monetary policy is one of the key tools that the Federal Reserve uses to maintain low unemployment and low inflation, specifically demand-pull inflation.

"The other key tool used by the government to manage the national economy is fiscal policy. Have you heard of Lord Keynes, Mr. Cooley?" Professor Dowers asked.

"Not really," said Jason, hoping to trade immediate embarrassment for prolonged embarrassment. He looked over to Samantha, who seemed to be enjoying this.

"I'll be covering Keynes on Wednesday. Perhaps you can join us then, Mr. Cooley," Professor Dowers suggested.

"I would like that," said Jason, starting to play along.

"Good. Now back to monetary policy. Monetary policy, as the name implies, has something to do with money. Tell me, what gives our money its value?"

"Because it is backed by gold?" one student yelled out.

"Not anymore," Professor Dowers answered. "Our money used to be backed by gold, but no longer."

"I knew that," Jason thought. Jason settled back into the lecture, starting to enjoy it. He looked over at Samantha. "More like a grizzly bear than a teddy bear, if you ask me," Jason said.

"That's his style to keep people interested," Samantha explained. "Everyone knows he's kidding. Except for you, of course."

"Miss Fletcher. Are you explaining the answer to your friend from Bloomington University?" Professor Dowers asked.

"No, he was just telling me that you were like a grizzly bear, and I was defending you," Samantha explained honestly.

Jason felt a little flushed. He was used to sleeping through classes, not providing the entertainment.

"For the students' benefit, this is Miss Samantha Fletcher. She took this class six years ago, and got an "A", I might add. She is interviewing students tomorrow for her company, *Switches.com*. And Mr. Cooley is her assistant."

"This guy doesn't let up," Jason thought. "But he is pretty funny," he admitted to himself. "And everyone in the class is paying attention."

"I realize that it has been a long time, Miss Fletcher, but perhaps you remember why our money has value."

"Because people think it has value," Samantha replied.

"This must be another joke," thought Jason. "I wonder where this one is going."

"Exactly correct. The U.S. dollar has value because people think it has value. It is not backed by gold or anything else of tangible value," Professor Dowers explained.

"That is incredible," Jason thought. He had never thought about it, but it was hard to believe the whole U.S. economy, and the whole global economy for that matter, was based on something that had value because people thought it had value.

"Let me tell you a story about Brazil," Professor Dowers said.

"Oh, this is a great story," said Samantha. "Professor Dowers has really interesting stories."

Jason couldn't believe that Samantha could remember a story from six years ago. He couldn't even remember what subjects he took six years ago.

"One year I spent a year in the interior of Brazil," Professor Dowers started. "While I was there, the Brazilian economy was going though hyperinflation, meaning the value of their currency was declining by something like 50% per year. One day a cheeseburger cost 1 unit. By the way, I won't confuse with the name of the currency, because they changed it. But anyway, a year later, a cheeseburger cost 2 units. Hyperinflation is simply very high inflation.

"The Brazilian government decided to recall all their currency and replace it with new money because, at the rate they were going, it was going to take a wheelbarrow full of money just to buy a pack of gum. The government decided it would take 1,000 units of the old money to get 1 unit of the new money. The government said that as of a certain date, the old money would have no value and only the new currency could be used.

"The day after the conversion was made, I went to buy some vegetables at the market. And you know what? Everyone at the market was still using the old money. Many of the people in the town were illiterate, and they had probably not read that the government had said the old money was worthless. They continued to use the old money for several months before the new currency was eventually phased in. The old money had value because people thought it had value. The government said that the old money was worthless, but because the people accepted the old money, it still had value.

"Of course, currency is not the only type of money. The U.S. money supply has three components: coins, currency, and checking accounts. The major component, about two-thirds of the total, is checking account balances. The Federal Reserve is responsible for managing the money supply. They make decisions, which I will explain in a second, to keep the economy growing and to keep inflation and unemployment low.

"Why do I care?" a student yelled rudely. "It's not like I'm going to be in charge of the Federal Reserve Bank one day."

"Good question, Mr. Spencer" Professor Dowers answered the student, not the least bit irritated. "Tell me, Mr. Spencer, does the sun revolve around the earth, or does the earth resolve around the sun?"

"Where is Professor Dowers going with this one?" Jason wondered to himself.

"The earth goes around the sun," the student answered correctly.

"Is it important to know that?" Professor Dowers asked.

"Well, sure," said Mr. Spencer.

"Why?" probed Professor Dowers.

"Because it explains the way the world works," the student answered.

"Do you think you will ever need to apply that information?" Professor Dowers asked.

"Probably not," John conceded, "unless I become an astronomer. I think I see where you are going, Professor Dowers."

"And where is that?"

"That learning about monetary policy helps explain how the world works, even if I won't apply it directly unless I become chairman of the Federal Reserve," Mr. Spencer added.

"And if you become chairman of the Fed, please remember who taught you your first economics class," Professor Dowers said with a smile.

"Now where was I at," Professor Dowers wondered aloud. "Oh yes, the money supply. Money is no different than potatoes."

"He talks in riddles, just like Samantha," Jason thought. "Maybe that's where she gets it from."

"There is a demand for money and a supply of money, just like potatoes. The demand for money comes from four sources. First, people need money to do their day-to-day business. This is called the transactional demand for money. Second, people like to have some money for a rainy day. This is called the precautionary demand for money. Third, people want to have money available to invest. This is called the speculative demand for money. Finally, people from other countries want our money to buy U.S. products. This is called the foreign demand for money. If you add up these four reasons why people want our money, the result is the demand for money.

"Does the demand for money go up and down?" asked a student.

"Absolutely," said the professor. "Transactional demand goes up with population, obviously, but it also goes up with income."

"Why is that?" another student asked.

"Tell me, Miss Updike," Professor Dowers said to the student who asked the question, "How much money do you have in your purse?"

"Not much," she laughed. "Maybe twenty dollars."

"And, not to get too personal, how much is your income?" Professor Dowers asked.

"Not much," she answered.

"I understand. You know, I just heard a story about Michael Jordan on the radio. He lost his wallet at a golf tournament. A spectator picked it up and looked inside. Guess how much money he had in his wallet?" Professor Dowers asked rhetorically. "He had over $10,000 in his wallet. This is an extreme example, but as people's income goes up, their consumption spending goes up, and they carry more cash for transactional purposes.

"Precautionary demand for money varies by income and how nervous people feel," Professor Dowers continued. "For example, I like to run my cars for a long time. The car I have now is pretty new; it only has 120,000 miles. My last car had over 200,000 miles on it when I decided to take it on a trip to New York. Needless to say, I carried a little extra money with me in case of car problems. Of course, with credit cards this isn't as important as it used to be.

"Speculative demand for money depends mainly on interest rates. If interest rates are high, you don't want a lot of money sitting in cash or in a checking account. You want to invest that money. If interest rates are low, people are less worried about having a lot of cash sitting around at no interest.

"So that's the story on the demand for money. Now let's talk about the supply of money. I've already mentioned that the Federal Reserve has overall responsibility for the money supply. The Federal Reserve Bank, or 'Fed', is a bank for other banks. The Fed manages monetary policy by working through the commercial banks. All commercial banks have deposits at the Federal Reserve Bank. The Fed manages the money supply mainly through what is called the fractional reserve system.

"Let's say that Michael Jordan decides to put his $10,000 in the bank so he doesn't lose it on the golf course. The Fed says that his bank needs to keep some of this money as a reserve, and they can loan out the rest. This is how a bank makes money. They get deposits from one group of people, and then they loan the money to other people and charge them interest. The Fed may decide that the reserve requirement, or the percentage of the deposits that the bank needs to keep on reserve, is 10%. So the bank keeps $1,000 of Mr. Jordan's deposit in their tills or in their account with the Federal Reserve, and they loan $9,000 to Miss Updike, who was recently approved for a car loan. Hypothetically," he said, smiling at Miss Updike.

"Miss Updike takes the $9,000 and buys a car at the Ford dealership almost immediately. Usually when people request a loan, they use the money right away. The Ford dealer then deposits the $9,000 in the bank. The bank needs to keep 10% in reserve, or $900, and loans the other $8,100 for a plastic surgery operation for Jason from Bloomington University."

"Come on," Jason yelled. "I've been good."

"I just didn't want people to forget our guests," said Professor Dowers.

"Anyway, you can see where this is going," Professor Dowers continued. "The original $10,000 deposit actually generates a money supply of $9,000 plus $8,100 and so on and so on and so on. Eventually, it generates a money supply of $100,000. The calculation is the original deposit divided by the reserve requirement of 10%. The Fed can alter the money supply by changing the reserve requirement. If they decrease the reserve requirement from 10% to 5%, the bank can loan out more money from each deposit, which increases the money supply. If they change the reserve requirement from 10% to 20%, that decreases the money supply in exactly the reverse way.

"The Fed has other ways to manage the money supply," said Professor Dowers. They can do open market operations. This means they buy or sell government securities. If they want to increase money supply, they buy government bonds from the public, putting more money into the hands of the public. If they want to reduce the money supply, they sell government securities, which means the Fed brings in money that is safely taken out of the money supply.

"The last way the Fed controls the money supply is through the discount rate. Earlier we talked about the reserve requirement. What if at the end of the day, a bank hasn't met their reserve requirement of 10%? They normally will borrow money from the Federal Reserve. The interest rate on these loans is the discount rate. If the discount rate is high, banks will be more careful to keep the required reserves and may even hold some excess reserves to be safe. If the discount rate is low, they will be more aggressive in their lending policies, knowing if they end up short on reserves they can borrow the money at a fairly low rate.

"This has been a very long introduction, but now I will get to the point. We've talked about the demand for money, and where this demand comes from. We've talked about the supply of money, and how the Fed manages the money supply. Now here is the key point. The price of potatoes depends on the supply of potatoes and the demand for potatoes. If there has been a bad crop of potatoes, meaning a small quantity supplied, the price of potatoes will be high. Potatoes are scarce, so people will pay more to get the limited quantity available. If there is a good crop of potatoes, the price will be low. If *McDonalds* runs a special promotion for french fries, the demand for potatoes will go up and the price of potatoes will go up. If people finally find out that french fries make you fat, the demand for potatoes will go down and the price will go down.

"The supply and demand for money works exactly the same way, but the 'price' of money is the interest rate. If there is a shortage of money, the price of money will go up. A higher price for money means a higher interest rate. You have to pay more to get the money, meaning you have to pay a higher interest rate. So a decrease in the supply of money means a higher interest rate. Conversely, an increase in the supply of money means that money is easier to get, so the interest rate will be lower. A lower demand for money means a lower interest rate, while a greater demand for money means a higher interest rate. You can change people's buying behavior by changing interest rates.

"The Fed can use the money market to influence economic growth, unemployment, and inflation. Let's say the Fed wants to increase economic growth. They just increase the money supply so interest rates fall. Maybe they decide to buy some government bonds from the public. With lower interest rates, people will be more willing to make investments which leads to economic growth.

"Let's say the Fed is concerned about high inflation. Since inflation means demand for goods and services is bidding prices up, the Fed will try to decrease consumption by raising interest rates. When interest rates are high, people are reluctant to buy new cars or borrow money to take vacations. To raise interest rates, the Fed decreases the money supply. Maybe they do this by selling government bonds or by raising the reserve requirement. I should say however," Professor Dowers interjected, "that Fed intervention is usually through open market operations or changing the discount rate. The Fed doesn't change the reserve requirement very often."

"Finally, let's say the Fed is concerned about high cyclical unemployment. They need to get the economy going. To do this, they increase money supply, which lowers interest rates, encouraging people to borrow money for consumption or for companies to invest in new equipment.

"Managing the money supply is a delicate thing. Usually the Fed wants to have enough money to encourage growth and to maintain low unemployment, but not too much money because that creates inflation. There is one school of economists called 'monetarists', led by Nobel Laureate Milton Friedman, who says the Fed should just maintain a consistent growth in the money supply equal to economic growth. Monetarists do not believe the Fed should try to fine-tune the economy to keep economic growth, inflation, and unemployment within certain targets.

"As a practical matter, the Fed has mainly concentrated on keeping inflation in check throughout the 1980s and 1990s, which may have led to a couple of brief recessions, but they have done a good job at keeping inflation low.

"What should you remember from today?" Professor Dowers summarized. "First, the demand for money comes from transactional demand, precautionary demand, speculative demand, and foreign demand. The Federal Reserve manages the supply of money through several tools: reserve requirements, open market operations, and the discount rate. The interaction between the supply and demand for money leads to a price for money, which is the interest rate. The Fed tries to manage the money supply to influence interest rates to keep our national economy in good shape. If they want more economic growth, they increase the money supply, called loosening the money supply in some magazine articles, to decrease interest rates. If they are concerned about demand-pull inflation, they reduce the money supply, or tighten the money supply, which increases interest rates. If they are concerned about unemployment getting too high, they increase the money supply, which reduces interest rates.

"That's it for today. Read the chapter on fiscal policy for next time. You don't want to miss that class, because we are going to teach our Bloomington University friend about Lord Keynes."

"Man, I thought he had forgotten," Jason said to Samantha. "Do we really have to go?"

"You promised," Samantha replied. "Plus, didn't you find him interesting."

"About a million times better than my econ professor," Jason admitted. "But I still prefer getting my economics lessons from you," he added romantically.

"I'm a little rusty on fiscal policy," Samantha confessed, "so we had better come for the next lecture."

Samantha and Jason looked to say good-bye to Professor Dowers, but he was answering questions from a group of students. They waved and headed out of the classroom.

Key Economic Terms – Chapter 10

Monetary policy
Macroeconomics
Fiscal policy
Keynes
Money
Hyperinflation
Money supply
Coins
Currency
Checking accounts
Federal Reserve
Economic growth
Inflation
Unemployment
Transactional demand for money

Precautionary demand for money
Speculative demand for money
Foreign demand for money
Interest rates
Commercial banks
Fractional reserve system
Deposits
Reserves
Reserve requirement
Open market operations
Government securities
Discount rate
Monetarists
Milton Friedman
Loosening the money supply
Tightening the money supply

Chapter 11
Another Lecture at WLU: The Fiscal Policy Chapter

The interviews went well. There were many fine students at West Lafayette University. Samantha and Jason identified 22 students between them to offer a site interview down in Indianapolis at *Switches.com*.

After the last interview on the second day, Jason and Samantha got a quick lunch at the Student Union and then went to Professor Dowers' class.

"Nice to see you again, Jason and Samantha," Professor Dowers started out the lecture.

"Always great to be the center of attention," Jason thought to himself.

"Today we are going to discuss fiscal policy," said Professor Dowers. "Jason, can you tell us what fiscal policy is?"

"I forgot to ask Samantha before I came," Jason thought to himself. "I should have known he would do this to me."

"No, Professor, I don't know what fiscal policy is," Jason answered.

"I know," said Samantha.

"I thought you would. Please tell us, Samantha, and show us how much smarter you are than your boyfriend," Professor Dowers said.

"Fiscal policy is the action that government can take to influence the national economy. For example, let's say the economy is experiencing cyclical unemployment. The government may try to increase government spending to get things going," Samantha explained.

"Exactly right," said Professor Dowers. "Let me explain this very precisely. Last time we talked about monetary policy, which is how the Federal Reserve tries to manage the money supply to help the economy grow at a sustainable rate with low inflation and low unemployment. The government can do the same thing with fiscal policy. They attempt to manage government spending and tax policy to achieve the same goals of sustainable growth with low inflation and low unemployment. Since monetary policy and fiscal policy are both tools that are working towards the same goals, it is important for the government and the Federal Reserve to have policies that work together, rather than working at cross purposes. Just this past week, for example, the chairman of the Federal Reserve was giving his views about a tax cut package being discussed by Congress. The Federal Reserve has nothing to do with tax cut policies, but they know that any tax cut passed by Congress will influence the national economy, and the Fed needs to make sure their monetary policy will work together with the tax policy that Congress establishes."

"Fiscal policy can be explained by one simple equation: GDP equals C plus I plus G plus X. In words, this says that the total output of the economy, GDP, is equal to the sum total of consumer spending (C), investment spending (I), government spending (G), and net exports (X). Net exports are exports minus imports. This explains how the total output of the economy is spent.

The total of C plus I plus G plus X equals how much people want to buy. There is also a level of GDP that shows how much our country can produce if it runs at capacity. This is called full employment GDP. If the total of what people what to buy is greater than what can be produced, that creates demand-pull inflation, and prices are bid up. If the total of what people want to buy is less than what the economy can produce, that means we will have cyclical unemployment because companies will lay off people to decrease production.

The main goal of fiscal policy is to institute policies so the total of what people want to spend equals what the economy can produce. If people want to spend more than the economy can produce, causing demand-pull inflation, the government may pursue a contractionary fiscal policy to reduce C + I + G + X. This means the government could spend less money, which lowers G, or taxes could be increased, giving people less after-tax money to spend which lowers consumption spending C. Either way, the total of C + I + G + X is reduced, and the total of what people want to spend can be brought into line with what the economy can produce. You may remember that the Fed could also try to solve the problem of demand-pull inflation by reducing the money supply. Reducing the money supply increases interest rates, and people are less likely to borrow money to buy things.

If the total of what people want to buy is less than what the economy can produce, the government could institute an expansionary fiscal policy to increase C + I + G + X by the government spending more money, which increases G, or lowering taxes, which gives consumers more after-tax income which in turn increases C. Alternatively, the Fed could expand the money supply and have the same effect. Expanding the money supply causes interest rates to fall, and people are more likely to borrow money to buy things."

"How do you know when the Fed should take the action and when the government should change the fiscal policy?" asked a student.

"A big factor is timing. The main tools of fiscal policy are government spending, which changes G; and tax policy, which indirectly changes C. I say indirectly for the following reason. If Congress votes in a tax cut, that will give people more after-tax income. If they have more after-tax income, which is the same as saying their take-home pay goes up, they will have larger consumption spending and C goes up.

"So a tax cut increases C by increasing take home pay, and more government spending increases G. But think how long it takes. Both tax cuts and government spending requires bills that are passed by Congress and are signed by the President. This can take a year or more. Then it takes time for the economy to feel the effects of the increased government spending or changed tax policy. This can take another year or more. Compare this with monetary policy, where the Federal Reserve can decide one day to increase the money supply. The next day they buy some government securities and they are done. Monetary policy works much faster."

"So why do we ever use fiscal policy?" asked another student.

"Well, you want to be close with fiscal policy. You want to have a government spending plan and tax policy that puts the economy close to where you want it to be. Monetary policy can be used to fine-tune," Professor Dowers explained.

"Why do I care about this?" asked another student. "How can I apply this?"

"You weren't here last time, were you, Sonya?" Professor Dowers asked.

"No, I had an interview. I'm sorry, did someone ask this last time?" Sonya inquired.

"Yes, but that's okay. It's an important question. Tell me, Sonya, is the earth round or flat?"

"It's round, of course," the student answered.

"Is this important to know? Will you ever apply this information?" Professor Dowers asked.

"Yes, it's important to know. I'm not sure how I apply it. Maybe if I sail around the world," she said.

"But it's still important to know?" asked Professor Dowers.

"Yes. Okay, I get it," she said.

"Good. And I'm glad we covered that again. Part of what we discuss in this class is very applied. Other things are to give you a better idea of how the world works. I call it the 'evening news' topics. Whenever you watch the news, you will hear about what the Federal Reserve is doing or different tax bills and government spending bills before Congress. Telling you about fiscal policy and monetary policy helps you understand how all these discussions fit together.

"One last topic. Remember last time we talked about how a $10,000 deposit grows to a $100,000 increase in money supply." There were some murmurings of agreement. "Well a similar thing happens with fiscal policy. Say the economy is suffering from high unemployment. The government decides to pursue an expansionary fiscal policy and increase government spending. Congress passes a new highway spending bill. Their first contract is for a new bridge over the Wabash River. The government pays Joe's Construction Company $10 million to build the bridge. Joe's Construction Company takes the $10 million dollars and buys $2 million in steel from Jane's Steel Company and spends $8 million in other raw materials and wages. Jane's Steel Company pays their workers $1 million and buys $1 million in raw materials. The Jane's Steel Company workers take their $1 million and spend money on food, cars, and other consumption items. You can see that the original $10 million will multiply throughout the economy. A $10 million increase in government spending may end up increasing total GDP by $30 or $40 million. This is called the multiplier effect.

"I'm going along pretty quickly here. Does anyone mind if we finish a little early today? I want to give you your money's worth," Professor Dowers joked.

"We'll get over it," one student yelled.

"Okay, let's summarize. Fiscal policy is actions that the government takes to keep the national economy at a sustainable growth rate at low inflation and low unemployment. Monetary policy has the same goals, and fiscal policy and monetary policy should be coordinated together for the best effect. You can look at fiscal policy as putting the economy in generally the right position, and then monetary policy can be used to fine-tune because monetary policy works much faster.

"The objective is to manage fiscal policy so that the total spending in the economy equals the total output that the economy can produce. The maximum that the total economy can produce is called the full employment GDP. When $C + I + G + X$ is equal to the maximum output that the economy can produce, the economy is said to be in equilibrium at full employment.

"If the amount that people want to spend is less than the full employment GDP, we have unemployment. The government may implement an expansionary fiscal policy and increase government spending or cut taxes. This will increase $C + I + G + X$ and get the economy up to full employment.

"If the amount that people want to spend is greater than the full employment GDP, we have inflationary pressures. The government may implement a contractionary fiscal policy and reduce government spending or increase taxes. This will decrease C + I + G + X and pull the economy back to the full employment level.

"If you remember one thing from the last two lectures, it is this," Professor Dowers summarized. "The goal of fiscal and monetary policy is to change peoples' behavior so that the amount they want to buy is equal to the amount that the economy can produce.

"Another big issue with fiscal policy is the national debt and the budget deficit. Have you ever heard any discussions about that on television?" Professor Dowers asked the class.

"I remember that guy with big ears talking about it?" yelled one student.

"Perhaps you mean Ross Perot," said Professor Dowers, "and you're right, he did a lot to bring attention to the national debt.

"Let's start with a couple of definitions. First, the budget deficit is the amount that government spending exceeds government revenues in any one year. Government revenues are mainly taxes. So the amount that the government spends above what it brings in over the course of a year is called the deficit. It's possible for the government to have a surplus, but that hasn't happened much lately.

"If you add up all the deficits and subtract the surpluses since the United States was founded, that is the national debt. Every year the government runs a deficit, that deficit is added to the national debt. The total national debt is about $6 trillion dollars. By comparison, annual GDP is about $9 trillion. So our national debt is about two-thirds of the final value of all the goods and services that we produce in a year.

"Whenever the government spends more than it brings in, it has to finance this shortfall by selling government bonds. People are willing to loan money to the government to finance the overspending."

"I thought the government could just print more money when it runs out," said a student in the front row.

"That's a common belief," said Professor Dowers, "but the U.S. financial system doesn't run that way. There are other countries that print money when they spend more than they bring in. These countries don't have a national debt because they don't need to borrow money, but they have problems with inflation. As you remember, inflation is rising prices. If you have a country that can turn on the printing presses whenever it feels like, that tends to cause lots of inflation.

"There are several reasons why the government may choose to spend more than it brings in:

- Part of our national debt came from expenditures on wars.

- Part of our national debt came from the wise use of fiscal policy, which is what we talked about today. If the economy is in a recession, it is good fiscal policy for the government to spend money to get things going, even if the government doesn't have the money to spend and needs to borrow it.

- Part of our national debt came from emergency spending, like hurricane relief. People need immediate help, and there is no time to raise taxes to pay for these emergencies.

- Unfortunately, a big part of the national debt has come from irresponsible spending. For the last 15 or 20 years, the government has run a deficit, even though the economy was strong and didn't need extra stimulus from deficit spending. Plain and simple, politicians just like to spend money.

"One other benefit of having a national debt is it provides a good, safe place to invest money. There are lots of people who own savings bonds or treasury bills, which is really a loan to the government. This is how the government finances the national debt.

"There are certainly some good reasons for having a national debt, mainly the flexibility for the government to spend money that it doesn't have to respond to wars, emergencies, or to stimulate the economy when needed. There are also some disadvantages:

- Psychologically, many people don't like the idea of having a debt that will never be paid off. We are taught to be responsible, and the idea of perpetually owing money with neither a plan nor the possibility of repaying it doesn't seem right to many people.

- The interest on the national debt must be paid every year, and it is now the third biggest budget item after welfare and defense. To keep paying the interest payments, the government needs to collect taxes. Because we have a national debt, taxes are higher than they would be otherwise. Most of the tax burden is placed on higher income people. We have a progressive tax system, meaning the higher your income, the higher percentage of your income goes to taxes. The bottom 50% of the income bracket pay almost no taxes. As a result, any tax increases fall on the higher income people, the same people who contribute the most to economic growth. The more you tax these highly productive people, the less incentive they have to work. Right now, a person in the highest income bracket pays about 40% of any extra income to the government as taxes. That discourages many high income people from generating more income, and that is harmful to the whole economy.

- A big problem of the debt is that it crowds out business investment. People save money, and then they go to look for good investments. Government bonds are very good investments because they are very safe. If people use all of their savings to invest in government bonds, there is no money left for businesses to borrow. Businesses then need to increase the interest rates on their investments to make them more attractive to investors. The national debt forces everyone to pay higher interest rates to borrow money to compete with government bonds because everyone is borrowing money from the same savers.

- Finally, the national debt can put a burden on future generations. Whether the debt puts a burden on future generations depends on who has lent the money, however, and this point is often overlooked. If the debt is owed to other Americans, it really doesn't hurt future generations of Americans. If government bonds are owned by Americans, the principle and interest payments paid by the government are paid to Americans. It's almost like borrowing from your parents. The money still stays in the family. If the money is owed to foreigners, the principle and interest payments paid by future generations leave America. This results in a lower living standard in the United States. This type of debt does put a burden on future generations. I heard one politician put it this way: 'In the 1980s, we borrowed a trillion dollars from the Japanese and had a big party. Now future generations will have to pay back that trillion dollars.'"

"So how do we solve this problem with the debt?" asked a student.

"Let we first reemphasize a national debt is not all bad. I gave you some reasons why it is good to have a debt: spending for war and emergencies, stimulating the economy, and providing good investment opportunities. On the other hand, the debt is troubling to some people's sense of responsibility, it crowds out business spending which leads to higher interest costs for companies and individual borrowers, it results in higher taxes, and it can place a burden on future generations.

"The main way to improve the situation is to stop wasteful spending. When extra spending is helpful and necessary, that's fine. But wasteful spending just makes the negatives of the national debt even worse.

"That's it for today. Now you can watch the evening news and understand what they are talking about, or you can debate your friends about the balanced budget amendment." Professor Dowers concluded his lecture.

Jason and Samantha waited in line behind a group of students to say good-bye to Professor Dowers. "Thanks for letting us come to your class," Jason told Professor Dowers after the last student left.

"Do you really mean that?" asked Professor Dowers.

"Yes, I do. As you might have guessed, I didn't do that well when I took economics at school. Since then, Samantha has showed me how important economics can be in a person's life. We even had our first big fight because of opportunity cost," Jason elaborated.

"Let's not get into that one," said Samantha. "I agree with Jason about the lectures, however. It was fun to come back and be a student for a few hours."

"It was good to see you again, Samantha. And Jason, make sure you don't lose this girl. She's a winner," Professor Dowers smiled in a fatherly way at Samantha.

"I know, Professor Dowers," Jason concurred while gazing approvingly at Samantha.

Key Economic Terms – Chapter 11

Fiscal policy
National economy
Consumption (C)
Investment (I)
Government spending (G)
Exports (X)
Imports (I)
GDP = C + I + G + X
Contractionary fiscal policy
Expansionary fiscal policy
Tax policy

After-tax income
Take-home pay
Multiplier effect
Economic growth
Inflation
Unemployment
Full employment GDP
Budget deficit
National Debt
Regressive tax system
Crowding out
Balanced budget amendment

Chapter 12
Marriage: The Financial Planning for Couples Chapter

Jason and Samantha have been working for *Switches.com* for over three years and, except for the one separation, their relationship was strong. It's approaching springtime and things are getting very serious. The past Christmas holiday found Jason and Samantha celebrating equally between their two families.

The phone rings at Samantha's house. It's 7:30 on a Tuesday night. "Hello," said Samantha.

"Hi Sam, it's me," said Jason. Jason, to his knowledge, is the only person Samantha ever permitted to call her Sam.

"Oh, hi. What are you up to?" asked Samantha.

"Well Sam, I need to talk to you. Are you free right now?"

"Are you okay, Jason? You sound really weird," replied Samantha.

"Yeah, I'm okay, I just would like to see you tonight," said Jason.

"I just finished picking up the house. Do you want to come over now?" Samantha asked.

"Sure, I'll be there in about ten minutes," said Jason.

Samantha hung up the phone and was truly puzzled with Jason's call. He'd been acting a bit strange for a couple of days, but she didn't make too much of it. "Maybe it's just a mood," she had told herself. She knew Jason had just been promoted to a managerial position and he had been working incredibly long hours getting up to speed with his new responsibilities. In fact, it was pretty clear that Jason had become a rising star at *Switches.com*. This, of course, was a far cry from his beginnings. The general consensus was, if you need something done quickly and efficiently, Jason was the man. Jason knew computers, he had good interpersonal skills, and Samantha helped him with the rest.

Samantha thought that something may have happened to someone in Jason's family. His father was getting old, and he was under a lot of pressure with his job in New York. He had to go into the office twice over the Christmas break when Samantha and Jason were visiting them.

Then again, maybe it was Jason and Samantha's relationship. Maybe Jason was getting nervous about that and wanted more space. "Wow, that's a chilling thought," she thought. Now, Samantha was really beginning to get worked up about what might be on Jason's mind. About that time, she heard a car door close. She went to the door and met Jason.

"Hi Sam, how are you doing?" Jason said.

"I'm okay. I just told you that on the phone," said Samantha. "But you've got me a bit concerned. Why were you so insistent that you needed to see me tonight? Is your father okay? Is your job okay?" Samantha left out the last possibility that was on her mind.

"Sorry about that, Sam. It's just that what's on my mind has been weighing heavily for some time, and I need to talk to you about it," said Jason. "But Dad's okay, and my job has never been better."

"What is that in your hand?" Samantha asked as Jason got up to the step, noticing a bag in his hand that he had been half trying to conceal.

"I thought we could open a bottle of wine and talk for a while. This is supposed to be a really good Merlot," said Jason.

By now Samantha was really wired. A phone call at 7:30, got to see you now, things weighing heavily on my mind, and now a bottle of wine. "A bottle of wine for what, to ease the pain?" Samantha wondered to herself. "I just know that he is tired of our relationship and wants to break it off," she prepared herself for the worst. As Samantha stood there, somewhat dazed and bewildered, Jason could see tears beginning to well up in her eyes. In all the time he had known Samantha, she has always been solid as a rock. She could be emotional over a good book or a sensitive movie, but he had never seen her get emotional for no apparent reason.

"I'm sorry, Sam," said Jason. "Is the Merlot a bad idea?" he continued cluelessly.

"No, that's not it," said Samantha. "I just feel like there is some bad news coming and I don't think I want to hear it."

"Man," Jason thought, "I've got this whole deal all screwed up. When I talked to Dad about this, he told me it would be a piece of cake. But somehow the train has jumped the track."

"Sam, I am really nervous right now," said Jason. "I called you and I bought this great bottle of Merlot because I wanted to surprise you when I asked you to marry me. There, I finally got it out."

Samantha nearly fainted and now she was really crying. "Jason, your timing and your presentation here tonight had me thinking the worst," said Samantha.

"Then why are you still crying?" asked Jason, looking very confused.

"Because this just might be the happiest moment of my life. And the answer is yes, yes, yes," Samantha said emphatically.

Jason wrapped his arms around Samantha and firmly embraced her, nearly forgetting that he was still holding the wine bottle. "You have made me the happiest man in the world," Jason told Samantha. "I promise that I will be the best husband in the world."

They finally got inside and opened the bottle of wine. They sat down on the couch. "Why all the cloak and dagger?" Samantha asked Jason. "You really had me confused."

"Well, you know we have plans to visit my parents this weekend in New York. When I told my dad that I planned to propose to you soon, he suggested we spend some time with his accountant while we were in town. Financial planning is a necessary step when talking about marriage," said Jason. "I was going to ask you last Saturday night but I got cold feet. This is really a little scary for me and I wanted it to be right."

"Let me get this straight," Samantha said. "You finally decided to propose to me so that we could meet an accountant this weekend to do financial planning?"

"Yes, I guess, if you want to put it that way," Jason said with some hesitation.

"Then I think I love you even more," cried Samantha.

"Just like Samantha to get all goo-goo about financial planning," thought Jason, glad that he had not messed up.

"By the way," Samantha suddenly remembered. "Aren't you supposed to be giving me an engagement ring?"

"Actually, my mother helped me pick out a diamond at Christmas. I wanted to get it wholesale in New York because you can get really good stones for a good price. I thought you could pick out the setting when we are in New York this weekend," Jason said. "As you know, the stone is the bigger part of the investment."

Samantha was so happy. She just knew that Jason would have picked out a good investment-grade diamond. It should appreciate quite well.

"I can't believe you have been planning this since Christmas!" Samantha exclaimed. "This is so exciting, I've got to call my Mom right now," said Samantha.

"Wait, said Jason. "I have a better idea. Why don't we visit them in Chicago after we get the engagement ring? I really should ask for your parent's blessing."

"You mean I have to wait until after New York to tell my parents?" Samantha complained.

"Hey, I've been keeping this inside since Christmas. You can go another couple of weeks. We can go to New York this weekend, and Chicago next weekend," Jason suggested.

"Okay," agreed Samantha. "It will be tough, but I will do it. Right now I'm for getting cozy and working on that Merlot you brought with you."

Samantha and Jason flew to New York on Friday night. Jason had cashed in a couple of frequent flier tickets, free airline tickets they had earned from taking business flights. Jason had set up a meeting with the accountant for three o'clock on Saturday afternoon. That gave them time to pick out a setting for the ring in the morning, and Samantha was wearing her new ring when they went in to meet the accountant.

"Hello, my name is Bob Allen," the accountant greeted them. "I've been expecting you. By the way, congratulations!"

"Thanks, Mr. Allen," said Jason. "This is Samantha. We appreciate you taking time on Saturday to help us with our financial planning."

"My pleasure, and it's 'Bob' to both of you. From what Jason's dad tells me," Bob said turning to Samantha, "I might learn a little about financial planning from you."

Samantha blushed. "I'm pretty good with personal financial planning, but I haven't had much experience in financial planning for couples."

"I'm still going to be careful," Bob said in a friendly way. "I made an informal agenda of topics. Here is a copy for each of you. Make whatever notes you wish and be sure to ask questions."

"Thanks," said Jason. The paper listed the following topics:

- Insurance Planning
- Investment Planning
- Budget
- Credit Cards
- Taxes
- Net Worth

"That seems to be a lot of ground to cover in such a short time," suggested Samantha.

"It will go pretty fast," said Bob. "Just make sure we don't have any confusion on any of the topics or issues.

"Insurance is a good starting point. Your dad told me that you have employer-provided life, health, and accident insurance. Is that correct and, if so, exactly what coverages are offered?" asked Bob.

Jason looked helplessly at Samantha. "We each have $20,000 term life insurance, and we can purchase at our own expense another $20,000 each," said Samantha. "Neither of us has any other life insurance, and we have not chosen to take the added $20,000 company-sponsored program."

"That's probably okay for now," said Bob. "However, your requirements are about to make a dramatic change. At some point, you probably are going to be thinking about a family." Both Jason and Samantha were visibly embarrassed with the family discussion. Bob could sense their discomfort. "It may seem premature to discuss such things now, but now is the time. I would recommend that each of you consider buying a $20,000 whole life policy as soon as possible."

"Wait a minute," said Jason. "Everyone I have talked to says that term is the way to go. Any purchase of whole life is a faulty investment. 'Buy term and invest the difference,' they tell me."

"You are right on track about the term insurance, Jason," Bob replied. "However, a modest amount of whole life makes sense this way. The cost will seem to be higher than term insurance is presently, but most whole life policies have a fixed premium cost. That is, the cost never changes regardless of your age or health. Term insurance costs fluctuate with age. As you grow older, term insurance is much more expensive. Term insurance also has no value other than the death benefit.

"On the plus side, term insurance can be purchased when there is a need. For example, families with growing children will usually have a substantial amount of term insurance in force, sometimes even a million dollars. The idea here is that should something happen to one or both of the parents, there is a substantial nest egg available to raise the children and provide for their education.

"When the children have grown and are on their own, the term insurance can be cancelled. The whole life policy you buy now will still be with you. A $20,000 policy is usually quite adequate to handle final arrangements and the like. It is never purchased to handle retirement needs; there are better investments for that. Unlike term insurance, whole life will typically pay an annual dividend. You can take the dividend as cash or you can take it as additional paid-up insurance. Doing the latter increases the face value of your policy, which increases the benefit. Let's say you let the dividends stay in the policy while your family is growing. It can happen that the $20,000 policy bought today may have a death benefit that has doubled or tripled in 30 to 40 years. I bought a $10,000 policy 35 years ago, and today it has a face value of over $43,000.

"When the kids are grown you can then choose to take the dividends, also called the return of premium paid, as cash. At that stage, it is likely that your annual dividend will be more than your annual premium cost. It's that way for me. So as you approach retirement, you can eliminate the budget item, insurance premium. Of course, the policy face value will no longer grow, but that's fine. There will likely be more than enough for the final expenses. Any questions so far?"

"Let me make sure I have this straight," said Samantha. "Don't buy any more company term insurance now but instead invest in a whole life policy. Any dividends declared should be left in the policy to buy more insurance. Buy term insurance as the family grows, making sure the amount is sufficient to raise the children including education. Cancel the term portion of your insurance program when the children are grown, and start applying the whole life dividends to the premium."

"That's a good summary, Samantha. Let's move on to health and accident insurance," said Bob.

"I have a question," said Jason. "Are the dividends declared by the insurance company taxable? I know dividends from securities are usually taxable."

"Great question. The answer is no," said Bob. "Remember, an insurance dividend is considered a return of paid premiums. That gets complicated, but the bottom line is that insurance dividends are not subject to taxation, at least at this time. IRS rules change, so you have to stay up-to-date all the time."

"I see. Thanks," said Jason.

"Health, accident, disability and hospitalization insurance is often misunderstood, and many people don't have adequate coverage for a variety of reasons. The biggest reason is cost. This insurance is expensive and it is not getting any cheaper," said Bob. "Since you both work at the same company, I need to ask a question: Can you tailor your program? What I mean by tailoring is this, are you permitted to select some coverage and decline others?"

"Gee, I don't know," said Jason.

"Yes we can," Samantha quickly responded. "We both have company-sponsored health coverage, that is, the company provides some coverage at their expense. Since their coverage is very basic, we can upgrade at our own expense. For example, the company provided program has a $500 deductible and after that, expenses are shared 60% by the company and 40% by the employee. It's called the 500/60/40 plan. The best plan is 100/90/10; a $100 deductible and then a 90/10 split, the company taking 90% of the expense. The cost is very high, however."

"That's right," said Bob. "But for the employees with families, a lower deductible and a smaller cost share may be cost effective. You will just have to run the numbers when the time comes. If you both work at the same company, you may have an option for one of you to give up the company-sponsored program and roll that cost savings into a family plan. Check on that when you get the chance. It may be another way to reduce monthly expenses.

"One last point before we move on," said Bob. "If one or both of you leave *Switches.com*, you will no longer be part of their insurance program, obviously. You do have an option. You can elect a program called COBRA to continue your health insurance. COBRA guarantees continued coverage in the former company program for 18 months, but you must pay the entire cost."

"Bob, we are in an HMO now," said Jason. "What is your opinion of that arrangement?"

"We have the option of declining the HMO and taking the traditional route," injected Samantha. "We obviously have to pick up the difference in cost if there is any, however."

"There is really nothing wrong with HMOs," said Bob. "In some instances they get a bad rap. There are horror stories on both sides of the issue, but typically a doctor will not neglect a patient just because of an HMO. HMOs are business organizations. Doctors, pharmacies and hospitals band together and sell their services. The more customers they have, the greater the opportunity to spread their cost. By doing so, they become very competitive and are usually less costly.

"Some people do not want to give up their freedom to choose their caregiver. The traditional approach has that advantage, but you pay for it. I have a friend who was diagnosed with cancer when he was young, and he was really glad that he had traditional insurance so that he could choose his own doctors. It's a trade-off between cost and flexibility.

"Do you pay for the other types of insurance, disability and so forth?" Bob asked.

"Yes, I have checked those, and the basic program from the company is pretty good," Samantha answered. "We have to pay extra for the disability insurance, but it doesn't cost very much. Health insurance is the big one."

"Good. Do you have any other insurance questions? I am sure you aren't ready for a Medicare pitch yet, are you?" Bob joked.

"No, we aren't ready for the rocking chair just yet," Jason said with a smile.

"The next item on the agenda is investment planning. Would you please summarize what you are presently doing?" asked Bob.

"Do you want to take that one or shall I?" replied Jason, motioning to Samantha.

"Oh, you go ahead," said Samantha.

"Each of us has managed to accumulate the equivalent of nine months take-home pay," said Jason. "We have the dough in a money market account. We earn in the neighborhood of 5% per year on the money, and we have avoided tapping that account for other purposes. Although I must admit I have been tempted at times.

"We also contribute $2,000 each year to an individual IRA, and we have directed the money be invested in an S&P 500 index fund. We have chosen a traditional IRA as opposed to the Roth style. I set aside 12% of my *Switches.com* pay in the company sponsored 401(k) program. Samantha contributes 10%, but she is also buying a house; I guess you could call that investing as well. We both have a little in certificates of deposit (CDs), but we think we want to put that to work in an investment that has a higher potential return.

"I am impressed," said Bob. "You both appear to be financially well disciplined. I suggest that each of you stretch your 401(k) contributions to the maximum allowable by your company. That will allow you to take full advantage of any matching funds from the company. Once married you will be able to eliminate one of your living quarters; the apartment I would imagine. Any savings you generate by doing this plus the money in the CDs gives you the opportunity to make a nice move into a securities-based investment program. Here you will encounter obvious risk but at your age the reward opportunity far outweighs any risk. You may want to start out with quality mutual funds. The nature of mutual funds is that a fund manager buys several stocks and bonds based on a strategy and then sells shares in his investment. Open any newspaper to the financial pages and you will see multiple pages listing mutual funds. Some are very specialized, such as funds that focus on the healthcare industry or perhaps stocks from Internet-related businesses, and others are more general, like your S&P 500 index fund.

"At your age, I would recommend you consider funds that are aggressive in investment growth opportunities. You can afford to accept some risk since history has shown the U.S. securities market will be a growth market over time. One caution: do not become discouraged with short-term losses. They will occur. You are in it for the long-term, particularly during your high-income producing years.

"The home that you own, Samantha, is also an investment," said Bob.

"Samantha did a lot of analysis when she bought the house," Jason said. "We have definitely decided to stay there. What do we do about the title in the house and our other investments? Should they be in both our names or individually held?

"Maybe I am going to have a prenuptial agreement and keep the house and money in my name," Samantha kidded Jason.

"I can't help you with that one," laughed Bob, "but I know a good lawyer. If you decide to forego the prenup, the question about title to the house and other investments is a good one. This brings up the necessity of beginning estate planning. Without a will, should anything happen to one or both of you, your estate will have to go through a process called probate. The law usually provides that the property of one spouse automatically passes to the survivor unless there is an express legal document that states otherwise. The legal transfer without a will can be time consuming and potentially expensive with lawyers, court costs and so on. Individual wills and powers of attorney short circuit the system and allow timely transfer of assets. A will becomes even more critical when children are involved. You can direct how they are to be cared for should you both not survive. Without a will, it can get ugly."

Samantha looked at Jason and said, "That's one I had not thought of. My dad's best golfing friend is a lawyer; I'll ask Dad about that next time I talk to him. I can also check on the prenuptial agreement," she added playfully.

"Good idea," said Jason. "On the will part, I mean."

"Might I suggest that you discuss wills, powers of attorney, living wills and health care representation as well when you talk to the lawyer," Bob suggested. "It is essential that you protect your joint net worth."

"If I remember correctly, net worth is that difference between what we own and the expenses or unpaid bills or contracts that we have accumulated," Jason said. Samantha and Bob nodded their approval. "We sure want to maximize that," said Jason.

"Is budgeting the next subject, Bob," asked Samantha.

"It sure is," said Bob. "Establishing a budget is likely not new to either of you, but you would be surprised at the number of people who live from paycheck to paycheck.

"Start with your savings and investment goals. I think you already know about paying yourself first: Automatically designate a portion of your take-home pay for investment, say 10%. It sounds like you are already doing that. Then detail your known expenses: food, utilities, home expense, transportation, church, clothing, and so on. Some of these items will fluctuate, but generally you can get a handle on the aggregate. Subtract that from the balance after savings and see if it works. If there is a positive balance, perhaps you may want to increase your savings.

"A budget is a flexible tool. It's sole purpose is to create a framework to live within. If you continually blow it on a monthly basis, then either you have missed some expenses or you have lost your ability to discipline yourself.

"Hand-in-glove with budgeting is the way you pay for expenditures. Today that includes cash, checks, credit cards, debit cards and direct withdrawals," Bob continued.

"I know about cash," said Samantha. "Jason rarely has any. I saw him use a credit card at the post office for three stamps. I was so embarrassed."

"Actually, that was a good move," said Bob.

"Right on! I hate cash. Besides, I earn rebate dollars with my credit card, Sam. You know that's why I do it," Jason said, looking at Samantha.

"Not so fast," said Bob. "Let's look at each payment method individually. Generally, I agree that you should use a credit card whenever possible. It avoids carrying large amounts of cash, it minimizes the use of checks–checks you often must pay for–and there are bonuses. The bonuses may be no-cost airline tickets, cash discounts on auto purchases or leases, and maybe just plain cash rebates. There is a downside, however. You must keep track of your purchases–keep the charge receipts. Make sure you verify all charges on your monthly bill; don't assume that your statement is error free. Second, use discipline when using your credit cards. Some studies have shown that people spend 20% more when they use credit cards instead of cash, because paying out cash seems a lot more real. And finally, *pay the entire credit card balance by the due date every month.* The interest and finance charges are very expensive.

"Debit cards are a different story. Debit cards are a great marketing tool created by banks. A debit card is an electronic instant check. Each time a debit card is used to make a purchase, the funds in a bank account are immediately deducted and transferred to the vendor. The advantage of a debit card is that it is difficult to overdraw your bank balance. For some that is an important characteristic. But debit cards earn no rebates and create no float. Float is that time that passes between purchase and the time the actual payment is made, or in other words, the time when you get to carry an interest-free loan.

"Checks are useful for those recurring bills that generally pop up monthly. If it is not possible to use a credit card, then a check is in order. There are vendors, however, that will accept an arrangement where your checking account will be tapped automatically to pay their bill. The best examples are utilities such as cable, gas, and electric. If a credit card is not possible, then this electronic transfer is a good system. The advantages are that the transfer is made on the due date and not before. You will never miss a bill or be late with a payment and you have no check costs. The disadvantage is that you have to remember that a deduction is coming and account for it in the checking account balance."

"How are you two doing?" Bob asked. "Do we need to take a break? Anybody want a *Coke* or *Pepsi*?"

"Do you have a *Diet Coke*?" asked Samantha.

"I sure wish you would get off those diet drinks, Sam. Don't you know they cause cancer," said Jason. "I'll take the real thing if you have it, Bob," Jason said. Bob returned with the drinks for Samantha and Jason, plus a *Diet Coke* for himself. Jason looked at him disapprovingly.

"This has been a good discussion," said Bob as they sipped their drinks. "You two are much more disciplined than most of my clients. And financial planning is more about discipline than how much money you have. Did you read about that cleaning lady who never made more than $15,000 per year, but she just gave millions of dollars to charities? People need to learn if they just consistently set aside some every month, it grows bigger than they could ever imagine.

Bob finished his drink and got back to business. "We can't have this conversation without some discussion about taxes. Have you set the wedding date yet?"

Samantha was ready to answer that one. "We are considering a December date, perhaps a couple of days before Christmas," said Samantha. "That's always a festive time of the year and we would like to travel to Belize or some place like that for a honeymoon. No firm date yet, however."

"I'm glad to see that you are also taking the opportunity to enjoy your money. I have other clients who get so caught up in financial planning, they forget that the point of good planning is to enhance their quality of life, not to live like a miser," Bob said. "But did you know that if you waited until New Year's Day, you could get the government to pay for your honeymoon night?" asked Bob.

"Now just how do you do something like that?" asked Jason, intrigued by the idea.

"Newly married couples usually have a tax problem," said Bob. "Let me explain. It is likely that this problem will be solved at some point with legislation, but as of now, it is a real issue.

"Each of you currently files an annual income tax return as a single taxpayer. Once married, you will likely file a joint return. Let's say that each of you has taxable income of $55,000. Taxable income is your total income after all deductions, write-offs and credits. Your individual marginal tax rate is 28%. Once married, your taxable income becomes $110,000 and the marginal tax rate jumps to 31%. You pay an extra 3% on part of your income, which probably will cost you an extra couple of hundred dollars."

"What happens if for the first year we choose to file separately?" asked Jason. "Can we escape the added tax?"

"I'm afraid not," said Bob. "You would then be classified as 'married filing separately' and the rate is the same as if you filed jointly.

"That's crazy," said Samantha. "I had heard about this, but I never paid much attention to it."

"It's called the marriage tax penalty," said Bob. "It wasn't meant to be that way, but something happened when the tax law was written and the language got screwed up. It now takes a change in the law that only Congress can legislate and then the President must approve. Everyone agrees it is wrong, but the system to change it is slow."

"Jeez," said Jason. "That's just not right. Thanks for filling us in."

"No problem. And I think that takes us to the end of the agenda," said Bob, referring to the paper he gave them when they first came in.

"We sure appreciate you taking the time to give us the benefit of your advice and experience," said Jason.

"Yes, thank you," Samantha added. "I think we generally have a pretty good handle on budgeting and the use of credit cards. I am particularly appreciative of the great explanation of the various insurance programs and the wide range of options available as investments. That marriage tax thing is a real disappointment. I think I will write to my congressman and my senator and tell them a thing or two."

"Good idea," said Bob. "I was happy to be able to help. Jason's father has been a good client for many years. I'm glad to help his son and new daughter-in-law start out on the right direction. Feel free to come back if you would like to review your post-marriage financial situation. This meeting is free, but depending on your net worth at the next meeting, I might start charging you," Bob said with a smile.

"Thanks for the offer. We just might take you up on that," said Jason.

"Thanks for the Cokes too," Samantha said as they got up to leave.

"Good luck to you both," replied Bob, showing them out of his office.

On the way back home, neither Jason nor Samantha spoke for some time. Finally, Samantha broke the silence. "You know, I really think we have established a good game plan for our individual financial programs. It kind of makes me feel sorry for those who never take the time to get good counseling."

"Yeah, you didn't know what a good catch I was, did you? Putting sound financial planning ahead of romance," replied Jason.

"Jason, you are crazy. Let's go back and review our notes or something," Samantha said with a suggestive smile.

"At my parent's house?" Jason smiled.

Key Economic Terms – Chapter 12

Financial planning

Frequent flier miles

Insurance planning

Investment planning

Budget

Credit Cards

Taxes

Net Worth

Term life insurance

Whole life insurance

Policy

Premium

Insurance dividends

Additional paid-up insurance

Return of premium paid

Health insurance

Accident insurance

Hospitalization insurance

Disability insurance

COBRA

HMO

Medicare

Mutual funds

Prenuptial agreement

Title

Probate

Will

Living will

Power of attorney

Health care representation

Net worth

Credit cards

Debit cards

Float

Electronic transfer

Marriage tax penalty

Chapter 13
Family Decisions: The Utility Chapter

It was a beautiful wedding. Jason and Samantha decided to have a New Year's Eve wedding in Chicago, saying "I do" one minute after midnight and beating the tax man. They spent one night at the Hyatt in Chicago before flying to Belize for their honeymoon.

When Jason and Samantha returned to Indianapolis, they moved Jason's things from his apartment to Samantha's–or we should say–their house, as the house title now listed both of their names as joint owners with rights of survivorship.

Jason and Samantha continued to move up at *Switches.com*. Jason was named Business Manager of the printers and scanners section, and Samantha was promoted to a newly-created position of Manager of Customer Satisfaction.

It was a late Wednesday afternoon when Samantha received a call on her direct phone line. "Hello, this is Samantha Cooley." Even after being married for almost a year, she still felt strange saying her new name.

"Hello, Samantha, this is Joe Perkins from Computer Management Recruiters. I was given your name by a former associate of yours, and I wondered if I could talk to you about an exciting management position that I have been retained to fill."

"My first headhunter call," Samantha thought. Management recruiters, commonly referred to as headhunters, are people who are hired by a company that is trying to fill an open employment position. The headhunter gets information about the requirements of the job, and then the headhunter will use their networks of contacts to find viable candidates for that position. Joe Perkins, from the sound of his company name, specializes in finding candidates for management positions in computer companies. He probably talked to his contacts and found out that Samantha is doing a good job at *Switches.com* in a position that is closely related to the job that he is trying to fill. Typically, the company who is hiring the new employee will pay a placement fee to the headhunter for finding a candidate who is ultimately hired. It is not uncommon for the headhunter to get 50% of the manager's first year salary. Another arrangement is for a company to have a management recruiter on retainer, meaning they pay the headhunter a flat fee to help fill any open positions that may come up. Bottom line: it can be very expensive for companies to recruit qualified, experienced employees, especially managers or people with specific technical skills.

"I would be glad to talk to you, Joe, but could you call me tonight at home?" Samantha requested. It is considered bad form to talk about a new job when you are supposed to be working at your current job!

"That would be fine," Joe replied. "Can you give me your home phone and a good time to call you?"

Samantha gave him her phone number and suggested that he call her after 8 p.m. That would give her time to talk with Jason first.

"Guess who called me today at work?" Samantha asked Jason when she got home. They usually drove separately because they never knew when one might have a late meeting. Today it was Samantha with the late meeting, and Jason had already started dinner.

"Bill Gates?" Jason guessed.

"No. But I wish he would call. I could tell him that all our customers are calling to complain about our computers, but their problems are usually caused by bugs with a new Windows release," Samantha said sharply. Jason knew Microsoft was a hot button with her. He smiled without her seeing him.

"Actually, the call was from a headhunter, my first one. Do you ever get calls?" Samantha asked Jason.

"Sure. Since my job takes me to a lot of conventions, the place is usually crawling with headhunters. How did you get rid of yours?" Jason asked.

"I didn't," Samantha replied. "I told him to call tonight."

"Why's that?" Jason asked. "You just got another promotion. Don't you like your job?"

"Sure I like it," said Samantha. "But I thought it wouldn't hurt to find out what positions are out there. Sometimes people stay in a position so long, their salary falls well below the market value, and they never know it."

"I don't think you have that problem," Jason said. "You make more money than I do." Samantha could tell that bothered him, but he only brought it up as a joke.

"Only a little bit more. And besides, I'm worth more. I'm a WLU graduate. You went to that glorified high school in southern Indiana, Bloomington University," Samantha explained, still fiercely loyal to her alma mater.

"Well, it should be interesting to hear what your headhunter has to say," Jason said, knowing it would be impossible to argue that he had the better college degree. "I guess I should have talked to those headhunters. Maybe I could be making more money than you right now."

Samantha and Jason had dinner, went through the mail, and promptly at 8 p.m. the phone rang. "Hello," said Samantha.

"Hi, Samantha. This is Joe Perkins calling back. Is this a good time?"

"Absolutely. You are very punctual," Samantha said.

"In my job, I have to be. In any case, let me tell you what I have. There is a company in Indianapolis that wants to hire a Vice President of Customer Service. As you can probably guess from the job title, the company that I represent is smaller than *Switches.com*. They are located in Indianapolis, so no relocation is required. The position has a solid base salary plus bonus possibilities that could potentially put your annual compensation in the six-figure range."

"What is the name of the company?" Samantha asked, a bit stunned by the six-figure comment. Even after her promotion, she was only making $60,000 per year.

"For confidentiality reasons, I can't reveal the company name at this time. That is pretty standard at this point in the discussions," Joe explained truthfully. "If you are interested, I will give them your résumé. If they think you are a good candidate, I then arrange an interview for you."

"Is there anything else that you can tell me about the position?" Samantha asked.

"Only that this is an aggressive, fast-growing company. They plan to go public in two years, and they want to be in a solid position for an IPO," Joe said. Samantha jotted down some notes on a pad.

"Okay," said Samantha. "Let me think it over and I will get back to you. Do you have a number that I can call you tomorrow night?"

"I'm traveling, but I could call you tomorrow night at this same time, if that's okay," Joe suggested.

"That would be fine," said Samantha.

"And remember, this is all confidential. There is really nothing to lose by sending them your résumé," said Joe. In his experience, some people tended to be very reluctant to even send in a résumé, probably because they felt like they were being disloyal to their current employer. Usually these people were the best candidates, because they were serious and took their careers seriously."

"I understand. I'll talk to you tomorrow night," Samantha said.

"So how did it go?" Jason asked. He was waiting anxiously in the next room.

"Pretty interesting. The headhunter represented a company who is looking for a Vice President of Customer Service," Samantha explained.

"A vice president position? Didn't he think you are a little young for that?" Jason asked.

"Well, he might not know how old I am. Plus he said this is for a small company, so maybe everyone is a vice president. But he did say the salary potential could be six figures with bonus," Samantha continued.

Jason whistled. "$100,000. Wow! That would make me interested," Jason said, forgetting his minor jealousy over his wife's higher income for the prospect of increasing the family income by something like $40,000. "How can they offer so much money?"

"I suspect the key word is 'bonus'. Small companies like this often offer smaller base salaries, but if the company does well, everyone gets a big bonus," Samantha speculated.

"What's this about an IPO?" Jason asked Samantha, looking over her notes.

"An IPO is an initial public offering. The headhunter told me they planned to go public in a couple of years, meaning they will make an initial public offering of stock. Your friend Bill Gates became a millionaire overnight when Microsoft went public, plus about 30 other Microsoft employees who joined the company in the early days."

"So you could be a millionaire in two years?" said Jason, half-joking.

"Maybe. It depends if they would give me an equity interest in the company, meaning I own part of the company rather than just being an employee. Some of these small companies might offer 1-5% of the equity in the company to entice employees to work for them," Samantha said.

"Combined with a really low base salary," Jason finished the sentence.

"Probably," Samantha agreed. "It is a high risk, high return situation."

"Does that sound interesting to you?" Jason asked.

"Maybe. We could then work at different companies," Samantha said. Even though they had not talked much about it, it was awkward having both Samantha and Jason working at the same company. In the cases where they had to interact on a professional basis, it was uncomfortable.

"That would be a plus," Jason agreed, not seeing the need to go into any additional detail.

"And we are in pretty good financial shape. We could probably afford for me to try something a little risky. We don't have any kids yet," she added.

"Yes, if there is ever a time to look at something like this, now would be the perfect time," Jason agreed, hoping to finish the conversation without getting into a discussion about kids.

"But if we decide to have kids in the next couple years, taking this position could be a terrible mistake. I would be in a relatively new job and the position probably has more responsibility and stress," Samantha said, projecting forward.

Since it was clear he couldn't avoid the children issue, Jason decided to confront it head-on. "Maybe we do need to decide on our plan for children," Jason said directly. "It seems like decisions like this would be much easier if we had already decided on that."

Samantha was surprised by Jason's initiative. Usually she was the one who initiated all of the "major life decision" conversations. And she did have a plan; she just hadn't talked to Jason about it yet.

"Maybe you should quit your job and we could start a family," Jason suggested. "Like you said, we are in pretty good financial shape. I think if you quit to have babies, we could still afford the house and remain financially comfortable."

Samantha wasn't expecting this suggestion. "Typical male attitude," she thought. "He thinks I should quit my job because the man's job is always more important."

"Why don't you quit your job?" Samantha said with a little anger. "After all, I make more money than you." She realized that comment wasn't fair.

"Well, you are the one always making comments about having babies. I just thought it was more important to you," Jason retorted.

"Look, I'm sorry," Samantha apologized. "I shouldn't have made that comment about making more money. We really both bring in a pretty good salary, and there is not much of a difference."

"Yes, and I want children too," Jason said, following Samantha's cue to cool off the conversation. "I just thought that you would be more qualified at taking care of children, so it would make more sense for you to stay home."

"Comparative advantage, you mean," Samantha said.

"Uh oh," Jason said. "I think I am about to get another economics lesson."

"You mean you don't remember comparative advantage?" Samantha said, genuinely surprised. "Comparative advantage is a key principle of economics. How did you miss that one?"

"Somehow I found a way," Jason admitted sheepishly.

"Okay, let me try to explain this, but don't get sensitive on me. Promise?" Samantha pleaded.

"Okay, I'll try not to," Jason agreed.

"Good. We are talking about who should go to work, and who should stay home with the kids," Samantha laid out the situation.

"Right," Jason agreed. "That is the basic question."

"Not to be big-headed or anything, but I think I could argue that I am better than you in both situations. I am better at work, because I make more money than you; and I would also be better taking care of children," Samantha stated as kindly as she could.

"I don't know why I would be sensitive about comments like that," Jason said sarcastically, "but I guess that is true. You do make more money than I do, at least for now, and I am more than willing to concede that you would be better than me taking care of kids. So where does that get us? You should do both things and I should do nothing?"

"Of course not," Samantha said. "We need to figure out how to take best advantage of our combined abilities."

"I don't think I understand," Jason said. "You just told me I am no good at either thing."

"Let me try a different example. Let's say that you can peel 200 potatoes in a day, or alternatively you can peel 500 carrots in a day. I can peel only 150 potatoes in day, or alternatively I can peel 100 carrots in a day," Samantha said, writing down the numbers on a piece of paper:

	Potatoes	Carrots
Jason	200	500
Samantha	150	100

"Gee, thanks. You made me better at peeling both types of vegetables," Jason said sarcastically.

"I'm trying to help you get your confidence back," Samantha said playfully. "So if you are best at peeling both types of vegetables, how can we best divide the work?"

"I don't know," said Jason, confused by the problem. "How many carrots and potatoes do we need peeled?"

"Let's see," Samantha said, looking over the numbers. "To make the numbers work out, let's say we need 600 potatoes and 2,000 carrots."

"Okay, so it would take me 3 days to do the potatoes or 4 days to do the carrots," Jason figured in his head. "And it would take you 4 days to do the potatoes and 10 days to do the carrots." He pondered the problem for a few minutes. "I guess we would be best if you did the potatoes and I did the carrots," Jason finally decided.

"Right, then we could get the whole job done in 4 days," Samantha confirmed. "That would be the best way to organize to get the job done as quickly as possible."

"Why does it work out that way?" Jason asked.

"In this problem, you have an absolute advantage in peeling potatoes and in peeling carrots. You can peel both types of vegetables faster than me. If you look at the numbers, however, I have a comparative advantage in peeling potatoes. In other words, you were way faster than me at carrots, but only a little faster than me with potatoes. I have a comparative advantage at potatoes; because compared to how bad I am at carrots relative to you, I am not nearly as bad at potatoes. We are going to get the most done if I specialize in the thing that I am almost as good as you in, and you specialize in the thing that you do much better than me. When you worked out the numbers, it showed that I should peel potatoes and you should peel carrots." Samantha thought that she had given a pretty good explanation, especially considered it had been seven years now since introductory economics.

"So what does this mean to our situation?" Jason asked. "Do I quit and stay home with the kids or do you?"

"You tell me," Samantha challenged him.

"Let's see. You are a little better at your job than me, or least that's what you seem to think," Jason thought aloud. "But I would guess that you are going to much better than me at taking care of kids. So you have a comparative advantage in taking care of kids, which means that you quit and stay home. Is that right?" wondering how he ended up with the answer that he wanted.

"That is what the principle of economics would suggest," Samantha said, smiling at the confused look on Jason's face. "But maybe you are evaluating the wrong choices," Samantha said.

"I knew there would be a catch," Jason said with disgust. "You are going to bring up real and nominal variables, or the time value of money, or something like that?"

"No, that's not what I was thinking," Samantha said. I'm just not sure that either one of us needs to quit. *Switches.com* is now letting people who spend a lot of time on the phone or on the computer telecommute, meaning they can stay at home several days a week and do their work on a more flexible schedule. I could possibly do something like that, and also have a nanny come during the day."

"That sounds like a pretty good option. Then you could be with the kids if there is an emergency," Jason said.

"Right, and to eat breakfast and lunch together. And I could take a break during the day to be with the kids and catch up on the work at night after they've gone to bed," Samantha continued.

"That sounds perfect. But why would *Switches.com* let you do that?" Jason asked.

"For the same reason these companies pay headhunters $50,000 to recruit a person like me. It is expensive to find good people. When a company finds a good person, they are willing to be flexible to retain that person. At least the more progressive companies," she added.

"Well, that sounds great if the company will go for it. Where does that leave you with that job that we discussed tonight?" Jason asked.

"If you are ready to go for kids, I think it would be better to stay at *Switches.com*," Samantha said, "at least if they will let me telecommute. They know me, and they are more likely to be flexible."

"That sounds like a good plan," Jason agreed. "And when do we start with kids?"

"How about right now?" Samantha said, taking his hand and leading him upstairs.

* * *

Apparently things were successful, because nine months later, Jason and Samantha's first child was born, Jason Junior. Samantha took one month off work and then started telecommuting. They also hired a nanny named Becky to take care of Jason Junior while Samantha was doing her work.

Although telecommuting was a very effective way to get the work done, it had the undesired effect of taking Samantha off the fast track. "Out of sight, out of mind" is how some explained it to Samantha. She didn't think this was fair, especially since her work performance was better than ever.

Jason, however, continued to do very well at work. On Jason Junior's second birthday, he was named Director of Sales for *Switches.com*. Samantha continued in her position as Manager of Customer Satisfaction. Things were sailing along smoothly for the Cooley family.

The company was growing as well. Instead of simply selling computer equipment, *Switches.com* had entered into several production agreements to make private label computer equipment.

One day several months after Jason took over his new job, he came home with a bottle of Merlot. "Good news or bad news," Samantha asked immediately.

"Not really either," Jason said unconvincingly.

"Try again," Samantha said.

"Okay, troubling news," Jason said, hedging his words a little. "Work stuff," he added, knowing that would keep Samantha from getting too worried.

"Let me get Junior to bed, and then we can talk about it," Samantha said. Jason kissed the baby, and Samantha took him up to the nursery. She returned in about ten minutes. Jason was sitting on the couch with the bottle of Merlot and two glasses on the coffee table. This had become their tradition when talking through difficult issues.

"So what happened?" Samantha asked, getting comfortable on the couch. Jason poured two glasses of wine and handed one to Samantha.

"One of the salespeople, Tom Charles, came to me today and said we have a problem with a customer," Jason started to explain.

"Which customer?" Samantha asked in a business-like tone. Customer satisfaction, after all, was her responsibility.

"*High Tech Labs*," Jason answered, "from Louisville."

"I haven't heard about a problem with them," Samantha said. "I could go check my database."

"No, that's not necessary. The problem just came up today. Tom brought the customer into the office today to see the new production line. The customer was having a problem with an invoicing problem, and he wanted to meet the person in charge. When the receptionist told him that you work out of your house, he went ballistic. He's a little old-fashioned, you see," Jason explained, trying to ease the pain. "He said the Director of Customer Service should be in the office taking care of problems."

"I'm sorry he feels that way. This is the first problem I've heard about this since I started telecommuting two years ago," Samantha said.

"That's not quite true," Jason said reluctantly.

"What do you mean?" Samantha asked, starting to get defensive.

"Other people talk about it in the office. Many people resent the fact that you work out of your house. There are other customers who don't like the fact that you don't work in the main office. Everyone tries to avoid saying anything to me, even though I am Director of Sales and customer satisfaction is a key part of my job."

"If I wasn't your wife, would you have brought up this problem to me?" Samantha asked pointedly.

"Yes, I guess I would have. I know how much you like the arrangement with the baby. When this happened today, however, I started thinking about how Jason Junior is getting older now, and maybe you would like to come back to the office. It would get you back on the fast track," Jason said encouragingly.

Samantha realized that Jason was trying to be considerate in this conversation, but it still burned her that people were saying things behind her back and she didn't even know it. "What if we have another baby?" Samantha asked Jason. "Then what?"

"I don't know," admitted Jason. "I just thought this might be the solution to the immediate problem. Do you want to have another baby?"

"I think I do," said Samantha. "Jason Junior is getting so big now, and he is ready for a brother or sister."

"That would be great," said Jason, genuinely excited about the prospect of another baby. "I guess things aren't that bad at work. There are complaints here and there, but you still get the job done."

"Actually, there is something else that I have been thinking about," Samantha said, now that she had a good opening. "I was thinking of quitting my job."

"Quitting your job?" Jason asked. "I thought you loved your job. And you bring home a pretty good income, too."

"I do love my job. There are just other things that I want to do. I just want to maximize my utility."

"Huh," said Jason. "Your utility?"

"I always forget that you don't know anything about economics," Samantha said. She took a sip of the Merlot and asked, "Jason, how do you measure your overall happiness and well-being?"

"I don't know. Net worth, maybe," hoping the economics reference was a clue to the right answer.

"So if you had a net worth of one billion dollars and were sickly and lonely, you would be better off than if you had a net worth of one million dollars and were healthy and had a beautiful wife?" Samantha posed the dilemma.

"Of course not," Jason objected. "Money isn't everything."

"So net worth isn't a very good measure of happiness and well-being. So which one are you going to pick?"

"I don't know. This is a hard one. There are so many things to be considered in a measure of happiness and well-being. Money is one, . . . health, family, . . . wine," he said, taking another sip of Merlot. "I don't know what I would pick."

"That's why economists came up with the idea of utility. A person's utility represents a person's happiness and well-being, however each individual person defines what he or she considers as overall happiness and well-being."

"Good concept. But why does quitting your job increase your utility?" Jason asked.

"Because it will give me more time with Jason Junior, and it will allow me to have another baby without feeling guilty that I might be shirking my work responsibilities. It would also give you more freedom to take business trips without worrying about coordinating my travel schedule, . . . you know, lots of things," she blurted out.

"But it seems like such a waste," Jason said. "You are so successful at work. You spent all that time at college and you know most business things better than me. Plus we give up your salary, which in turn changes all of our savings calculations, retirement plans, budgets, and so forth."

"I've already calculated all those things. We will have less money, but we will still be fine. I just want to concentrate on more important things," Samantha said softly. She took him by the hand (again) and they went upstairs.

* * *

Nine months later Stephanie was born. One year after that came another boy, Alex. With three kids Samantha was working harder than ever. But she was also very content and happy that she was maximizing her utility.

Key Economic Terms – Chapter 13

Management recruiter (headhunter)
Retainer
Initial Public Offering (IPO)
Base salary
Bonus

Equity
Risk
Absolute advantage
Comparative advantage
Utility

Chapter 14
The Promotion: The Managerial Economics Chapter

It's 8 p.m. Thursday night when the phone rings. Jason Junior, now a freshman in high school, has just finished a homework assignment and is in the kitchen looking for a snack.

"I'll get it," Junior yelled. "Hello. Hi Dad. I'm okay. I just finished my math assignment and I am working up the energy to tackle English. Yeah, football practice is going great. I've got an outside chance to start Saturday's game. Are you going to be there? Good, I know I'm only a freshman, but I am ready.

"Mom's upstairs with Stephanie," Junior continued. "I think they are going over her dance recital routine. Man, you should see how stupid it looks! Wait a minute; I'll get Mom. Hey Mom," Junior yelled without covering the phone, "Dad's on the phone and wants to talk with you."

"Okay," said Samantha, "I'll take it up here. Hello, Jason, how are you doing?" asked Samantha. "Hang up the phone, Junior. Junior! Just a minute, Jason, I think Junior set the phone down and forgot it." Samantha went to the top of the stairs and called for Junior again.

"Yeah Mom, what's up?" Junior answered.

"How about hanging up the phone in the kitchen?"

"Oh yeah, sorry about that Mom. I'll get it now," said Junior.

"There," Samantha said to Jason. "Sometimes it is a real zoo around here. Let's start over. How are you, Jason?"

"I'm fine, Sam. Junior just told me that he might start Saturday. It must be going well for him. I think Jake Roper, the starting quarterback, is either sick or has an injury."

"I am not sure which," said Samantha. "All I know is that it's hard to get a word in edgewise right now. I have no clue as to what Blue 46 or Red 23 mean. I am sure it has nothing to do with art class."

"All the rest of you guys getting by?" asked Jason. "Steph is excited about her junior high recital on Sunday. You haven't forgotten, have you?" inquired Samantha.

"Certainly not," said Jason, as he visualized three hours of video and camera work. "What about Alex?"

"Well, he is a mess; you are going to have to deal with him when you get home. He apparently got into it with a bunch of girls at recess and was sent to the principal's office again. How is it going in New York City? When will you be home?"

"Larry sent everyone home tonight but asked Steve Berg and myself to stay with him," said Jason. "We'll get a charter out of Teterboro tomorrow afternoon. That's why I called. Can you arrange something with the kids for tomorrow night? I want to take you out to *Ruth's Chris*. I've got a couple of things to go over, which are all good, by the way." Every since the botched proposal, Jason had been careful not to make good news sound like bad news.

Samantha thought to herself, "If Larry Johnson, the CEO of *Switches.com*, sent everyone home from one of the biggest meetings in company history a day early, but kept Jason onsite, something must be brewing."

"Did you get the deal put together?" asked Samantha.

"That's just it," said Jason, showing obvious excitement. "It looks like we are the new owners of *Egos Materials*. This increases our company size by 40% and really steps up the action in our semiconductor business. Larry is now planning a restructuring and he wants me to take a newly created position of Chief Operating Officer (COO). He will continue as CEO and Steve Berg will move from Director of Finance to Chief Financial Officer (CFO). Things are moving at light speed, and I am right in the middle. Larry wants to have an executive meeting Tuesday afternoon," Jason continued. "The former owner of *Egos* and his management team will be in town all day Monday to meet with us. On Tuesday, Steve and I are to make a presentation to Larry describing how we see the total operation coming together. He knows we won't have all the details, but Larry does want our best economic evaluation of what lies in store for the new *Switches.com.* I plan to work late tonight on some ideas, and I want to try them out on you tomorrow night at dinner."

"I can make that work," said Samantha. "Tell you what. I'll even go out and find a good bottle of Merlot for us to drink when we get home from dinner."

Sam always knew the right buttons to push. "Great, Sam. See you tomorrow," said Jason. "Tell Alex to get his act together. Good night, love you."

* * *

The group arrived by taxi at Teterboro, a small general aviation airport just over the river in New Jersey, at 2:45 p.m. on Friday. Their charter was scheduled for 3:15 p.m., so it appeared everything was on schedule.

Just then a tall and distinguished man greeted them. "Are y'all the *Switches.com* guys?"

Larry replied "Yes" at which time the stranger introduced himself as J. D. Sharp.

"I'm your pilot," said J. D. He looked like a fighter pilot from *Top Gun.* There was no doubt that he was in charge. "I've got that Falcon 50 over there," said J. D. "The weather is perfect and we'll be at Angels 40, that's 40,000 feet to y'all, in no time. Gonna have you home safe and sound before you know it." From that J. D. went through a safety briefing and told them more about the Falcon 50 than was probably necessary, but it did seem like J. D. was the right man for the job.

Once aboard, Larry asked Steve and Jason to sit across from him. The seats were arranged in groups of four, with pairs facing one another. As they reached cruise altitude, Larry began to provide some planning guidance regarding the *Egos* visit and the executive session planned for Tuesday.

"I know that Tuesday is pushing the timing a bit," said Larry, "but I want to see how you two see the economics of the new business. Then, we will put together a formal program that we can announce to the company. We will do that simultaneously with your promotion announcements. I really don't want anyone other than the three of us to know of the promotions or our plans with *Egos* before we have a solid game plan."

"Oh man," thought Jason. He sure hoped Samantha didn't say anything about their conversation last night before he could tell her of the confidentiality of the matter.

"Jason, are you okay?" asked Larry. "You look a little green. Is the airplane bothering you?"

"No, I'm fine, Larry," replied Jason, just thinking ahead.

"Okay," said Larry. "Why don't you two make some notes? Here are the topics I want you to expand on in our Tuesday meeting. If there are matters I have overlooked, please include them." Larry gave them a sheet of paper with the following topics:

- *Communications. How do we get the word out? How do we control our operations and how can we tell if everyone understands what's going on?*

- *People. How do we make sure we have the right partners both inside and outside the company?*

- *What are the cost categories? Which are the most significant?*

- *How do we maximize revenue and minimize cost?*

- *What about the relationship between price and volume?*

- *I am interested in the cost of money. How do we raise cash when we need to?*

- *We are going to have to increase our effort. Do we need to acquire more space for plant activities? Do we need to expand our present production facilities? What about new facilities?*

Larry continued after Jason and Steve had a chance to look over the paper. "Not only does that sound like a great deal to hash over, it is. But, gentlemen, we are on the brink of an incredible opportunity. This kind of opportunity comes around only rarely. I want to make the most of it. Don't worry about being overwhelmed; just break each piece into its smallest increments and then study and report on the basic economics of it all.

"Hey, it feels like we are beginning our descent. Does anyone have any questions?" Larry asked.

Jason wasn't sure if it was the whirlwind week, the successful acquisition of *Egos*, the promotion opportunity, the corporate jet flight, or just plain fatigue. In any case he offered no questions. Neither did Steve Berg.

"Good," replied Larry. "I hope you have a great weekend. Call me over the weekend if you have any questions." It was clear that Larry did not expect either Jason or Steve to just hang out until Monday. Saturday and Sunday looked like regular workdays with a recital and a football game thrown in for a little variety.

"Hi, Sam," Jason announced as he made his way to the refrigerator for a cold *Sam Adams*.

"Hi," Samantha replied. "You look really tense. Did everything go okay since we talked last night?"

"Frankly Sam, I'm really wired," said Jason. "Did you say anything to anyone about the promotion?"

"Yeah, I sent an e-mail to the entire neighborhood." She paused for effect. "No, of course not. Why?" asked Samantha.

"Thank the Lord," Jason sighed as he successfully emptied half of the *Sam Adams*. "Well, I wasn't supposed to mention it. I didn't find that out until after I talked to you."

About that time, the back door closed with a resounding bang. "Hey, Dad, Mom, I did it! I am the starting QB!" said Junior with great excitement. "I think I will go on a quick count for the first quarter and use a delayed cadence in the second quarter. I saw John Elway do that and he ate the Packer's lunch."

"Okay, tiger, slow down," Jason said. "The best thing you can do is just relax."

"How can I relax, Dad? This is my big chance," replied Junior. "Haven't you ever wanted to do well your first time with a new assignment?

Jason thought of his own situation and considered the similarity of his new assignment from Larry Johnson as he replied, "I think I know what you mean, Junior."

"Junior, you'd better get your head about you. You're in charge while your Father and I are out this evening," said Samantha.

"Gee, Mom, how does that look? The starting quarterback has to baby-sit the night before the big game," lamented Junior.

"Well, it will give you a chance to study the playbook, won't it?" Samantha said, more of a statement than a question.

"I guess so," said Junior. "Have a good time."

Jason planned to say a quick "hello" and "good-bye" to Stephanie and Alex, anxious to get to dinner and talk with Samantha. Stephanie was practicing for her recital. She hardly noticed that Dad had come back after being gone for a week. "Typical 13-year old girl," Jason thought.

Alex, however, was very glad to see his dad. "Can I come with you tonight?" Alex asked.

Jason felt guilty since he had been away all week, and he knew he would have to do a lot of work over the weekend. "Okay," Jason agreed, knowing that Samantha would probably not be too happy. She liked to have some husband/wife time alone each week. "Date night," she called it. Jason and Alex headed downstairs together. Samantha didn't look too upset. She knew how much Alex missed his dad.

"Thanks for making the arrangements for dinner Sam," said Jason as they arrived at *Ruth's Chris*.

"My pleasure," said Samantha. "Are you going from memory or do you have some notes?" Samantha knew he would want to talk business. She liked it too. After spending most of her time with the kids, she liked to talk about business issues. Alex had brought a portable video game with him, and he occupied himself while Jason and Samantha talked.

"I stayed up late last night and wrote a few things. And then Larry gave us a list of questions on the flight home. Please, Sam, critique me. This is a huge deal."

"No problem," said Samantha, never being shy about critiquing Jason. "Let's get on with it."

"I think it is essential that we communicate a strategy to all parts of the organization, the old and the new. After we combine the companies, my recommendation to Larry is that we create focus groups comprised of the various functional areas like sales, marketing, production, and so forth from people with *Switches.com* and *Egos*. This way we can get people from both companies working together on their specialty areas," Jason began. "We will follow with a written letter of instructions that details how the various functional areas fit into the overall plan.

"I also think we should retain our functional organizational setup long-term. I see no reason to dismantle what already works. We should retain the financial department, the administrative department, maintenance and repair as organized and assign them to Steve Berg. I'll take engineering, production, sales, marketing, and corporate development. I'll recommend that all *Switches.com* functional vice presidents submit their proposals as to how they will integrate the *Egos* operation in one month, taking into consideration the comments from the focus groups."

"Okay," said Samantha, "I understand. But how are you going to be able to be sure that everyone–and I mean all employees and team members–know what their role is? More importantly, how will you make sure everyone is in the information loop?"

"Perhaps we should try some attitude surveys," replied Jason. "We can supplement that with work councils and the like. I think most importantly, we have to make sure people are comfortable with the corporate leadership. If we have glitches there, we should fix them now.

"To be successful in this venture, we must have the right people in the right place. I was really impressed with the *Egos* Director of Engineering. We are weak at that position at *Switches.*"

"Do you mean that you think Sandy Andrews is weak?" asked Samantha.

"Yes. I know he is a long-time employee, not to mention that Sandy is Larry's brother-in-law," replied Jason. "Placing the *Egos* person in charge with Sandy as his assistant is a good fix, I think. Sandy is great with the detail and the *Egos* people will see this move as a plus if we install one of their leaders as a Vice President."

"That sounds fine as long as Larry will go for it," agreed Samantha. "It also gets complicated when relatives work together," thinking about the problems that they had.

"I want to discuss costs with you for a bit, Sam," Jason continued. But first we should probably decide what we want to order for dinner." They looked over the menus and placed their orders. Then they got back to business.

"I see our main cost categories as either variable or fixed costs. Our variable costs include people, materials, and promotional expenses. The main fixed costs include people, plant, and administrative overhead. These categories are not meant to be complete, Sam, but they do give us an agenda to discuss."

"You said 'people' twice, Dad," said Alex, not even lifting his eyes from his video game.

"He doesn't miss a thing," thought Jason. He had even forgotten Alex was at the table.

"That's because people expenses can be either fixed or variable. Variable costs are those expenses that increase or decrease based on business activity. Production workers are variable costs. The more you make, the more production workers that you need. Managers are fixed costs. You have them regardless of how much you produce."

"So you're a fixed cost, Dad?" asked Alex.

"Right, I am a fixed cost. Whether we make 5,000 units or 20,000 units, they still have to pay me," said Jason.

"Unless you produce zero, and then you are fired," Alex observed.

"Right, thanks for that happy thought," said Jason to his son.

"Alex reminds me of a good point, however," Jason said to Samantha. "We should performance base as many of our people as possible. This would keep much of our people cost as variable cost."

"What's performance base?" asked Samantha, who had never heard that term before.

Jason answered, "If we tie individual productivity to individual pay then our people will be rewarded when the company is successful. However, if we stumble, we are not faced with a horrendous fixed people cost."

"The employees have to eat, Jason," Samantha said with some authority. "Are you saying that if production falls and the sales team does not sell, no one will be paid?"

"No, not at all," said Jason. "A proper performance-based pay program has two parts. One is a fixed salary or hourly rate, the base pay. The second part is a bonus for superior performance by skilled labor or commissions for the sales people based on their sales. The senior management like me should have a base salary coupled with a bonus opportunity based on the profitability of the function the person manages. Performance-based pay helps turn part of our people cost into variable costs, as opposed to strictly fixed costs.

"You know, Samantha, any time we start up a new line or offer a new product; our short-term production costs will be high. The integration of *Egos* is a costly proposition. If we don't get our products and technology in sync early on, short-term production costs will eat our lunch. Now, as we move out over time–the long term–many of our startup and changeover activities will become fully amortized or written off. That's when we hit the cruise control button. We likely have core products that will pay the way initially for our startups. The important thing is to recognize any non-winners and not succumb to an escalation of commitment."

"What's 'escalation of commitment'?" asked Alex, still engrossed in his game but obviously listening to the conversation at the same time.

"Look at it this way," said Jason. "Let's say you spent $60 of your own money to buy a new computer game. You start playing, but you find out it's no fun. Do you keep playing it?"

"Maybe. I don't want to waste my $60. Can I get a refund?" Alex asked.

"No, the game is no longer made, and the store won't give you a refund," Jason said.

"I'll probably play it once in a while," Alex decided.

"At the company we can have the same situation. If a product is not selling and we are sure we have properly educated the customer, no amount of marketing money will improve its acceptance. But it's still tempting to keep the product alive because we have invested time and effort in developing the product. It's probably best just to eat our cost and start over, however, just like you would probably be better off putting the boring game on the shelf and playing with one that you like better."

Alex seemed satisfied, so Jason continued his discussion with Samantha. "*Egos* has a very important new product that will come with the acquisition. Because of limited production facilities, the cost to produce this product actually goes up with higher production. To get to higher quantities, we have to pay overtime to the production workers.

"It goes without saying that if the costs to produce a product exceed the revenue, we shouldn't make it. Here are the numbers for the new product from *Egos*." Jason pulled out a printout from an Excel spreadsheet and handed it to Samantha.

Product Quantity (units per month)	Production Cost (Total dollars)	Marginal Cost ($ per unit)
1	$10,000	
2	15,000	$5,000
3	20,000	5,000
4	40,000	20,000
5	100,000	60,000

"Can I see that?" Alex asked.

"Sure," said Samantha, glad he was taking an interest.

"I understand the first two columns," said Alex. "What does the third column mean, marginal cost?"

"Marginal cost is the extra cost for making the next unit. It costs $10,000 to make the first unit," Jason said. "A unit, by the way, is a shipment of 20,000 semiconductors. It costs $15,000 to make the second unit."

"Why is the second unit so much cheaper?" Alex asked.

"Well, we talked about all the fixed costs that a company has. If you make only one unit, all the fixed costs are charged to that first unit. If you make two units, you spread the fixed costs over both units. Your fixed costs for each unit cut in half."

"That makes sense," Alex agreed. "And where does marginal cost come in?"

"Marginal cost is the extra cost for making one additional unit. Our total costs went from $10,000 to $15,000 when we went from one unit to two units, so the extra costs of making the second unit are $5,000.

"That's easy," said Alex. "You can really see that overtime kick in at around the 4th unit," showing a very good understanding of the table for only being in sixth grade.

"Yes, but here is the question. If we can sell this product for $25,000 per unit, how many units should we make?" Jason asked, impressed that his son was picking this up so easily.

"Let's see. I can make 5 units for $100,000, which is $20,000 per unit. So I guess I should make 5 units and make a $5,000 profit on each," Alex calculated.

"Nice try," said Jason to his son. "That's the way most people would answer. The key, however, is to look at the marginal cost. If it costs you $60,000 extra dollars to make the 5th unit, then why make that unit when you will only get revenue of $25,000 when you sell it?"

"I guess I wouldn't. But when I calculated the average price of each unit, it seemed to make sense to produce 5 units," Alex said, a little confused.

Samantha looked proudly at Jason and Alex. She must have been a good mother. Both of her men at the table were talking about economics.

"It might be easier to look at total profit." Jason pulled out a pen and wrote on the other side of the first table. "If I can sell my product at $25,000 per unit, here is my total profit." He wrote out the whole table.

Product Quantity (units per month)	Total Revenue (Total dollars)	Production Cost (Total dollars)	Profit (Total dollars)
1	$25,000	$10,000	$15,000
2	50,000	15,000	35,000
3	75,000	20,000	55,000
4	100,000	40,000	60,000
5	125,000	100,000	25,000

"Hey, that does work!" said Alex "The highest profit is with 4 units. Does it always work that way?"

"Yep. You maximize profits when you set marginal costs equal to marginal revenue. Marginal revenue is the extra money you get from selling one additional unit. If you are selling something at a constant price, the marginal revenue is the same as the price. And it makes sense if you think about it. Whenever you make a effort to do something, you need to get more in return for the extra effort that you make, or it's not worth it," Jason explained. "Take grades, for example."

"Don't say it," Samantha said sternly.

This made Alex even more interested. "Tell me, Dad," he pleaded.

"Let's say I told you that if you did 100 hours of math homework this semester, you could get an 'A'," Jason said, ignoring his wife's warning.

"That sounds about right," Alex said.

"Now what if I told you that if you did 20 hours of homework this semester, you could get a 'B'," Jason continued with the example.

"So an extra 80 hours of work moves me from a 'B' to an 'A'. That's not worth it," Alex decided. "I'd take the 'B'."

"Thanks a lot," said Samantha.

"But he now has a firm grasp of marginal thinking," Jason said, "which is a key concept of economics."

"What if you raise the selling price to $60,000?" Alex asked. "Then you could afford to make that 5th unit."

"Well, maybe," said Jason. "That might work until a competitor undersells us, and then we won't sell any units. In fact, price and volume is the next topic I was planning to talk to your mother about."

"Let's talk about price and volume, Alex," Samantha jumped in, excited that Alex had so much interest in economics.

"Here's a quiz, Alex. When I shop for meat next week, let's say that pork is on sale at a 50% discount. At the same time, beef prices did not change. What will I do?"

"You will probably buy pork," Alex answered. "Even though I hate pork."

"That's just what the meat manager wants to happen," said Samantha. "By making the price adjustment, volume goes up hopefully enough to increase total revenue. If price goes down and total revenue goes up, that's called elastic demand. Think of a rubber band. Price down, total revenues up, elastic demand," Samantha motioned with her hands like Marcel Marceau, really getting into it. "If price goes down and total revenues go down, that is inelastic demand," Samantha continued.

"That's what Uncle Mitchell does every year," Jason continued the story. "He lowers the price of current model year new cars when the new models arrive. He's hopeful that the lowering of price will spark a demand for the current model year new cars and trucks. He gets rid of last year's inventory and since his volume is up, he suffers no loss in profitability."

"Whatever," said Alex, his interest in economics waning. He went back to his video game.

"You sure have a lot of ideas, Jason," Samantha said, a little disappointed that Alex had lost interest. "What else did Larry want to know about?"

"I guess I forgot to show you his list. Here's what Larry gave to Steve and I on the plane." Jason pulled out a folded sheet from his pocket and gave it to Samantha.

- *Communications. How do we get the word out? How do we control our operations and how can we tell if everyone understands what's going on?*

- *People. How do we make sure we have the right partners both inside and outside the company?*

- *What are the cost categories? Which are the most significant?*

- *How do we maximize revenue and minimize cost?*

- *What about the relationship between price and volume?*

- *I am interested in the cost of money. How do we raise cash when we need to?*

- *We are going to have to increase our effort. Do we need to acquire more space for plant activities? Do we need to expand our present production facilities? What about new facilities?*

"I guess we've discussed the first five subjects. That brings us to the cost of money. What are your ideas there?" Samantha asked Jason.

"The cost of money is a major issue for any business," said Jason. "The best way to raise cash is through operations, obviously. That is not always possible, especially with new startups," explained Jason. Samantha listened quietly through this conversation, even though she knew these things better than he did. After 12 years of being an at-home mom, Jason sometimes forgot how intelligent Samantha was.

"There are several other ways to raise capital," Jason droned on. "They include: bank borrowing, revenue bonds, and sale of company stock."

"Oh, well," Samantha thought to herself. "Maybe Alex will learn something from Jason's lecture."

"Bank borrowing is the simplest, but sometimes the most expensive," said Jason. "The loan may be a precise sum, such as several thousands of dollars, or more frequently, a line of credit is established with a cap. The cap will vary based on the credibility of the company and its solvency. My guess is that *Switches.com* could qualify for a several million dollar line of credit if necessary."

"That's a lot of money," said Samantha. The carrying costs, interest that is, will be expensive."

"No doubt," said Jason, remembering now that Samantha knew all this better than he did. "That's why we must be careful with our borrowing practices.

"We may wish to create a bond issue. By doing so, we create company debt that ordinary people or financial institutions may buy into. Bonds are normally secured by the business as collateral and they pay a fixed amount of interest for a fixed period."

"How do you know what interest rate to attach to the bonds?" asked Samantha. She had never been involved with bond financing before.

"Likely the rate will have to be competitive with government bond issues which are the most secure. In consumer terms, they are virtually guaranteed," said Jason. "If we offer an interest rate similar to government bonds, no one will buy them since there will be some perceived risk investing in our company. Therefore, we must offer a rate with a premium. What I mean is that we will offer a rate that equals the government rate plus an additional fraction of a percent or maybe even a full percent. We will watch what other companies similar to us do and set our rates to be competitive."

"I guess bonds are like selling stock," Samantha said.

"Not exactly," replied Jason, who obviously had done some homework on these financing options. "If we plan to sell stock publicly, we will change the ownership of the company. Right now, Larry Johnson and his family own the company. If we decide to make an IPO, then we are taking the company public. There are a host of things that happen when we do that. The biggest change is that we will have individual and institutional investors or more generally put, new owners."

"Are you going to recommend issuing stock?" asked Samantha.

"Perhaps," said Jason. "Likely the Johnson family could retain the majority of the stock and therefore maintain control. Over time however, Larry's control could erode and his family would lose control. I seriously doubt whether Larry is ready to take the company public at this point. The company is very successful and there is no good reason to share that with anyone else. Now, if money gets tight and borrowing and bonds are not the answer, he may change his mind. You know, this is why Bill Gates of Microsoft, Steve Jobs of Apple and Mike Dell of Dell Computer took their companies public."

"Hey, I've heard of those guys," Alex chimed in. "They are all really rich. Are we going to be like them?"

"Probably not," said Samantha, and Alex lost interest.

"The last item on the list is to talk about expansion. That must be a real consideration now with the acquisition of *Egos*," said Jason. "We have our two plants in Indiana and *Egos* has a plant in Ohio and another plant in Kentucky. Our production capability is pretty well centralized while our customers are mostly on the West Coast and in the Southeast. With all of our growth, we need to decide if it might be necessary to build new plant facilities and, if so, where."

"What are you going to recommend to Larry about that?" asked Samantha.

"My first choice is to increase output with current facilities," said Jason. "We work a full day shift now and a partial night shift, but the night shift just completes packaging and makes sure all production from the day shift is shipped. We manage production so there is no carryover to the next day.

"I think we could go to a second full shift and even a third if necessary. That means more people, but I believe the facilities can handle it. We also have an option to purchase several hundred acres near the northern Indiana site, but land acquisition saps critical cash. What I would really like to do is strike a lease with the owner of the land for say 40 years, with an option for an additional 40 years. That way we don't spend cash and we don't have to borrow to buy the land. Actually, it may be possible to lease the acreage for the equivalent of what the interest cost would be on a purchase. That way we have the land but no debt. I'm even thinking about striking a lease deal and then cash renting the land to farmers for crops. That income will cover part of the costs of owning the land while we consider our options. Of course, we should only do that if we really intend to build on the property."

"There may be a better way," said Samantha. "Since our customers are in the Southeast and on the West Coast, we might be able to find idle plant facilities available for leasing in our customer's backyard. If we need more plant space, that could be very cost effective. Being close to your customer means we could be more responsive than competitors and our shipping costs will be lower."

"You are really creative, Samantha," said Jason. "We miss your ideas at work. I wish we could capitalize on all of your organizational skills. Maybe we should start our own company one day."

"Maybe," said Samantha. She was proud of how Jason had mastered the economics of the business. And she was doubly proud that Jason would soon become the number two man at *Switches.com*.

"Jason, let's skip dessert here," said Samantha. "I have something special at home. Besides, that's where the Merlot is."

"You guys are gross," said Alex, understanding their code words. Jason and Samantha were embarrassed.

Key Economic Terms – Chapter 14

Restructuring
Task forces
Focus groups
Functional organization
Variable costs
Fixed costs
Performance base
Amortize
Escalation of commitment
Marginal cost (MC)
Marginal revenue (MR)
Maximize profits at MC = MR
Marginal thinking
Price

Volume
Total revenue
Elastic demand
Inelastic demand
Line of credit
Cap
Solvency
Carrying costs
Bonds
Government bond issues
Stocks
Ownership
Public company

Chapter 15
The International Assignment: The Economics of LDCs Chapter

"I think we have that production facility issue solved," Jason told Samantha one night at dinner.

"Did you decide to expand an existing plant, or are you going to build a new plant closer to your customers in the Southeast and West?" Samantha asked, recalling the discussion at *Ruth's Chris* several months before.

"Before I tell you, I need to get something," Jason said, getting up from the table.

"May I be excused?" said Alex. Junior was at football practice, and Samantha was trying out for a play, so Alex was the only kid at home.

"Sure," said Samantha, knowing that she and Jason could have their discussion in peace.

Jason came back with a bottle of Merlot.

"Oh, no," said Samantha. "What is it this time?"

"It's nothing bad," said Jason. "It's an opportunity."

"I am not moving to California," Samantha said immediately. "I don't want my children growing up on the West Coast."

"It's nothing like that," Jason said.

"Good," said Samantha. "I don't want to move. There is no place better than Indiana."

"How do you feel about Southeast Asia?" said Jason.

"Southeast Asia! You've got to be kidding. I just said I didn't even want to go to California."

Jason realized he had not managed this conversation well. "How did Samantha always know what he was going to talk about?" he wondered.

"Let's back up a second," Jason said.

"I'm not moving," Samantha repeated. "We have one child in high school and our daughter will be going to high school soon. This is not a good time to move. And Southeast Asia? You're crazy." She folded her arms and stared at Jason.

"So much for backing up for a second," Jason thought.

"Look, let me just explain the situation," Jason said calmly. "If you are not interested, I will just tell Larry and that will be the end of it." That wasn't quite true. When Larry told Jason about starting up a plant in Southeast Asia, he pretty much said that Jason would run the operations. He didn't give Jason much choice in the matter.

"Okay, I'll listen to you. But I refuse to go," Samantha reiterated.

"Good. Here's the story," Jason began. "Our financial analysts have been doing a lot of 'what-if' cases to see how best to combine *Egos* and *Switches*. One scenario they considered was what if we build a plant in Southeast Asia and shut down our U.S. production facilities. The economics are so much better in Southeast Asia, and all of our component suppliers have moved there. It's just too expensive to make computer equipment in the U.S., especially with the way prices have been falling."

"Well that certainly makes sense. I just don't know why you need to get involved. You are a sales and marketing guy. What do you know about production?" Samantha demanded.

"I'm the number two person at *Switches.com*," Jason said firmly. "The Southeast Asia production plant is the most important project that we have. Unless we can improve our production costs, we will be out of business in less than two years, at least at the current rate." He paused a moment to let that point sink in. "Larry trusts me, and he needs someone that he can trust. Plus it will only be for one year, eighteen months tops. Just enough time to set up the plant and hire a local production manager."

"What if it takes longer?" Samantha asked. "You could end up being stuck there for 20 years."

"Unlikely," said Jason. "You should see what it costs to keep an ex-pat–you know, an American on temporary assignment in a foreign country–in Southeast Asia. The company pays all of our expenses to keep our house in Indiana, they pay all of our expenses in Southeast Asia, they pay my regular pay and bonuses, plus–and here's the good part–I will get 2% ownership in *Switches.com* when I come back."

"Wow, Larry really wants you to go," Samantha said. "He has never talked about giving any ownership to anyone outside of his family. And I have to admit, it makes good business sense, and it certainly wouldn't hurt our financial picture either. But if it's only going to be for a year or so, maybe you should just live there temporarily, and I will stay here with the kids."

"I thought about that. I even talked to Osman, who lived overseas without his family for a while. He said it just doesn't work. You can't concentrate on the job, the trips home take a lot of time, and most importantly," Jason said, watching Samantha's body language, "I would miss you too much."

"Okay, you overdid it on the last point, but those reasons make sense." Samantha was resisting less, but she clearly was not convinced yet.

"What about the kids?" Samantha asked.

"That's the good part," Jason said. "You will love this. It turns out there is a new American school there," Jason said.

"Where is 'there', by the way?" Samantha interrupted.

"It's a country called Jabodia," said Jason.

"Never heard of it," Samantha replied immediately.

"Well, you will soon. It is a small country that is very favorable to business, should we say, especially foreign currency regulations and taxes. Many of the companies starting up in Southeast Asia are building factories in Jabodia," Jason explained. "That's why they have this new American school. Many of the new companies are sending in American executives like me."

"So there is a new school. That's good," said Samantha, not understanding why that was such a big deal.

"Right, but you haven't heard the best part yet. They are looking for an American administrator to get things going. I think you would be perfect," Jason said confidently.

That really threw Samantha for a curve. Move to Jabodia and start a job as the administrator of a school?

"I've haven't done anything in education since college. What would I know about that?" Samantha asked.

"You would be perfect. You are a mother who has the same concerns as the other mothers who will be moving to Jabodia. You understand the computer business, and it's computer companies that are funding the school. And I think you are ready for a new challenge," Jason said.

"Jason always knows the right buttons to push," Samantha thought. She was looking for a challenge. The kids were getting older, and they didn't need her as much any more. The idea of going back to work was very appealing. She just had never thought about being a school administrator in Jabodia until ten minutes ago, so it was a bit much to take all at once.

"Why do you think they will hire me?" Samantha asked.

"Maybe because *Switches.com* is part of the American school consortium, and Larry is responsible for finding a school administrator. He said he mentioned your background to the rest of the consortium, and they thought you would be perfect."

"How long have you know about this?" Samantha asked, raising her voice.

"I just found out today, Honey," Jason said. "Honest. But it seems like Larry has been thinking about it for some time. Probably even before the *Egos* acquisition."

"Okay, sorry," said Samantha. "I just didn't want to think that you had been scheming about this."

"Of course not," said Jason.

"Have you talked to the kids about this yet? I have a feeling this news will devastate the kids," said Samantha in an anxious tone.

"No, I didn't want to say anything to them until we had talked about it," Jason replied.

"Let's do some market research," Samantha suggested. Jason nodded.

"Alex," Jason yelled. "Could you come down here for a minute?"

"I'll be right there," Alex yelled back. Three minutes later, still no Alex.

"Alex," Jason called again. "Please come down."

"Okay, just a second," Alex yelled.

"Right now," Samantha yelled with conviction. Alex was downstairs in 15 seconds.

"How do you do that?" Jason asked Samantha admiringly.

"It's all in the voice," Samantha said. "You have to mean business."

"Not really," Alex thought. It's just that Mom takes away the Nintendo if you don't come down, and Dad doesn't.

"We have a serious question for you, Alex," Samantha said. "What would you think about living in Southeast Asia for a year or so?"

"You mean like Korea?" Alex asked.

"Close to there," Jason said. "It would actually be a country called Jabodia, which is really close to Korea."

"Sweet!" exclaimed Alex. "That would be awesome."

"Why do you say that?" Samantha asked.

"My friend Rodney V. went to Korea and learned Tae-Kwon-Do and everybody thinks he's cool! Plus," he added, "I'm sick of all the corn around this place. It is boring."

"But what about your friends?" Samantha asked.

"Well, it's only a year. And I'll come back a Tae-Kwon-Do expert! Hi-ya!" Alex began to dance around the room doing karate moves. "Besides," he added between punches, "kids at school mess with me. Boy, will they be sorry when I come back a Tae-Kwon-Do expert! Hi-ya! Hi-ya!" He did some pitiful looking kicks.

Jason made a mental note to ask Alex later about what the kids at school were doing to him at school.

Just then, Stephanie came in. "What's wrong with Alex?" she asked. "Why is he dancing?"

"I'm not dancing! I'm doing Tae-Kwon-Do!" Alex yelled.

"Whatever. Anyway, Junior's coming soon. He's saying good-bye to his immature friend outside." Stephanie dropped her books down on the coffee table.

"How was play tryout?" Samantha asked.

"Okay. My voice got messed up a little when I was starting, but I fixed it. I think I might get a part."

"Good job." Samantha smiled at her.

"Hi-ya!" Alex soared across the room and into the coffee table. Stephanie's books flew everywhere.

"Alex!" Jason roared. "No more karate!"

"Not karate, Dad, Tae-Kwon-Do."

"Whatever it is, stop it."

"Okay, okay."

The door opened and Jason Junior walked in. "Boy, what a great practice! Coach said my passing was great! This season is really going great for me!" He pretended to pass a football. "Touchdown!" he yelled, throwing his hands up.

"Stephanie, Junior, could I talk to you guys for a minute?" Jason said. "I'll make it quick; I know you have homework."

"Sure, sure," Junior said, still pumped up.

"Yah, whatever." Stephanie sat down on the couch.

"Can I leave?" Alex asked. "I think I know what's gonna happen here."

"Sure," Samantha said, not sure what he meant.

Alex ran up the stairs into his room and slammed the door. You could hear a faint "Hi-ya!" as the door shut.

Jason and Samantha turned to face them. "Well," Jason said, "This is a very important matter, so please give me your full attention."

"Okay," Junior and Stephanie said in unison.

"Well, kids, we are thinking of moving to Southeast Asia for a year. It's a place called Jabodia, near Vietnam."

"WHAT?!" Stephanie yelled. "This has got to be a joke! Uh-huh, no way. I am, like, so staying here!" She sat down. "I am not leaving this chair. You can go to that foreign place, but I will just stay right here. Right here in this chair. Nope, I'm not leaving." She crossed her arms.

"I'm with Stephanie on this one," Junior said coldly. "They probably don't even know what football is in Jabodia, or whatever it's called. They probably do sumo wrestling or something weird like that. No way." He sat down next to Stephanie. "I'll stay right here next to Steph."

"Come on, guys," Jason said. "Open your minds up a little bit. I may have a new job there starting up a new factory. Plus I will get a big bonus, and we could use some of that to go to Hawaii on the way," Jason said, hoping to bribe them a little.

"We seem to be doing fine with money right now, Dad." Stephanie said. "Why do you need a stupid new job?"

"You'll be going to an American school. I might even be the administrator of it," Samantha added.

Jason was surprised that she had joined him in convincing the kids. "Maybe she is warming up to the idea," he thought.

"Doesn't help," Junior said.

"Well, we might be going no matter what you think," Jason said, getting mad.

Stephanie ran up the stairs to her room. "You guys are so unfair!" she screamed, slamming her door.

Junior ran up the stairs after her and went into his room.

The house was silent.

"Well, I guess one out of three isn't bad," Samantha said.

"So do you think this is a good idea?" Jason said to Samantha.

"Yes, I guess so. I need to know more, but it would be a great experience for the kids. Plus if you say 'no', I'm not sure what Larry will think. I think he is already counting on this," Samantha correctly surmised.

Jason didn't have to say anything. He wasn't sure that he really had a choice, at least if he wanted to keep his job. And it did have lots of benefits. He was glad that at least Samantha and Alex were open to the idea.

* * *

"We need to leave," Jason called to Samantha. "The seminar starts in 45 minutes."

"Okay, I'm coming," yelled Samantha, coming down the stairs. "Let's go."

The last couple of weeks had not gone well. Junior had effectively argued that Jason got to stay at his old school when his parents moved to New York, so why shouldn't he get to stay in Indianapolis. He even called Uncle Mitchell and pleaded his case. Uncle Mitchell and his wife had agreed to live in Jason and Samantha's house for the year, and Junior would continue at his current high school. Jason figured that Uncle Mitchell didn't want Junior to interrupt his budding football career. Junior would go to Jabodia for the summer.

Stephanie also wanted to stay home. Since she had not entered high school yet, her case was not as convincing. Jason and Samantha promised her that they would return home before she started high school. Stephanie still wasn't happy, but she got over it.

Jason and Samantha were attending a workshop for people who would be living in less developed countries, LDCs, or sometimes called Third World countries. The workshop was offered a few times per year, and people paid about $400 to hear a three-hour lecture on living in a new culture. In most cases, the employers like *Switches.com* picked up the tab.

"How many people are scared?" John Schultz, the seminar leader, started out.

Many people raised their hands.

"You probably haven't had much time to get used to the idea," Mr. Schulz said. "Moving to a LDC can seem very intimidating. Many of the things we take for granted here in the U.S. are non-existent in the LDC countries. And it doesn't really matter which specific country is your destination. This seminar is designed to help you understand the mindset of the locals that you will meet in your new homes. Many of you have probably signed up for other seminars that discuss the specific country where you will be living."

Jason and Samantha nodded silently in agreement. They would attend another seminar about Jabodia offered by a relocation consultant later that week."

"Here is the critical point that you need to understand about LDCs," Mr. Schulz said. "The difference in per capita income between the United States and the countries that you are going to simply boggles the mind. Almost everything flows from this point."

Mr. Schulz turned on his projector and the room automatically dimmed. "Here is a table with the per capita income in the U.S. compared to some of per capita incomes of the countries that you will be going to," Mr. Schulz said, flashing the first slide. "The per capita income, or GDP divided by population, is over $33,000 in the United States. By comparison, the per capita income of many of the poorest LDCs is $100 or $200 per year. In other words, many of you spend more money in one day than a person in this country earns in an entire year. And as I said, everything flows from this.

"If a person in Jabodia, for example, had a sick child, they would likely give as much thought to taking that child to the doctor as we would be likely to plan a trip to the moon. It simply is not an option that most people consider in these countries.

"I was living in a poor country in Africa a few years ago. I knew a farmer who was fairly wealthy, at least by this country's standards. He even had a corn grinder that was operated by a waterwheel. One day I was walking around on his property, and the belt had fallen off the waterwheel. I tried to fix it, but I couldn't figure out how to stop the waterwheel so I could put the belt back on.

"I went to look for the farmer, but he had gone to town. His wife said she knew how to stop the water, but she wasn't strong enough to do it by herself. I agreed to help. She showed me that I needed to roll over a rock to stop the water, which I did, and I slipped the belt back on. Then I rolled the rock back. This was a pretty heavy rock, and by the time I was done, I was pretty sweaty.

"On the way back, I told the farmer's wife, 'It sure is hot today.'

"'No it's not,' she told me, 'you are just fat.'"

"'What a rude thing to say,' I thought at the time. I was trying to help her, and then she goes and insults me. But then I realized she was trying to pay me a compliment. Most people in LDCs don't have enough to eat. If a person is fat, that means they are important enough to make a lot of money. They can buy enough food to get fat. What we consider an insult in the U.S. can actually be a compliment in a LDC.

"This is what I am trying to impress upon you before you go to your new homes. The income difference is so great, people in LDCs think about the world totally differently. They worry about having enough food for their next meal. When was the last time you worried about not having enough food for your next meal? Hunger is a powerful driving force."

Mr. Schulz continued the lecture, showing more income comparisons. The numbers didn't mean much to Samantha. She was thinking about the example of the sick child. "Can you imagine not being able to take a sick child to the doctor?" she thought. "As likely as me planning a trip to the moon." That story said it all to her.

After a short break, Mr. Schulz started a discussion about birthrates and death rates. "One of the things that will amaze you when you get to your new homes is the number of young children and teenagers. In most of these countries, the birthrate is very high and life expectancy is low. It's not uncommon to have half of the population of some of these countries under the age of 16.

"Now, let's talk about birthrates. The birthrate is the number of births for every 1,000 in population. Many of these LDCs have birthrates as high as 35. Now that might not seem like much, but when you figure half of the population is worthless for bearing children—these people are called men—and then subtract all the old women, the very young girls, and then the women who have recently had babies, a birthrate of 35 is pretty much running flat out. The death rate is also high, around 25 in many of these countries. That means the population growth is 10 out of 1,000, a population growth rate of 1%. By comparison, the U.S. population growth rate is about the same, with both the birthrate and death rate in the U.S. lower than the LDCs.

"Many people and organizations make efforts to help LDCs. The biggest effect is usually on the death rate, at least initially. There are some very positive effects that organizations can make to reduce the death rate in LDCs. It is fairly easy to improve the sanitation conditions in LDCs by separating human wastes from the water supply. Vaccinations and nutrition can also make a big difference. So death rates can drop immediately down to about 10.

"It is much more difficult to influence the birthrate. If you lower the death rate to 10 and the birthrate stays at 35, now the population growth rate is 2.5%. Since economic growth is measured by GDP per capita, if the population is growing at 2.5%, it really slows down the growth of GDP per capita.

"With birthrates you are dealing with something pretty personal, and many people say, 'Stay out of my business.' There is also a strong bias in LDCs to have more children. Since 90% of the people in LDCs work in agriculture, having more children means having more farm labor, which increases the amount of food the family can raise. There is also a bias towards big families because eventually the children will take care of the parents. There is nothing like Social Security in LDCs, so parents' security comes from having children who will take care of them in their old age. And since many children die at a young age in LDCs, parents have a boatload of children to make sure there is someone left to take care of them in their old age. It's just a different way of thinking than in the U.S.

"Even if you convince people that lowering the birthrate is a good idea, it is difficult to implement. Many birth control methods cost money. If your total annual income is $100, you are spending almost all of your money on food, not birth control. Other birth control methods require planning, and planning is not something that most people in LDCs have much experience with. That choice is not always very effective.

"Many countries have started aggressive birth control programs, and I could really tell you some horror stories. In some countries, the government forces a woman to have an abortion if she gets pregnant after already having two children. In other countries, an IUD is automatically inserted when a woman delivers her first baby. In still other countries, the government requires all doctors to do at least six sterilizations per month or lose their privilege to practice medicine.

"Countries try to reduce the birthrate in an attempt to raise the per capita income of their people. This is a reasonable objective, but it may be more humane to work on the income side of the equation rather than the population side. Since per capita income is real GDP divided by population, you can either increase real GDP or reduce population to increase per capita income. As it turns out, once per capita income rises to about $600 per year, birthrates usually start to reduce by themselves, even without draconian birth control measures.

"I've gone into detail on this section because population growth is a major issue in LDCs. It is something that you will personally observe, and I don't want you to be surprised. Let's take a break."

"Maybe it's lucky Junior is staying at home," Samantha said. "If we only bring two children, maybe the government will leave us alone." It was an uncomfortable effort at a joke. To think that governments could do those things without permission. It really is a different world.

After a short break, Mr. Schulz started the third and last section of the workshop. "In the previous section we talked about increasing per capita income, focusing on the denominator of the equation, or population. Now let's look at the numerator of the equation, or real GDP. How can countries increase real GDP? How can we help them? As Americans in these LDCs, locals will look to you as a source of help for their problems.

"One way to increase real GDP in LDCs is simply to send them foreign aid, typically money or food. People have been less willing to send money to LDCs in recent years for whatever reason, so this part of a LDC's income is actually declining. Some have suggested that we send more food to LDCs. After all, the U.S. often has a surplus in food. Why not send some of that surplus to LDCs?

"Even though this approach is well intentioned, there are a few problems. There are logistics problems. Many countries do not have the roads or trucks to transport the food around the country. More important, food shipments depress the food prices in the LDCs. If the prices are lower, it is less profitably to invest in farming. You end up discouraging food production in LDCs, which is exactly the wrong policy.

"A better approach is to help LDCs develop their own food production and production of other goods and services. Many of the people in this room will be involved in expanding the productive capacities of LDCs. While newspaper accounts may say that you are exploiting the local population, the local population is glad that you are coming. Incomes are very low in these countries, but you are helping to narrow the gap between the developed countries and underdeveloped countries.

"And let me just finish today by elaborating on that point, the issue of narrowing the gap between the per capita income of developed nations and the per capita income of LDCs. The per capita income of the U.S., as mentioned earlier, is about $33,000. It is growing at about 1% per year, or $330 per year.

"The per capita income of LDCs, and let's be generous, is $500 per year. These countries are growing faster, maybe 5% per year. That means that per capita income is growing $25 per year. Simple arithmetic says that the gap is getting bigger, not smaller. If you work out the numbers, it will take 100 years before the gap starts to narrow.

"This is a good point to remember. The gap between the per capita income of LDCs and countries like the United States is large and growing. This can be very frustrating to the poor countries. We need to do what we can to help them, not just for altruistic reasons, but for the very practical reason of maintaining order in these countries. This may be a blunt statement, but it is the truth.

"I want to thank all of you for coming to this seminar. I hope I have helped you understand a little more about the culture of the less developed countries. I think you will have a very interesting experience in your new assignments."

"That was an eye-opener," Jason said to Samantha on the way out. "I had never thought about things in those terms before. It helps explain some of the things that you read about."

"Except now we won't just be reading about them. Soon we will be living them," Samantha said, expressing both excitement and trepidation.

* * *

The Cooley family, without Junior, moved to Jabodia. Samantha immediately got involved with the American school. She really liked seeing Alex and Stephanie during the day. Alex, of course, started Tae-Kwon-Do lessons. And Jason immersed himself in the job. There was a whole new culture to learn and new ways of doing business. After a slow start, he started up the new plant and trained a Jabodian national to take his place. After 14 months, things were in shape and the Cooley family was ready to return home.

"Larry," Jason said over the phone, "I just got the production report for January, and we are up to 97% efficiencies. Lu Thu is doing a good job running the plant, and inventories are built up to the required levels. All in all, I think my job here is done."

"I'm glad to hear the plant is running so well," said Larry. "You have done a good job, and I hope it gave you some valuable experience. Your foreign assignment has really given you some good résumé value."

"Yes, maybe even *Switches.com* will hire me," Jason joked. "So what do you think? Should I start making plans to move back?"

"We have a slight problem with that," Larry said.

"Look, I know Lu Thu has only been on board for six months, but he had a lot of experience with other computer companies before joining us and I have complete trust in him. And I'm not just saying that so I can come home," Jason quickly added. "Actually, we have started to like it here. Samantha likes her job, and the kids are doing well."

"That isn't the problem," said Larry. "I know this isn't going to sound fair to you, and I don't know a better way to say it, so let me just say it straight. My son has decided to get into the business, and I plan to name him the COO."

"But that was going to be my position," Jason retorted, feeling both angry and confused.

"I know," said Larry. "But you know *Switches* is a family business, and eventually my son Rob will be taking over. He has never shown much interest in the business, but now that he has, I would like him to work under me for a few years.

"You have done a good job, Jason, and I want to be fair to you," Larry continued. "You can stay in Jabodia for another year, or you could come back home as a Vice-President reporting to Rob."

"And what about the equity position that you promised me?" Jason asked.

"I'm sorry," Larry said. "That was if you came back in the number two position. Now we don't really want any ownership outside of the family."

Jason couldn't believe this. He took this international assignment to help the company, and now he was taking a downward move. He thought about pushing the equity issue, but decided to pursue that another day after he got some legal advice.

"I find this very disappointing," Jason finally said. "I have been very loyal to you and this country, and now you do this to me."

"I don't blame you," Larry said with some sympathy. "But it's a family thing." Larry did feel guilty, but he rationalized that it was his company and he could do what he wanted.

That evening Jason showed up at home with a bottle of Merlot.

"Larry said we could go home?" Samantha said excitedly.

"Not quite," Jason confessed. "I'm afraid this is not good news."

"We have to stay here?" Samantha guessed.

"Your perception is usually pretty good, but you're probably not going to guess this one. Where are the kids?" Jason asked.

"They are still at school. They are having a movie party tonight," Samantha responded.

"Good, because I need to talk to you alone. Today I told Larry that my job was done, and we were ready to come home. Larry said we have a problem. I thought he might have thought Lu Thu wasn't ready to take over. But that wasn't it. In fact," Jason said, recalling the conversation, "he didn't say anything about that."

"Jason, please hurry. You are killing me here," Samantha pleaded.

"Anyway, Larry said that his son Rob was getting into the business, and Larry is going to make him the COO."

"But that was your position!" Samantha exclaimed. "Rob doesn't know anything about the business."

"I know, but Larry thinks that he should work under him to learn the business," Jason explained.

"And what are you supposed to do?" Samantha asked.

"Either stay here for a while or come back as a Vice President working for Rob," Jason said disgustedly.

"And what about the equity position?" Samantha asked, duplicating Jason's thought process from earlier.

"No deal. Larry doesn't want to give away any ownership now," Jason said.

"You had a deal," Samantha said sternly. "He can't do that. I can't believe Larry is doing this."

"Well, he is, and we need to decide what to do about it. I have no intention of giving up easily," said Jason.

After a long discussion, Jason and Samantha decided they were not interested in being a part of the "new" *Switches.com*. Over the next several weeks, they made their arrangements to return. *Switches.com* gave Jason a "golden parachute" worth about $300,000 mainly to avoid any problems with the verbal agreement to give Jason a 2% equity position when he came back. In return, Jason signed an agreement promising not to pursue any legal action.

Finally the entire family was back together and ready to start a new phase in their lives.

Key Economic Terms – Chapter 15

"What if" analysis

Ex-patriot (ex-pat)

Foreign currency regulations

Less developed country (LDC)

Third World country

Birthrate

Death rate

Population growth

Per capita income

National

Efficiency

Chief Operating Officer (COO)

Equity position

Golden parachute

Chapter 16
Planning to the End:
The Funeral and Estate Planning Chapter

Jason and Samantha spent much of the first week at home meeting with lawyers and accountants to finalize the severance agreement with *Switches.com*. It was both stressful and sad. Both had felt like they had given part of themselves to the company, and now it was all ending with a technical, legal agreement.

Jason returned home one afternoon after handling a few errands to find Samantha in tears. He knew that she was feeling a lot of stress from the breakup with *Switches.com*, but this was too much.

"What's the matter, Sam?" asked Jason.

"There has been a terrible automobile accident involving Uncle Mitchell," sobbed Samantha. "The details are sketchy at this point; I only know that Uncle Mitchell was by himself in his car when he was struck by a pickup that apparently ran a stop sign."

"Where is Uncle Mitchell now?" asked Jason, as calmly as he could.

"Saint Vincent Hospital. I just got a call from Aunt Jackie, and Uncle Mitchell is in the emergency room. I told her we would come as soon as you got home."

"Good," said Jason. "Let's go." Jason took a moment to call his parents to let them know of the accident. It was unclear what Uncle Mitchell's condition was, but Jason promised to call as soon as he could get more complete information.

Uncle Mitchell and Aunt Jackie had no local immediate family. Although they had been married over 40 years, they had no children. Samantha and Jason were their closest geographic relatives. Consequently, Mitchell and Jackie had grown close to Samantha and Jason over the years.

Neither Jason nor Samantha spoke on the way to the hospital. Each was lost in thoughts and memories of the good times with Uncle Mitchell. He was an unbelievable person. He worked virtually all the time, and he had built a business that was the envy of his peers. He was more of a father to his employees than a boss. Uncle Mitchell had no enemies.

As they arrived at the hospital, Samantha broke the silence. "What do we do now?" she asked.

"I'm not sure," replied Jason. "I guess we should see what we can do for Aunt Jackie. Uncle Mitchell is a tough old bird. I'm sure he'll be on his feet in no time. Let's see if we can find them."

As they found their way to the emergency room, Jason remembered the many times they had visited just such a place as the kids were growing up. A broken arm here, a broken collarbone there, not to mention the scrapes, bumps and viruses. They looked around but there was no Aunt Jackie. Jason asked the receptionist if she knew where Mitchell and Jackie Cooley were. The receptionist, in a very quiet voice, answered, "Check the intensive care unit (ICU)."

That doesn't sound good," Jason said as they entered the elevator enroute to the fourth floor ICU wing. When the elevator doors opened to the fourth floor, they saw Aunt Jackie sitting alone by the window.

"Aunt Jackie," Samantha said as she rushed over. "We got here as soon as we could. How is Uncle Mitchell?"

Aunt Jackie was barely coherent, and she began to cry. "Your Uncle Mitchell is hurt badly and the doctors are not optimistic."

"Do you know what happened?" asked Jason.

"Well, according to the police, someone ran a stop sign and hit Mitch in the driver door. There were no skid marks. They think the driver was drunk. Mitch has several broken bones, but more significantly, he has a severe head injury and he is in a coma. The doctor has told me that the next 12 hours are crucial. They let me in with him for short periods, and I can see that he is not responsive."

"Jason, I know this sounds crass but I need you to do something for me as soon as possible," said Aunt Jackie.

"Sure, anything," answered Jason.

"Here is my house key," said Aunt Jackie. "Upstairs in the master bedroom closet is a built-in fireproof safe. Please go to the safe, open it, and in the top left hand drawer, you will find a package of labeled documents. Bring me the two that are marked 'Living Will' and 'Healthcare Representative' with Mitch's name on them. Here's the combination."

Jason was somewhat stunned. He knew of such things, but until now, they were just documents prepared by lawyers. He never thought about people actually using these documents. For a moment Jason couldn't respond. After what seemed to be an eternity to Samantha, Jason finally answered, "Okay."

"Go on now, Jason," said Aunt Jackie, "there is nothing you can do here now anyway." It seemed that Aunt Jackie had, all of a sudden, become very controlled and businesslike. Aunt Jackie noticed how Jason was looking at her. "The one thing Mitch drilled me on was preparation," Aunt Jackie said to Jason. "He frequently said that we should never be unprepared to meet any circumstance."

Jason understood his instructions, but his actions were almost in slow motion. He knew why Aunt Jackie needed the documents, but somehow he wanted to delay any action.

Jason knew Uncle Mitchell was a good businessman and, as such, Jason knew he likely was a master at planning. He thought about his own situation and realized for the first time that he was almost totally unprepared for a personal disaster. It was clear that his priorities must change immediately.

Jason got to the house and went into Uncle Mitchell's and Aunt Jackie's master bedroom. He opened the safe as instructed and was struck by the neatness and organization. At a glance he could see a file marked 'Property' that probably contained deeds and insurance papers. There was another file labeled 'Certificates of Deposit'. Still another file marked 'Health, accident and life insurance policies'. There were two videotapes marked 'Personal property' and 'Household goods'. Apparently Uncle Mitchell actually went to the trouble to videotape the interior of his home complete with jewels and other valuables. There were what appeared to be stock certificates, keys, credit cards and several interesting heirlooms. All these in a safe built to withstand fire, wind, and water.

Jason found the drawer mentioned by Aunt Jackie. Here again, things were neat and orderly. On top was a folder marked 'Final wills', 'Durable powers of attorney', 'Trust agreements', 'Living wills' and 'Healthcare representatives'. He knew the purpose of each but somehow their importance and relevance to him always seemed distant. His head was spinning. He was on a mission for Aunt Jackie, but he also realized how poorly prepared he was from a personal planning point of view. All the way back to the hospital, he was consumed with his woeful planning for Samantha, Alex, Stephanie and Jason, Jr. He made a pledge that he would correct the travesty without delay.

As he returned to the ICU, Samantha met him. "Any change?" asked Jason.

"No, nothing yet," Samantha replied. "Aunt Jackie is in with Uncle Mitchell now. I know Aunt Jackie is under maximum stress, but I am in awe as to how controlled and calculated she seems to be."

"Yeah, I know," said Jason. "I was completely blown away at what I found in the safe. Everything was labeled and it seemed like every base was covered. It is almost as if they both knew something was going to happen. You just can't believe how organized they are, Sam. You and I are in the dark ages when it comes to preparation. But you know what, Sam? Preparation has just moved to the top of my priority list."

"You mean ahead of getting a new job?" asked a startled Samantha.

"Yep, I'll get a job, that's a given. But if something were to happen to me or you, for that matter, having a job means little if we aren't prepared for the worst," said Jason.

"Jason, did you find the papers?" asked Aunt Jackie, coming back from Uncle Mitchell's room in ICU.

"I have them right here," said Jason. "Is there any change with Uncle Mitchell?"

"No," replied Aunt Jackie. "Jason, it's late, who is watching the kids?"

"They are fine," Samantha quickly offered. "Jason, Jr. and Stephanie have things under control. I called them while Jason was over getting the files."

"Well, I think you should go home now. I'm fine here," said Aunt Jackie, "and they will not allow any other guests now anyway. I'm going to stay here tonight; the nurses made a bed for me in the room next to Mitch."

"We can't leave you alone, Aunt Jackie," said Samantha. "We'll just wait out here."

"I appreciate that, Samantha," said Aunt Jackie, "but you can't do anything here at the moment. Save your energy for when Mitch is awake."

"Okay," said Jason, "but I'll be back first thing in the morning."

"And I'll be with him," said Samantha.

"In that case, maybe one of you can go with me to see the hospital administrator when I deliver these papers," said Aunt Jackie.

"Of course," said Jason. "Here's my cell phone number, Aunt Jackie. Call if you need anything."

Samantha and Jason were quiet a good bit of the way home. Finally, Jason broke the silence. "Sam, this situation is a wake-up call for us in a sense."

"What do you mean?" asked Samantha.

"Well, the fact of the matter is, we are a long way from being prepared should tragedy strike us," said Jason.

"Where do we start?" asked Samantha.

"I think the contents of Uncle Mitchell's safe are a good place to start. After we get the kids in bed, I'll tell you what I found," suggested Jason. The kids were very concerned about Uncle Mitchell. Jason and Samantha told them everything that they knew, and then the kids went to bed. Samantha went in to talk to each of the kids individually in bed while Jason went to his office and looked over their personal financial files. Jason and Samantha then sat down at the kitchen table with a piece of paper.

"If you remember, our lawyer told us we needed to do some planning in the event of the death of you or me," Jason began. "I had almost forgotten about it until I pulled out my notes from our last meeting with her."

"I know," agreed Samantha. "It's just that we are both fairly young, and I guess I didn't like thinking about it."

"Me neither," Jason agreed. "But anyone can get hit by a car, so we should be prepared all the time. Uncle Mitchell's safe reminded me of the documents that we need to have prepared. Our lawyer told us we should have four documents done immediately and eventually prepare two others." Jason took out a piece of paper and started writing. "The immediate documents were:

1. Update last will and testament.
2. Prepare durable powers of attorney.
3. Appoint healthcare representative.
4. Prepare living wills.

"Secondarily, our lawyer said we should consider:

1. Trust agreements for each of us.
2. Funeral arrangements.

"I found some guidebooks that our lawyer gave us. Here is a brief description of each document." Jason put the guidebooks between him and Samantha so they could read it together. Jason described each document aloud as they were reading it.

"*Last will and testament*: This is a legal document that stipulates or declares what actions are to be taken regarding family possessions in the event of death. When someone dies, the legal process that follows is called probate. This is the event that takes place that determines how the assets and the liabilities of the deceased are handled. When there is a properly executed will in place, the probate procedure is usually an administrative procedure that is taken care of by a qualified lawyer. With a proper will in place, the probate process is of little consequence. If someone were to die without a properly executed will, the courts are charged with the authority to make judgments on behalf of the deceased. In this case, the probate process may be time consuming and traumatic. Most people see the function of a will as one that divides assets according to some plan or program. That is accurate, however, in the case of dependents, children or elders, a will can instruct those who remain what actions to take. For example, if a mother and a father die together in an accident and leave dependent children, the courts would be called upon to prescribe care for the children. Proper planning on the part of the parents can provide a bridge. The parents may name a person or persons in their will to assume guardianship. Obviously this needs to be prearranged with the named guardians. Furthermore, the will may stipulate a portion of the estate be apportioned to the guardian for support of the dependent children. The ultimate guardian decision still remains with the court.

"*Durable power of attorney*: This is a legal document that gives authority to another to act on one's behalf in the event of permanent or temporary incapacitation. Husbands and wives normally prepare an individual power of attorney that grants their spouse the authority to act on their behalf if something should happen that renders one incapable of acting independently. This document handles those situations short of death. For example, if a spouse were to have a stroke and be unable to take care of his or her affairs and unable to conduct legal business, a power of attorney grants the able survivor full authority to carry on. This includes entering into contracts such as asset purchase and sale on behalf of the disabled spouse or dependent. Some powers of attorney may have only limited provisions. They may even act for people who are fully capable of acting for themselves but for some reason there may be a limitation. A good illustration is a power of attorney granted by one spouse to the other to convey property like selling a house. It may happen that a wife is traveling overseas and will be unable to attend the closing of a jointly owned property that is being sold. In that event, the husband is granted a limited power of attorney to act for his wife in her absence. There are other uses but the rules remain the same.

"*Healthcare representatives*: In some respects the preparation of a document that appoints a healthcare representative resembles a power of attorney. A healthcare representative document is a very specialized legal stipulation. It states in clear terms who makes the healthcare decisions for another. In Uncle Mitchell's case, he is unable to make healthcare decisions, but he had previously prepared a document that gives this authority to Aunt Jackie. Now, you might say it is only reasonable that spouses may speak for one another. Some situations may require life-threatening procedures by doctors or other medical staff, and these people are sometimes reluctant to act based on a decision by a spouse for fear of an ensuing liability. Consulting a documented healthcare representative bridges that gap. In some cases these documents are part of a person's medical file; other times they are provided when necessary. Aunt Jackie intends to file the document with the hospital, thus documenting her authority to act.

"*Living wills*: A living will is a legal document that states the author's wishes in the event the author may only be kept alive by artificial means. In most states today, medical people will go to extreme measures to maintain the life of another. A person may choose to short-circuit those activities if there is no chance of recovery. Most living wills state that a person does not wish to be kept alive by artificial means if there is no chance of survival. A living will is designed to limit unnecessary family suffering and expense. The author of a living will sees no purpose in artificially maintaining body functions simply to prolong the dying process. Living wills are seen by some as a blessing.

"Sam, that is the basic four," said Jason. "There are two more issues that should be addressed depending on the desires of the spouses. One is a prearranged funeral. Some make such arrangements in advance for two reasons:

1. Doing so usually fixes the costs. Funeral arrangements are expensive and sometimes paying early saves extraordinary expense later.
2. Convenience. Some just want to get it over with and behind them. Doing so also ensures the arrangements are in keeping with one's own wishes.

"The second issue is that of trusts. The federal and state governments heavily tax the estates of those who have died. In some cases marginal estate tax rates may exceed 50% of the estate after funeral expenses and retirement of debts. Many people fail to properly recognize the full value of their estates. Today, IRAs and 401(k) programs are exploding in value because of the success of the securities markets. Add to that the equity in a home, other property and the value of life insurance. Soon a person's estate becomes a big number.

"Now, I should make clear that one spouse may pass their entire estate to the surviving spouse tax free. That's right, there is an unlimited marital tax deduction between spouses. The problem occurs when the surviving spouse dies. At that point, the entire estate, less any exemption and funeral expenses, is subject to tax.

"A trust established by both spouses, that is, both have their own trust, bypasses estate taxes up to a point. In 1999, $650,000 of any single estate is exempt from taxation. This exemption climbs to $1 million in 2006. Assume two people live until 2006, and then one dies. Assume further that together they have a joint estate valued at $2 million. Upon the death of one spouse, the survivor becomes the owner of the total estate with no death tax liability. Now, if the survivor should die in 2007 with the estate still worth $2 million, the dependent children would receive much less since $1 million is subject to estate taxes. That is the value of the estate in excess of the second spouse's exemption of $1 million.

"If, however, each spouse would have created separate trusts of equal value, $1 million each, the tax burden is significantly lessened. Here is what happens. At the death of the first spouse, the trust manager named in the trust document then administers the $1 million trust established by the deceased. The surviving spouse does not become the owner of the deceased's $1 million trust. Instead, the survivor receives all the income produced by the trust of the deceased, however the principal is retained for the remainder beneficiary named in the trust. When the second spouse dies, the remainder beneficiary, normally the children, receives the value of both trusts exempt from taxes up to $2 million.

"Trusts may be tailored in many ways. If the owners of the trusts want charities to receive part of the estates, that may be so stipulated. There are many ways a trust may be configured. The key is that trusts are a legal way to reduce estate taxes.

"Anyway you look at it, Sam, we have a lot of work to do to get our affairs in order," said Jason.

"It's so hard to think about us right now with Uncle Mitchell and Aunt Jackie on our mind," replied Samantha.

"I know Sam, I know. We need to get the kids squared away if we are going back to the hospital in the morning," said Jason.

"You should plan to go early, Jason," said Samantha. I will make some arrangements for the children and follow later in the other car."

"Good plan," Jason replied.

When Jason arrived at the ICU the next morning, Aunt Jackie was waiting. Jason could sense something had changed since last night. "What's the matter?" asked Jason.

"I just had a long, detailed conversation with the doctor," said Aunt Jackie. "The doctor explained that Mitch will never recover and that he is essentially brain dead. The only thing providing life is the machine. In keeping with Mitch's request, he is now off life support. I fully expect him to pass this morning. I called your father and Mitch's sister in California before I made the decision. We are all at peace with the decision and I am confident Mitch would agree."

Jason and Samantha stayed very close to Aunt Jackie over the next few weeks. Aunt Jackie had decided to keep the business and continue the operation. She was fortunate that Uncle Mitchell had hired and schooled good managers. Aunt Jackie became very creative in the manner in which she compensated the most senior managers. She created a program whereby each of the key people could earn shares in the business based on the total business success. Each of the managers had made a commitment to stay on and it appeared the business would continue to be successful.

About eight months after Uncle Mitchell's funeral, Jason and Samantha were visiting Aunt Jackie. "Jason," said Aunt Jackie, "I can't begin to describe how smoothly things have gone considering. The business seems to be on track to continue its growth and the prior financial planning done by Mitch has taken the uncertainty out of what could have been a very difficult transition for me. The wills, power of attorney and the trust have all worked according to the plan. The Third National Bank is acting as the trust manager for Mitch's trust. I am comfortable with the investment decisions they have made thus far.

"It's a difficult time for me," said Aunt Jackie, "but Mitch made it much easier. And I will always love him for that. He was a great husband to the very end, and then some."

Key Economic Terms – Chapter 16

Living will

Healthcare representative

Deeds

Certificates of deposit

Durable powers of attorney

Trust agreements

Last will and testament

Guardian

Estate

Limited power of attorney

Probate

Wards of the state

Prearranged funeral expense

Estate taxes

Chapter 17
The Decision: The Entrepreneurship Chapter

Everyone was happy to be back home again in Indiana. Even Junior seemed to enjoy being together with the family once again. While everyone felt a little uncertain that Jason needed to find a new job, their aggressive savings program plus the $300,000 settlement from *Switches.com* gave them more than enough money to live without feeling financially strapped for several years. Of course, they would prefer not to use up too much of their nest egg, but their significant savings certainly took the pressure off and would allow Jason the time to find the job that he wanted.

Junior was beginning his junior year in high school. Samantha was looking forward to being more involved with Junior for his last two years at home, especially after the overseas separation. Stephanie was just starting high school and she was excited to be back with her friends. Alex was starting eighth grade. All three children had changed a great deal in the past two years. Junior had held onto the position of starting quarterback, and college recruiters were already coming to watch him play. Stephanie had developed a new compassion for people, mainly from seeing the living conditions in a less developed country. Alex was also effected by the time in Jabodia, and he was talking about studying agriculture to 'help feed the world,' as he put it. Alex also had earned his black belt in Tae-Kwon-Do, giving him a new sense of confidence, even against his football star, older brother.

Samantha and Jason agreed that Samantha would handle the school registrations and Jason would concentrate on his job search. Jason wanted to find a position that would take advantage of his wide-ranging experience, but he wasn't sure if he wanted to go back into the computer hardware business. This seemed to be the time to take a fresh look at the opportunities and Jason's interests and find the best fit.

Jason set to work updating his résumé and beginning to research the available opportunities. He armed himself with Sunday editions of the *Chicago Tribune* and the *New York Times*. He also bought a copy of the *Wall Street Journal Employment Guide*. These were all good printed sources for employment and career opportunities, and there was also an almost limitless amount of information on the Internet.

Jason even considered contacting a headhunter. Since he wasn't sure what industry he was interested in, he decided to postpone that option for now. In the meantime, he would send résumés to those opportunities that appeared to present a good fit with his capabilities.

After several weeks and too many "no thank you" responses, Jason began to seriously ponder the fact that he may be significantly overqualified for most career positions. The fact that he was a very senior former executive out of a job did not improve his marketability.

Jason had noticed many franchise opportunities in his research. They ranged from donut shops to mail distribution centers, and even coin-operated Laundromats and car washes. "Perhaps I should start my own business," Jason thought to himself. The success statistics of many franchises is very good, but Jason couldn't see himself running a donut shop or car wash.

Jason continued to ponder the possibility of being his own boss and how that would fit with his background and interests. Late one night, he had an idea. He found a copy of the local telephone book and began to look through the Yellow Pages. Something was missing, so he did a quick search on *Yahoo.com*. Again, he was unable to find what he was looking for.

There was nothing in either source that focused on computer-based education and educational support. There were plenty of sources for supplies for students and teachers. There were references for testing services. But there seemed to be a major void when it came to educational software systems.

"Hey, Samantha," Jason called. "Do you remember many customer service calls from schools when you were at *Switches.com*?"

"Tons of them," Samantha called from upstairs. "Teachers didn't seem to be very good at putting their software and hardware together. And they would always ask me about good software."

Jason decided that he would visit the Board of Education and find out where they found software that provided lesson plan outlines, aids to assist both the gifted and the challenged students, and also software for class scheduling. "That should cover all the bases," Jason thought to himself. "There must be a host of functions at the teacher and the administrator level that had to be automated in today's environment."

The next morning he called the local Superintendent of Schools, Bill Frank, and arranged an appointment for later that day. He did not mention this appointment to Samantha.

Jason walked into Bill Frank's office at the appointed hour. "It's nice to see you, Jason. I remember you and Samantha from your involvement with school activities before you transferred overseas," said Bill. "It's nice to have you and your family back in the community. I hope you plan on getting involved again. What can I do for you today?"

"I'm curious," began Jason. "Where do you get your educational software support for your school system?"

"Boy, talk about a headache," answered Bill. "With all the advances in computers, you would think there were be lots of good choices. Unfortunately, there are thousands of educational software programs but it's tough to find out which ones are any good. There are a couple of national sources that we have used in the past. We take what we want from the various suppliers, and our tech support people put together a package that works, at least most of the time. At the rate we are going, we will soon be employing more tech support people than teachers."

Jason sensed some apprehension and dissatisfaction in Bill's tone. "Does that mean that the vendors do not tailor a system to support your specific requirements?" asked Jason.

"Heavens no," said Bill. "They must have enough business, because they are totally unwilling to offer any customer support. We are lucky to even get anyone on the phone. We have never been able to find anyone who would take the time to create a program that suits our individual needs. What is your interest here, Jason?" Bill asked, wondering where Jason was going.

"I have a fair amount of experience in the computer business," said Jason. "Information systems are an area of specific interest to me. I have given some thought to launching a business that would provide computer support specifically for schools."

"Well, someone needs to," said Bill. "I think you've identified a real market need. We've had some students from the university come in and set up routine systems as part of their computer technology coursework, but that's the only outside help that we've ever received. I suppose we could hire a general computer consulting company, but they would charge too much for a school district."

"Thanks for your time today, Bill," said Jason. "You have been very helpful. There may be something here. I think I will look into it further." Jason shook Bill's hand and said good-bye.

Over the next few weeks, Jason visited a dozen different school systems in central Indiana. The situation never varied. Everyone was relying on a patchwork system that created a great deal of frustration.

"Sam, we need to talk," said Jason one afternoon.

"What is it?" asked Samantha. She had been leaving him alone on his job search, knowing that he would come to her when the time was right.

"I have spent several weeks researching educational software and the different networks that schools are using. I think there might an opportunity here. And since I can't seem to interest anyone in my credentials, I think maybe I'll hire myself."

"Oh, come on Jason," said Samantha. "Have you taken leave of you senses? It sounds to me as if you want to start your own business."

"Nope, that's not it," said Jason. "I want to start 'our' business. We've got some money set aside. I think we can do something here."

"What would I do?" asked Samantha.

"You, Sam, have the best organizational skills of anyone I have ever known," replied Jason. "I think if I can come up with the ideas, you can play a major role in helping me put it together and run it. I have already got the name. It's *The Indiana Educational Software Support Company* or *TIESS* for short. What do you say? Are you in?"

"This is a bit sudden," Samantha said tentatively.

"Come on," Jason said. "It will give us a chance to work together again. Don't you remember how you loved working at the American school in Jabodia, and you learned a lot about what type of computer systems are needed in schools."

"I must admit that your idea is a perfect combination of our skills. But to be truthful, I am a little nervous about going out on our own, confessed Samantha. "I guess I would consider it under a few conditions. I propose we spend some quality time reviewing all the economic aspects of a new business startup. If, after we finish that task, we still feel good about it, we might do some market testing."

"Great," said Jason, happy that Samantha had been so receptive to the idea. "I'll start tomorrow with a draft pro forma, then we talk some more," Jason proposed.

"Make sure you include some sort of a timetable of critical incidents for us to review," counseled Samantha.

"No problem", said Jason. Samantha was already organizing, just as Jason had predicted.

Jason visualized that the pro forma, or more correctly, the business plan for *TIESS* should assess these major areas:

- Market Research
- Financing
- Staffing

With a basic understanding of what the business would be all about, he and Samantha could concentrate on the details of starting a private business venture.

"Sam, I have some planning information I think we should review," said Jason a few days later, giving her an outline of his business plan.

"That's okay with me. I just put on a fresh pot of coffee," replied Samantha.

"First off," Jason began; "we need to make sure we have done a credible job with market research. Specifically, who are our customers, how large is the potential, what are the risks, and why will they need us.

"I see our primary customer base being school administrators. The superintendent is a key player, and he or she will always be interested in ways to improve efficiency within budget constraints. There are at least fifty school districts within a one-hour drive of where we live. It does not appear that there are any local players in the software engineering business. Quite honestly, I think most of what is now offered comes from publishers and vendors who provide text and study material. Each vendor apparently has its own system, which leads to frustration at the teacher and administrator level."

"There are probably several orders of magnitude more opportunities if we expand to the entire state or even a multi-state area," observed Samantha.

"You're right, Sam," said Jason. "But I think we should concentrate locally and develop a real workable product before we think about expanding our business too far. When we are successful locally, we could expand or even franchise the idea.

"We know a lot about software integration, Sam," Jason continued. "I am not sure what our customers know. Not much, from what I've seen. Therefore, I can see our technical support activity becoming very costly in terms of time. In other words, let's focus the effort initially. If it doesn't work, we can pull the plug before we become too committed to too many customers." Samantha nodded her approval.

"What about financing?" asked Samantha "We really don't have the cash or the collateral, and we don't have any customers yet."

"Yes we do have collateral, Sam," said Jason. "We have our house, those two small parcels of land that we bought several years ago, and we have our investments."

"Jason, you are not suggesting we cash in our investments, are you?" said a startled Samantha.

"No, that won't be necessary, Sam," answered Jason. "We have eight months of living expenses in my money market account that should be adequate until we get our first paycheck. We have the $300,000 from the settlement from *Switches.com*. I judge we have about $250,000 equity in the house. It should be no problem to get a home equity loan for nearly 90% of that amount, or roughly $225,000. We won't take that as cash; we will view it as a first tier line of credit.

"I checked our IRA accounts and they have a value of about $450,000. I believe we can pledge those assets and generate a second tier line of credit."

"What does it mean to pledge assets?" inquired Samantha.

"It means we hand over control of the accounts to the bank. They do nothing with them without our approval; however, the asset is in their possession as collateral. The $150,000 or so that we have in mutual funds plus those two small parcels of land will be left alone since that is the education fund for the kids.

"There is also the SBA, the Small Business Administration. They provide loans as well. We'll just have to look at that alternative and then make a judgment about applying for a loan."

"You are talking about a lot of money here?" said Samantha. "Do we really need to have this much money available?"

"The number one reason that new businesses fail is because of under capitalization. I don't want to make that mistake," said Jason.

"I am sure glad you are not putting the education fund in jeopardy," remarked Samantha with some relief. "But then again, virtually everything we own will be mortgaged or pledged. That's an uncomfortable feeling."

"That's our risk, Sam. Nothing ventured, nothing gained," said Jason cheerfully. "The real opportunity lies with a sponsorship," continued Jason with a smile. He had clearly thought his business plan out.

"What's that all about?" asked Samantha.

"If we make a sale or two and begin to build a client base, I believe there will be software companies who will want to get involved with our product. We will do some research and conduct some trials, and then we select the one who appears the most competent. I think we should enter into a relatively short contract period with our partner, say two years. We ask for an upfront payment of perhaps 20% of the first year's revenue as part of the contract negotiation. We use that revenue as operating cash, thus lowering the demand on our lines of credit.

"And the reason we'll limit the initial contract to two years is to test the marriage?" asked Samantha.

"Exactly, Sam," said Jason. "A long-term deal with someone who cannot produce would be a disaster.

"Let's talk about the third part of our business plan, staffing," said Jason. "Initially, we're it."

"You mean just you and me?" Samantha asked.

"Yep, it's just us," continued Jason. "There are two major reasons. One, we want absolute control at the outset. We have to be able to act quickly when necessary and besides, if we do all the work ourselves for a while, we will know how to educate and train our employees. The second reason is probably more cogent. If the venture bombs, there is no one else involved."

"Yeah, I'd hate to have to lay someone off due to a lack of business success," said Samantha.

"You know what, Sam? When the venture gains momentum, we'll have people at the doorstep looking for a chance to ride with a winner. We will need to find some really good technicians for our business. Selling will be important, but our technical support will carry the day.

"Well, Sam, that's the outline of a brief business plan. There is more but that gives you a flavor for how we get started."

"I'd be less than truthful, Jason, if I didn't level with you and tell you I am very apprehensive about this," said Samantha.

"Fear is a good thing, Sam;" said Jason, always looking at the positive. "It will keep us focused.

"Tell you what. Let's take a break now, and tomorrow I want to lay out some of the economic factors that we will have to cope with," said Jason.

The next day Jason gave Samantha another outline of his ideas. "Sam," Jason began. "As we look at the economics of operating a business, I would like to establish three categories:

- People
- Pricing issues
- The Customer

"When we talk about people, the first issue is compensation or pay plans," Jason explained. "I know this seems a bit early to be concerned about people, but people expense is going to be our biggest financial cost, so we need to think ahead. There is more to compensation than just salaries or hourly pay. A pay program includes company benefits and, while some of these benefits do not appear as cash outlays, they all affect the bottom line. For most companies there are insurance programs that offer both term and health and accident programs. I think we ought to fund the basic coverage for both. However, the cost for any additions or upgrade is at employee expense.

"Then there is the matter of time off. There are national holidays, sickness, funerals, and, of course, vacations. If the employee is not at work, someone else must pick up the slack or the customer goes unattended. An unattended customer will cost revenue."

"So the cost impact is doubled any time we continue an employee's pay while they are absent," said Samantha. "I know you like performance based pay systems, Jason. Are you proposing that's the way we organize?"

"Yes, Sam," said Jason. "You know we will be unique in the company. As the owners, we are 100% performance based in our pay. Sure, we can draw a salary or an hourly wage, but anything we take from the company is out of our pockets. As the business matures, we want to make sure we are properly rewarded, economically speaking. No matter if our compensation is salary plus a bonus or all bonus; it should be representative of our effort and investment. If the company is making money, our compensation becomes a business expense that shelters income from taxes. We want to maximize such shelters, staying within the law, of course.

"Sam, there is a phenomenon we will experience as we begin to increase staff. Whenever we bring a new professional on board, that new employee often needs to be paid more than our current employees," continued Jason. "We won't want to hire just anyone. We will likely target people who are employed and who are successful. We want them to increase our success. It will take an attractive pay program to entice them to leave a position where they are well paid and successful. On top of that added expense, we then have to consider our own people. If their compensation is not made comparable to the new hires fairly quickly, we will have discontent.

"Another big issue will be how many supervisors we will need as we get larger," said Jason.

"I think we should consider a fairly wide span of control," responded Samantha. "Managers and supervisors are expensive, and if we can, I'd like to see us minimize that cost. I think one manager for every 6 or 7 employees would be a good target."

"I agree," said Jason. "At least in the beginning, it does not seem prudent to overwhelm us with a lot of overhead. If we grow the company to where we cannot personally be involved in the day-to-day operations, we may have to add supervisors to ensure quality control.

"Let's get into pricing issues," said Jason. "As a general statement, I don't believe we should be nervous about charging what we are worth. Many startup operations begin with bargain basement prices to get their foot in the door and then they can't understand why they lose business when they raise prices.

"Since our competition is from large national companies, we can probably price competitively and make a profit, especially since we will offer better service. The larger companies have more overhead cost to amortize. The flip side is that these large companies can afford to sell at a loss to make a profit."

"That sounds a bit screwy," said Samantha.

"Look at it this way, Sam," said Jason. "Many of the large national companies perform the software service as an add-on to their book sales. Books are their business. They could well decide to virtually give away their software business to retain a book account. Of course, in the long run, the books are priced such that the software business is not a net loss to their operations.

"You see this technique in action every day at the grocery store. Think about the one product that most grocery stores use to attract customers. Grocery stores are not alone in the use of this universal product to draw customers. Gas stations and convenience stores use it as well."

"I'm not sure what the product is," said Samantha. "No, wait. I do know. Is it soft drink products?"

"You've got it, Sam," said Jason. "You know I have seen 24 can cases of soda pop advertised as low as $3.99 per case. Do the math, that's less than 17 cents per can! When was the last time you saw a can of pop for 17 cents? When you factor in the entire store overhead and then add the cost of the pop from the supplier, they have to be losing money." Jason continued, "But how many people only buy the carton of soft drinks. Usually they buy other items, items at full price with a full profit."

"Well then, what's to stop the big guys from giving away the software and drive us from the business?" asked Samantha.

"No problem," said Jason. "We have something the big guys don't have or at least they can't offer it without charging for it."

"What's that?" asked Samantha.

"Us," said Jason. "The large booksellers are not that close to the customer. They can't provide custom service and there is no way they can match our response time. That's our niche. And you know what? The customer will pay for that kind of service. I don't see the big guys trying to match what we can do; it is just too costly for them. We don't sell books and they are not in the software business. We can co-exist. I'll tell you one more thing. If we become credible in the market place, the book people may knock on our door one day and offer to buy our business. The publishing business is very competitive. If a publisher had a subsidiary operation like ours, they could set themselves apart from their competitors. Anyway, if they come calling, it could get interesting.

"There may be a time when we will offer coupons, discounts or rebates," said Jason. "Those techniques become valuable tools if we want to close out a particular product line or just reduce idle inventory. Reducing selling prices also may be very effective to move products when next generation technology products are available. Do you remember what Uncle Mitchell used to do when he closed out last year's models?"

"Sure do. The people across the street won't buy a car at any other time," said Samantha.

"Okay," said Samantha. "What do you see as our expense for advertising? I know it is going to be important to get the word out to as many prospective customers as possible."

"Sam, the conventional thinking in business today is that advertising equals more business. That, in turn, means more revenue and more profit," said Jason. "You know, just to challenge you a little, I don't believe that is always the case.

"Not too long ago, Uncle Mitchell gave me a lesson in the economics of advertising. Did you know that his car dealership did virtually no formal advertising? You didn't see those annoying and foolish commercials coming from his place when he was in charge. His advertising costs were a fraction of his competitors and he outsold them, hands down."

"How did he do it?" asked Samantha.

"Uncle Mitchell said it was simple economics," said Jason. "He used to sell about 2,400 new and used vehicles each year. Uncle Mitchell said that most dealerships his size spent a minimum of $30,000 per month advertising their products."

"Sure, all car dealers advertise. Just look at today's paper," Samantha responded.

"Let me tell you what Uncle Mitchell used to do," said Jason. "Several years ago on January 1st, Uncle Mitchell just pulled the plug on all advertising. Instead of spending $30,000 each month on advertising, he invested the money in an interest-bearing account. Next he had his office manager make a list of all new and used car sales, by customer, complete with address and phone number, that took place during the month exactly 18 months prior. He chose 18 months because that is about the halfway mark to a customer repurchasing or releasing another vehicle. Since he was selling about 2,400 vehicles each year, he had a list of about 200 customers.

"He then instructed his sales staff to contact all 200 customers and invite them to the dealership to pick up a gift. That first calling netted about 100 customers. He then had the sales staff call the tardy 100 customers and invite them in again to pick up their gift. In all, I think he had about 160 responses that first month."

"What was the gift?" asked Samantha.

"Cash," responded Jason. "A check for $150 for each customer, no questions asked. It made no difference to Uncle Mitchell if the customer had gone somewhere else in the 18-month interlude to buy another vehicle. The customer still received a check for $150. Uncle Mitchell enclosed a short letter with every check. He told each customer how important he or she was to his business success, and he just wanted to share his good fortune."

"People thought he had lost his mind, didn't they?" asked Samantha.

"No question about it," said Jason. "But guess what? These people began to talk about this crazy car dealer at work, at parties, on the golf course, and some even discussed it at church.

"The bottom line is this," said Jason. "He was going to spend the money anyway, why not spend it on his present customers instead of spending the money on advertising just to lure new customers to his business? It's part of the golden rule of business, 'Take care of your customers, because if you don't, they may become someone else's customers.'

"Uncle Mitchell continued the practice every month. The surprise is that it didn't always cost $30,000. Typically, there would be no shows, but on average he was able to reach 90% of his customers. Plus, the money on account was earning interest. In the end, Uncle Mitchell actually invested less and less each month."

"Why can't we do the same thing?" asked Samantha.

"We can and I think we should," replied Jason. "We will have to create a different scenario since our business is different, but I am convinced that we should reward our loyal customers and not waste valuable resources chasing new customers. Our customers will be our advertisers."

Samantha sighed. "I don't know whether I am overwhelmed or whether I am just worn out. I do know one thing, however. We should commit ourselves to TIESS and set the wheels in motion to become our own business owners."

"I hoped you would say that," said Jason.

Key Economic Terms – Chapter 17

Franchise	Collateral
Market testing	Pledge assets
Pro forma	Client base
Business plan	Span of control
Market research	Startup operations
Financing	National companies
Staffing	Quality control
Customer base	Loss leaders
Technical support	Advertising

Chapter 18
The Next Generation: The Welfare Economics Chapter

After a slow beginning, the new business started to do well. The kids grew up. Junior went on to be a star quarterback at West Lafayette University, breaking all the passing records of Sketch Wind. He then became an insurance agent in Indianapolis, cashing in on his name recognition and did very well. Alex also went to WLU, majored in Agricultural Economics, and became a commodity trader on the Chicago Board of Trade.

The only problem, at least in Jason and Samantha's mind, was Stephanie. Despite her parent's advice, she decided to go to Bloomington University. "Only dumb people go there," Samantha tried to tell her daughter.

"What do you mean?" Stephanie argued back. "Dad went there."

"Look, I hate to tell you this, but your dad was no genius when I met him," Samantha said as kindly as she could. "I pretty much taught him everything that he knows. He certainly didn't learn very much at Bloomington University."

In the end, Stephanie decided to go to Bloomington University and major in liberal arts, and her parents grudgingly supported her decision. Stephanie graduated from BU and decided to spend a few years with an overseas relief agency in South America. When she returned to the United States, she got a job as a social worker in Chicago. One weekend, Jason and Stephanie decided to visit Alex and Stephanie in Chicago.

"This is a great place that you have, Alex," Jason said admiringly from the apartment on Lake Shore Drive. "It's too bad your sister didn't get a real job."

"Are you going to start on that again?" Stephanie said. "Because if you are, I'll just leave now."

"I'm sorry," said Jason, "I was just teasing. You have to admit that your brother has done very well for himself."

"I have done very well for myself too," Stephanie retorted. "Just because I don't make $100,000 like Alex doesn't mean that what I do isn't important."

"Why don't we talk about something else?" suggested Samantha. "We always get on this topic, and it's not very pleasant."

"No, I think it's time we resolve this issue," Stephanie said assertively. "I'm tired of these jokes. Do you even know what I do?" she asked her parents.

"Of course we do," answered Samantha. "You try to help people in the inner city find jobs and things."

"And don't you think that is important?" Stephanie asked.

"Yes we do," Jason answered. "It's just that we want you to enjoy life. It must be difficult living in that dangerous neighborhood and never having enough money. And for what? It's not like poverty is getting any better."

"But I am making a difference. I don't just sit around and trade pork bellies all day long. I don't see how that makes such a great difference for society," Stephanie said.

"Hey, leave me out of this," Alex complained. "I just want to sit back and enjoy the fight. Plus, with all the taxes I pay, I'm helping lots of people. I think your friends in the inner city probably make more than I do with all the welfare payments."

"This is exactly what I am fighting for," said Stephanie. "You say 'welfare' like it is a bad word. It just means the government is meeting the needs of people who are unable to take care of themselves, either for a short time or for a long time. People don't understand welfare, both on the giving side and the receiving side. But it is a huge issue. If a country can't deal with the welfare issue, all of society can break down."

Jason and Samantha had never seen Stephanie so passionate about anything before. "What do you mean, honey?" Samantha asked.

"I have been reading a book about how societies make decisions. Generally, there are three inputs to any decision: facts, principles, and values. These are the three inputs needed to make solid policy on welfare. But everything is so distorted, it is hard to make good policy.

"Take facts, for example. Alex just said that people on welfare probably make more money than he does."

"I was just kidding," Alex interrupted. "And can't you leave me out of this?"

"Maybe you were kidding," Stephanie said to Alex, "but you would be surprised at how many people think that welfare is the ticket to riches. And on the other side, you would be surprised at how many people on welfare think money magically comes from the government. They forget that welfare payments come from somebody's tax dollars. There is a real problem with facts."

"What were the other two inputs?" Jason asked, trying to be supportive.

"The next is principles. When it comes to welfare, we have really distorted the principle that working hard will get you a better standard of living. If everyone is guaranteed a minimum standard of living, there is no reason to work. We need to strengthen the connection between productivity and reward."

"Now you're talking," said Jason. "That's my girl," he said to Stephanie.

Stephanie smiled. "I'm glad you liked that one, Dad, but now let's talk about the third input, values. This book said that everyone values seven things:

1. More economic freedom
2. More job security
3. More growth
4. Stable prices
5. More income fairness–not necessarily equality, but fairness
6. Consumer protection
7. Peace

"I would buy that," said Samantha. "That's a pretty good list."

"It is a good list. But you can't get all seven of these at the same time. There are trade-offs. For example, more freedom sometimes conflicts with consumer protection. More growth through high technology may threaten job security.

"If we want to make good welfare policy, first we have to get the facts and principles straight. But then we have to decide on the trade-offs between these seven values," Stephanie summarized.

"You have really thought about this," Jason said admiringly.

"Of course I have," Stephanie said indignantly. "What do you think I do, pass around welfare checks all day long?"

Jason didn't answer because that is really what he thought she did all day.

"So why is what you do so important?" Alex asked, worried that he would stop being the favorite.

"Because we have so much potential to do better," Stephanie said. "At a lower cost," she added for her father's approval.

"Back in the old days, welfare was primarily done by families, supplemented by churches and communities. The people in charge used to use their judgment about who really needed help. They also used to make people work for it, thus maintaining the link between productivity and reward." Jason beamed again at that one.

"Now most of welfare is administered by rules and bureaucracy, not judgment," Stephanie continued. "We have so many people that need to be processed for welfare, there is endless red tape and forms. The cost of all this bureaucracy takes away from money that could get to the people that really need it. It is expensive to figure out who meets the rules.

"Many of the rules promote dependency. People learn how to play the welfare game, and they forget a main objective is economic freedom. On the trade-off between the seven values, some people are putting more emphasis in the security that comes from welfare rather than economic security.

"The most devastating effect is the effect on families. Some welfare programs actually discourage two parent households. Some programs give bigger welfare payments to single parent families compared to families with two parents. Basically the welfare system pays the father to leave.

"There is also a negative effect on the children of a family on welfare. Children see how their parents are dependent on welfare, and they don't learn the principles of working hard to make a better life.

"If I can get some of these children away from the dependency of welfare, I think I am making a pretty big contribution—not only for these children, but for society as a whole.

"I am working to change the welfare system so it doesn't give the wrong incentives, especially destroying families. At the same time, we need welfare. There are people in our society who are really hurting. Our society needs to have compassion for these people." Stephanie finished and waited for a reaction.

Jason, Samantha, and Alex all felt pretty guilty after Stephanie's soliloquy. "We're sorry," Jason said, feeling pretty confident that he spoke for everyone. "You are doing wonderful work. I guess we all get caught up in the outward appearances of success, and we don't appreciate the things that you are doing. I'm proud of you, Steph."

"Me too," said Samantha.

"Me too," said Alex.

Stephanie was happy that her family finally understood her passion for helping other people improve their lives. She knew that the people she worked with appreciated her, but having her family's support was very special.

* * * * *

Late that night, Jason and Samantha talked about the day. "Stephanie has really turned out all right," said Samantha.

"Yes, I'm very proud of her," Jason agreed.

"In fact, thanks to understanding the principles of economics, our whole lives have turned out well," Samantha remarked. "We have great kids, a very large 401(k) plan, and a successful business."

"You're right," said Jason. "I guess we are going to live happily ever after–until, of course, we need to execute our living wills or our last will and testament."

"Yes, Jason. Economics is wonderful."

Key Economic Terms – Chapter 18

Commodities trader

Chicago Board of Trade

Pork bellies

Welfare

Inputs to decisions by society: facts, principles, and values

Income fairness

Income equality

Dependency

Conclusion
The Essential Economic Principles in Life

We hope that you enjoyed our fictional story of Jason and Samantha. Of course, the true measure of whether we have succeeded with this book is to see if you grasped the key economic principles presented in this fictional setting. In this final chapter, we will review the essential economic principles in life illustrated by the story in this book.

In the Introduction, we said that economics is how we allocate our scarce resources to satisfy our unlimited wants. Economic decisions can arise in many different situations: in your personal life, in organizations, in individual markets, in the national economy, and between countries.

We dealt with many personal issues in the fictional story of Samantha and Jason. The car buying chapter, the house buying chapters, the financial planning chapters, and the funeral and estate planning chapter covered many of the basic terms and strategies of personal finance. The most important principle to remember from the personal finance chapters is this:

- **Planning is essential.** For example, setting aside 10% of your income starting with your very first job will give you security during bad times, and this plan will probably allow you to retire as a millionaire. Spending everything you make puts you in a very vulnerable position.

We also talked about making decisions in organizations. The merger of *Egos* and *Switches.com*, the international assignment, and the chapter on starting a business gave you some insights into how decisions are made in companies. There are two key principles to remember from our discussion about company decisions:

- **Use marginal thinking to make decisions.** You should look at the additional costs and benefits, not the total costs and benefits or the average costs and benefits, when making decisions.

- **Sunk costs don't matter.** This principle is a further emphasis on marginal thinking. If you have a lot of money or effort invested in a project, that is immaterial to a new decision. All that matters is the additional costs and benefits from the point of the decision forward.

We also covered two key principles of economic theory:

- **Maximize utility.** When making a decision, don't just look at the financial impact. Consider overall satisfaction.

- **Allocate resources according to comparative advantage.** Do not simply assign tasks by absolute advantage, or that could lead to suboptimal results.

We also discussed the economics of the national economy or society as a whole. A good foundation in these topics is necessary to understand the world around you. The discussion on the three questions that face all societies and the three ways countries answer these questions, the GDP chapter, the unemployment and growth chapter, the debate about politics, the welfare economics chapter, and the monetary and fiscal policy chapters all dealt with issues of the national economy or society as a whole. There are four key principles to remember from these chapters:

- **The key variables of the national economy are growth, price stability, and unemployment.** Of these three variables, growth is the most important for the standard of living of a country.

- **Growth is driven by investment.** Investment allows a country to expand its means of production.

- **Monetary policy is controlled by the Federal Reserve Bank, and fiscal policy is controlled by Congress and the President.** The goal of both monetary policy and fiscal policy is steady growth while keeping inflation and unemployment low. The policymakers do this by trying to equalize the amount that people want to buy with the amount that the economy can produce.

- **Politics is usually not a disagreement on the end objectives, but a disagreement on the means to reach the end objective.** At the most basic level, conservatives have more faith in the ability of the market to solve our problems efficiently, while liberals have more faith in the ability of the government.

We also discussed how different countries interact and trade with each other. The chapter about Jason wanting to buy a *Honda* described the mechanism of international trade, and the chapter about the international assignment raised many of the issues of the economics of less developed countries. There are two key issues to remember from these chapters:

- **Floating exchange rates automatically correct imbalances in trade.** If a country is importing more than it exports, its currency will eventually depreciate, making it more expensive for that country to buy goods from other countries. This is a very long-term effect, however, especially in the United States due to the flows of international investments.

- **Most of the world's countries are very poor.** The United States and the developed countries essentially live in another world than the less developed countries.

This book has covered the major principles of introductory economics. For many people, this is the end of the road. Hopefully this book has provided you with a good foundation. For others, there is plenty more to learn. Maybe you will consider taking some advanced courses in economics.

Glossary

401(k). A savings program offered by employers and savings institutions. Most contributions made by employees are before the levy of any taxes; however, withdrawals are taxable. 401(k) programs were created to help individuals better provide for retirement.

Additional paid-up insurance. Insurance that adds to the original policy face value.

Advertising. The act of encouraging a person to buy a product or service.

After-tax income. The income remaining after the Federal Personal Income Tax has been paid.

After-tax savings. Earnings that may be invested after the application of any taxes.

Appreciation. The increase in value for an asset that is held over time.

Asking price. The initial price established for the sale of an asset or service. Sometimes called the first price or the negotiable price.

Base salary. The amount of money paid to an employee before bonus, commission or other incentive.

Before-tax savings. Earnings that may be invested before the application of any taxes.

Birthrate. The number of live births annually per 1000 population.

Bonds. Debt instruments that companies and governments may issue to generate cash.

Bonus. A sum paid to an employee in addition to the base salary.

Broker. A licensed individual that is permitted by State law to buy and sell real estate.

Burial benefits. A payment made from the Social Security Trust Fund to help offset burial expenses. The benefit is available to those that have contributed to the Fund.

Buy American. An attitude that implies that buying foreign goods hurts Americans.

Cap. The maximum amount of money that may be drawn on a particular line of credit.

Certificate of deposit (CD). A savings instrument offered by a financial institution.

Charity tax deduction. The Federal Personal Income tax contains a provision that certain gifts to eligible institutions may be subtracted from the taxpayer's income before he calculates the tax he owes. Gifts to churches and Scouts are examples.

Checking accounts. Money on deposit with commercial banks that may be withdrawn at will by the depositor, sometimes called demand deposits.

Chicago Board of Trade. A major exchange for commodities.

Chief Operation Officer (COO). The individual in an organization that has responsibility for all day-to-day organizational operations.

Client base. Customers who regularly do business with a company or business.

Closed-end Lease. A lease that fixes the residual value at the inception of the lease.

Closing. The event that completes the paperwork and the exchange of money in an asset purchase.

COBRA. A provision in the law that permits an employee to continue his health and accident insurance coverage for 18 months after terminating employment.

Collateral. Something of value that is offered to be forfeited in the event of a default on a loan.

Commercial banks. Businesses who hold money for individuals, with or without paying interest, and who lend part of this money at interest.

Commission. The fee, generally represented as a percentage, charged by an agent that is assisting in the sale of an asset.

Competition. The recognition that what someone else does will influence my behavior and that my behavior will influence others.

Conservative. One who believes that the individual or business has a comparative advantage over the government in deciding what ought to be produced, how it ought to be produced, and who gets it.

Consumer Price Index (CPI). An indicator of how the prices of what consumers buy have changed from a base period, weighing items in proportion to their part of the typical consumer's spending.

Consumption (C). Spending by consumers for food, clothing, entertainment, etc.

Contractionary fiscal policy. Government tax increases or spending decreases with the objective of decreasing GDP, usually to fight demand-pull inflation.

Cost-push inflation. A rise in prices caused by changes on the part of the producer, or supply changes.

Counteroffer. An offer made by a buyer or a seller that replaces the last offer of the other party.

County (income) tax. The amount levied against earnings that are paid to support county government operations.

Credit cards. A rectangular piece of plastic that substitutes for cash in a purchase of goods and services.

Currency. Coins and paper money, a responsibility of the Fed.

Customer base. The core customers recognized by a particular business.

Cyclical unemployment. Temporary drop in spending and jobs (After this, people are rehired at old jobs when the economy picks up.)

Death rate. The number of deaths annually per 1000 population.

Debit card. A rectangular piece of plastic that when used causes an immediate withdrawal from a checking account.

Demand. A series of price-quantity combinations showing how much consumers are willing to buy at various prices.

Demand-pull inflation. A rise in prices caused by changes on the part of consumers, a demand increase.

Dependency. People relying on society to take care of them, usually associated with welfare.

Deposits. Amount of money entrusted to the bank for safekeeping.

Disability insurance. Insurance that provides payments in the event a wage earner becomes unable to work due to a physical disability.

Discount rate. The rate of interest charged by the Fed to commercial banks for loans to meet the reserve requirement.

Discouraged worker. No job, stopped looking after a long unsuccessful job search. Not a kind of unemployment since the person is not looking for a job.

Earnest money. A sum that is deposited by a prospective buyer of an asset, in conjunction with an offer to buy. This money is forfeited if the person does not come through on the offer.

Economic growth. The annual percent increase in real GDP per person.

Electronic transfer. The movement of money using an electronic means.

Equity position. Ownership in any enterprise.

Essential industries. In times of war it may be impossible to buy some products in a free world market. The production of these products is done by essential industries.

Excess miles. The miles accumulated over the term of the lease that are in excess of the stated allowable miles.

Exchange rate. The amount of one currency that it takes to buy another currency.

Expansionary fiscal policy. Government tax decreases or spending increases with the objective of increasing GDP, often to fight cyclical unemployment or increase growth.

Exporting jobs. A pejorative term referring to the fact that the importing country will lose employment when it begins to import a product. Rather than saying we are importing radiators from Mexico, we say that we are exporting radiator production jobs to Mexico.

Exports (X). Goods and services sold to another country.

Externalities. A person benefits or suffers as the result of the actions of another.

Federal Reserve (the Fed), or The Federal Reserve Bank. A bank for banks with the responsibility for managing the money supply and credit in the US to promote economic growth and minimize cyclical unemployment and demand-pull inflation.

Federal (income) tax. The amount levied against earnings that is paid to support federal government operations.

FICA. The abbreviation for the social security deduction levied against earnings. The letters stand for Federal Insurance Contributions Act.

Financing. A technique that employs borrowing to purchase an asset.

Financing. The program that generates operating capital for a business.

Fiscal policy. Deliberately changing federal spending and taxation in the country to cause the GDP to move so that there will be more economic growth and less cyclical unemployment or demand-pull inflation.

Fixed exchange rates. The government sets the amount of foreign currency that will be traded for one unit of its own currency.

Float. The period of time that passes from the time a person buys a product or service and the time that person must make a cash equivalent payment.

Floating exchange rates. The value of one currency in terms of another as determined by currency traders. Values are market determined.

Foreign demand for money. The desire for our currency by foreigners.

Fractional reserve banking system. A system of banking where the bank does not hold all the money deposited with it, but keeps only a fraction of it, lending out the rest as the basis for it earnings.

Franchise. A business arrangement where a private individual or company pays a fee to use the name, product or technique owned by someone else. An individual *McDonalds* facility is usually privately owned, however, the private facility owner pays a franchise fee to the *McDonalds Corporation* for the right to sell *McDonalds'* products.

Frequent flier miles. A bonus paid in miles by an airline as an incentive to purchase travel space. The accumulated miles may be traded for free air travel according to an established program.

Frictional unemployment. People who choose to change jobs before finding a new one.

Full employment GDP. A level of GDP representing how much can be produced in the economy when all resources are being used at capacity: all workers working, all land cultivated, all factories busy, and so forth.

Gap insurance. Insurance that is either provided or purchased in a lease. The insurance stipulates that if the asset is damaged beyond repair (total loss), the owner of the lease is not responsible for any deficiency that may occur between the residual value and the unpaid lease payments.

Gold standard. International trade is based on payments in gold for imported items. Usually the country will set a conversion rate of how much of its currency is equal in value to an ounce of gold.

Golden parachute. A negotiated agreement that provides a termination benefit (usually substantial cash or cash equivalents) to someone should that individual be asked to resign their position by a higher authority. Such a provision is usually reserved for very senior executives as an incentive to leave a company's employment.

Government securities. Financial instruments sold by the government indicating an amount that will be paid to the bearer at a specified date.

Government spending (G). Government purchases of goods and services. When included as a part of GDP it does not include transfer payments, outlays for which no concurrent good or service is required, such as social security payments.

Gross Domestic Product (GDP) The value of the final goods and services produced in the country in a year.

Gross National Product (GNP) The value of the final goods and services produced by the country's businesses in a year

Gross pay. The value of the pay and all benefits.

Health and accident coverage. Insurance protection that provides money to subsidize expenses related to health care.

Health care representative. The person that has the legal authority to make decisions for another who is unable to make their own decisions due to a medical disability.

HMO. An organization of care givers that band together to offer health related services. The banding together is designed to minimize medical costs. The acronym stands for Health Management Organization.

Home equity loan. A loan of money from a financial institution to a property owner. The loan is usually based on the owned portion of the property. In the event there is a mortgage on the property, the money loan will be based on the difference between the property value and the mortgage value (the equity).

Hyperinflation. Prices increasing at more than 10% annually.

Imports (I). Goods and services purchased from another country.

Incentives. A provision that encourages someone to behave in a certain way.

Income equality. Everyone's income is exactly the same.

Income fairness. Some people deserve to have a higher income than others, a value judgment.

Individual retirement accounts (IRA). Savings programs established by wage earners. Contributions may be made with earnings before taxes, which means that withdrawals will be subject to taxes. Withdrawals may not begin before age 59 ½ or a penalty is incurred. There is a new IRA, termed Roth IRA, which permits contributions with earnings after taxes. In these cases, the withdrawals are exempt from tax at withdrawal. The withdrawal age requirement remains 59 ½.

Inefficient producers. Producers whose cost of production is higher than that of other producers either in the country or abroad.

Infant industries. Producers who have recently started production and have not yet expanded their output to be able to get the economies of scale to get their costs down to be competitive with producers in other countries, but there is hope that they can become competitive in a reasonable time.

Inflation. The annual percent increase in prices.

Initial public offering (IPO). The initial offer of company stock (ownership) for public sale.

Insurance dividends. Money returned to insurance policyholders. May be taken as cash or used to purchase additional insurance. Normally considered a return of premium and not a taxable event.

Interest rate. The price of money. If the interest rate is 6%, it costs 6 cents to use a dollar for a year.

Investment (I)—(a) Spending by businesses to increase the stock of manmade goods and services used for production such as factories and machines. (b) Investment is the key to growth. Investment is the creation of manmade goods and services used for production including factories, machines, education, research and infrastructure (things that facilitate increased productivity such as roads, market reports, airports, weather forecasts, cellular phones, and so forth). (c) The purchase of something in hopes that it will earn income or increase in value, such as government bonds, common stock, antiques, farmland, and so forth.

Keynes. John Maynard Keynes, the author of fiscal policy.

Lease term. The duration of the lease.

Leasing. A technique used to pay for the use of an asset. There is no ownership. Leasing is different from renting in that there is usually a purchase option available at the end of the leasing term, such as with automobiles.

Less developed country (LDC). A country whose GDP per capita is below the world's average.

Liberal. One who believes that the government has a comparative advantage over the individual or business in deciding what ought to be produced, how it ought to be produced and who gets it.

Line of credit. A negotiated amount of credit with a financial institution. This "line" may be drawn on at any time without further notice.

Liquidity. A term that describes the amount of cash that may be raised immediately. This normally includes cash, savings accounts that may be liquidated and any other asset that may be instantly turned to cash. Fixed assets such as real estate and other property are generally excluded.

Listing agent. The person that lists an asset for sale.

Living will. The legal document that directs action in the event a living person can continue to live by means of artificial life support.

Local (income) tax. The amount levied against earnings that are paid to support local government operations.

Loosening the money supply. Increasing the money supply so that interest rates will decline.

Loss leaders. Products or services that are offered by businesses or companies at less than their cost. The offering of these loss leaders is designed to bring customers to the business so that the customers may purchase other products or services that will earn a profit.

Macroeconomics. A study of the decision making about resource use by an economy as a whole.

Management recruiter (headhunter). A professional who is paid to find and convince people to make a job change.

Market testing. The technique used to place products or services into the market on a trial basis to test customer acceptance.

Marriage tax penalty. The increase in income taxes a married couple must pay. Generally, filing an income tax statement as two singles creates a lesser tax obligation than filing as a married couple. Legislation is often proposed to correct this situation.

Matching contributions. Normally a term applicable to 401(k) accounts. Many employers will make contributions to employee accounts as an incentive to encourage savings.

Means testing. In order for a person to be eligible for a certain benefit, he must show that he is in need of it; that his income is below a certain standard.

Medical insurance. Purchased protection used to offset the cost of medications, physician care and hospital expenses.

Medicare. The term used to describe government provided insurance for health and hospitalization.

Minimum wage. Employers are not permitted to pay an hourly wage less than the minimum wage. It is designed to keep employers from exploiting workers. It causes unemployment because it causes people worth less than this arbitrary wage to be excluded from work.

Monetary policy. Deliberately changing the money supply by the Federal Reserve Bank to cause the GDP to change so that there will be more economic growth and less cyclical unemployment or demand pull inflation.

Money market accounts. Savings accounts where the interest rates are parallel with secured government securities. These accounts normally function like checking accounts with larger interest returns.

Money supply. (M1) The checking account balances and the currency in the country.

Multiplier effect. A small change in C, I, G or X will cause a much larger change in GDP. Each dollar spent initially will cause its recipient to spend a fraction of it and that will be income to its recipient, resulting in a much larger change in GDP after many iterations from a small change in spending.

Mutual funds. A combination of securities offered as a package. The intent is to spread investment risk.

National companies. Companies that have a presence generally recognized in the majority of the nation.

National reasons for unemployment. Cyclical or structural unemployment.

Natural rate of unemployment. Usually considered as 3-4% unemployment. These are people that are switching jobs or are unemployable.

Net pay. Gross pay less all deductions.

Net worth. The amount left after subtracting all liabilities from all assets.

Nominal GDP. The GDP in current dollars. When nominal GDP increases, part of the increase may be from increased production and part may be from higher prices.

Nominal interest rates. The rate of interest that the lending institution declares it is charging to borrowers, usually an annual percentage.

Offer. An overt act to purchase.

Open market operations. Purchases and sales of government securities by the Fed in order to change the money supply. When the Fed buys government bonds, the payment for the bonds is deposited in the seller's bank account, increasing the money supply.

Open-end Lease. A lease that permits negotiation of the lease end residual value at the end of the lease.

Opportunity cost. The value of the opportunities foregone because one chooses to take a certain action. It is what could have been earned from a resource used for something else in its next best use. A recognition that the value (opportunity cost) of an item is not what was paid for it but what it could be sold for today.

Ownership. To hold or possess property.

Pay yourself first. The phase that describes the act of putting money into savings or investments before any expenses are satisfied.

Payroll deductions. Those items that are deducted from an individual's aggregate pay. Examples are taxes, insurance premiums and savings.

Per capita income. The nation's GDP divided by the nation's population.

Performance based. The majority of an employee's pay is based on some increased effort. Exceeding a sales objective, minimizing rejects in an assembly operation and exceeding a safety standard are examples.

Personal reasons for unemployment—frictional unemployment, voluntary unemployment, or unattractive worker.

Pledge assets. A form of collateral. Asset ownership is retained, however, should a loan default occur, the lender has the authority to call for the pledged asset to be sold to satisfy the debt.

Policy. The document that contains the insurance provisions.

Population growth. The percentage increase in population arising from births over deaths as well as immigration over emigration.

Pork bellies. Unsliced bacon, a commodity that is traded on the Board of Trade.

Power of attorney. A legal document that gives another the authority to act for oneself.

Precautionary demand for money. The desire for money by individuals and businesses in case of an emergency.

Premium. Two meanings. When used in conjunction with life insurance, the premium is the cost of the insurance policy. When used in conjunction with interest rates, the premium is the amount added to a base interest rate (the cost) as profit for the lending institution.

Prenuptial agreement. A legal document that stipulates who gets what in the event the subsequent marriage does not last.

Prime rate. The interest rate charged by the bank to its good customers on large loans.

Probate. The legal process of satisfying the debts and dividing up the assets of an individual who has died.

Producer Price Index (PPI). A weighted average of wholesale prices, somewhat comparable to the Consumer Price Index except at the wholesale level.

Property taxes. An amount levied by a local government that an owner of real estate must pay as a share of the cost to operate the appropriate government.

Public company. A company that has issued stock to private individuals or institutions is considered a public-owned company.

Quality control. The procedure employed by a business or company that is used to minimize errors.

Quotas. A limit placed on the annual amount of an item that may be imported from one country to another.

Real GDP. The GDP that has been adjusted for inflation. When real GDP increases 5%, it means that there are 5% more goods and services produced.

Real interest rates. The nominal rate of interest less the rate of inflation, both stated annually.

Realtor. A businessperson who assists buyers and sellers of real estate.

Recession. A decrease in real GDP two quarters in a row.

Renter's deduction. A deduction that is allowed on a federal or state income tax return. The deduction is sometimes equal to the total monthly rent payments. This deduction is allowed as a fairness gesture by the taxing governments since the interest on home mortgage payments is allowed as a deduction.

Renting. Paying for the use of an asset with no ties to eventual ownership.

Reserve requirement. The amount of money that a commercial bank is required to have in its till, in the vault or on deposit with the Fed, often stated a percent of a kind of deposit.

Reserves. The amount of money held by the bank in order to be able to meet the needs of its customers and to operate safely.

Residuals or residual value. A leasing term. The residual is the value assigned to the leased asset at the end of the lease.

Retainer. A fee paid to entice someone to provide goods and services as needed.

Roth IRA. See IRA.

Securities investments. Corporate stocks and bonds. There are also instruments called mutual funds that are included as securities. Mutual funds are aggregates of stocks and bonds offered as packages.

Security and damage deposit. A sum, usually equal to one month's rental payment, charged to a renter at the inception of the rental term. The owner holds the sum until such time as all repairs, if any, are made at the termination of the rental period. The deposit is also used on property leases.

Selling agent. The person that assists in the sale of the asset.

Social Security Trust Fund. The fund that receives FICA contributions. This is also the fund that disperses social security payments.

Social security. A governmental program established in 1935 to provide wage earners a retirement benefit. The program requires an equal payment from wage earners and employers at each pay period. Presently full benefits are available at age 65, although payments, at a reduced rate, may begin as early as age 62.

Span of control. The number of people reporting to one supervisor.

Speculative demand for money. The desire to hold money instead of other assets so that one can move quickly to take advantage of opportunities.

Staffing. The procedure of placing people in positions in organizations.

Standard and Poor's 500 (S&P 500). 500 company stocks that are aggregated as a group and tracked on the New York Stock Exchange.

Startup operations. The activities associated with the opening of a business.

State (income) tax. The amount levied against earnings that is paid to support state government operations.

Stocks. Securities issued by companies to create cash. The issue of one or more shares of stock entitles the stock purchaser an ownership position in the issuing company.

Structural Unemployment. Jobs permanently lost. Perhaps a worker is replaced by a machine or a new worker.

Sunk cost. Money spent in the past that does not impact a future decision.

Supply. A series of price-quantity combinations showing how much producers are willing to sell at various prices.

Take-home pay. The pay in cash or check from one's employer after all the deductions have been taken out, such as income tax, social security, insurance costs, and so forth.

Tariffs. A tax placed by the importing country and collected at the border on imported items.

Tax cuts. Reductions in the amount of tax owed by an individual or a business.

Tax freedom day. The fictional calendar date when a wage earner has earned the equivalent of his annual federal tax liability using all gross wages. The date usually falls in May of each calendar year.

Tax policy. The overall federal government attitude toward taxation in collecting money from the public.

Taxes. Payment to the government to finance public purchases.

Technical support. The providing of expertise to a customer as part of a business arrangement.

Term life insurance. A life insurance instrument that accumulates no cash value other than the death benefit.

Third World country. A country with a low GDP per capita. The first world countries are the Western, developed, capitalistic countries and the second world counties are the communist countries.

Tightening the money supply. Decreasing the money supply so that interest rates will increase.

Title. The legal document that proves ownership.

Trade. The people of one country buying goods or services from the people of another country. Over time trade always has to be reciprocal, imports must equal exports.

Trade deficit. The country is importing a greater value of goods and services than it is exporting.

Trade war. A situation where one country puts a trade barrier (prohibition, tariff, or quota) against another country's product and the second country responds likewise.

Trade-in value. The allowance, usually in dollars, assigned to an asset that is being traded for another asset.

Traditional IRA. See IRA.

Transactional demand for money. The desire for money by individuals in order to do business, buy lunch, pay tolls, and so forth.

Types of unemployment: cyclical, structural, frictional, voluntary, unattractive employee.

Unattractive Employee. Cannot land or hold a job due to education, attitudes, character, prejudice, discrimination, productivity, location, or motivation.

Unemployment insurance. A sum that is contributed by wage earners and employers to state agencies. The agencies may then provide subsidies to employees that lose employment through no fault of their own.

Unemployment. Looking for work and not finding it. If a person has a job, part-time or full-time, he or she is employed. If a person is looking for work and has not yet found it, that person is unemployed. If the person is not looking for work and not working, that person is not in the labor force.

Vesting. The period of employment that must be met before the employer 401(k) matching contributions are fully earned. The uninterrupted period is usually five years. Leaving the employment short of the five years results in less than a 100% earning of the matching contributions.

Voluntary unemployment. Has a job offer but chooses not to work, very picky about job.

Warranties. The term used to describe any guarantees offered by a seller. The original manufacturer of an asset or the original provider of the service may only offer a warranty. Any other offering that resembles a guarantee is termed a Service Contract.

Welfare. Society providing money or services to individuals unable to care for themselves.

Whole life insurance. A life insurance instrument that accumulates cash value. The cash value may be left with the insurance company to build in value, the policy can be surrendered for the cash value, or a policyholder can take a loan up to the cash value.

Will. The legal document that stipulates the decisions of a deceased.

Withdrawal penalties. Some savings instruments like CDs, IRAs and 401(k)s may not be withdrawn before a particular date. Early withdrawal may result in a reduction in interest (the penalty).

Index

401(k) · 169, 172, 175

A

Absolute advantage · 117
Accident insurance · 108
Additional paid-up insurance · 108, 169
Advertising · 160, 169
After-tax income · 97, 169
After-tax savings · 62, 169
Allowance · 78
Amortize · 130
Appreciation · 51, 169
Asking price · 78, 169

B

Base salary · 117, 169
Before-tax savings · 62, 169
Birth rate · 141, 169
Bonds · 128, 130, 169
Bonus · 117, 169
Broker · 78, 169
Budget · 101, 108
Burial benefits · 62, 169
Business plan · 160
Buy American · 44, 169

C

Cap · 130, 169
Carrying costs · 130
Certificate of Deposit (CD) · 32, 44, 51, 169, 175
Charity tax deduction · 69, 169
Checking accounts · 89, 169
Chicago Board of Trade · 161, 164, 169
Chief Operating Officer (COO) · 120, 141
Client base · 160, 169
Closed-end lease · 38
Closing · 78, 169
COBRA · 103, 108, 169
Coins · 89, 170
Collateral · 160, 169
Command system · 22
Commercial banks · 89, 169

Commission · 78, 169
Commodities trader · 164
Comparative advantage · 112, 117
Competition · 69, 169
Compound interest · 51
Conservative · 69, 169
Consumer Price Index (CPI) · 11, 14, 169
Consumption (C) · 97, 169
Contractionary fiscal policy · 97, 169
Counter-offer · 78, 169
County tax · 62, 169
Credit cards · 108, 169
Credit Cards · 101, 108
Currency · 89, 170
Customer base · 160, 170
Cyclical Unemployment · 170

D

Death rate · 141, 170
Debit cards · 106, 108
Deeds · 150
Demand · 17, 18, 19, 22, 38, 170
Demand curve · 22
Demand schedule · 22
Dependency · 164, 170
Deposits · 89, 170
Disability insurance · 108, 170
Discount rate · 89, 170
Discouraged worker · 30, 170
Durable powers of attorney · 145, 150

E

Earnest money · 78, 170
Economic growth · 89, 97, 170
Economics · 1, 5, 6, 7, 8, 13, 39, 46, 67, 119, 131
Efficiency · 141
Elastic demand · 130
Electronic transfer · 108, 170
Equilibrium price · 22
Equilibrium quantity · 22
Equity · 117, 141, 170
Equity position · 141, 170
Escalation of commitment · 130
Essential industries · 44, 170
Estate · 71, 143, 150
Excess miles · 38, 170

Exchange rate · 44, 170
Expansionary fiscal policy · 97, 170
Ex-patriot (ex-pat) · 141
Exporting jobs · 44, 170
Exports (X) · 97, 170

F

Federal Reserve · 10, 13, 14, 85, 86, 87, 88, 89, 91, 92, 93, 170, 172
Federal Reserve (the Fed) · 10, 13, 14, 85, 86, 87, 88, 89, 91, 92, 93, 170, 172
Federal tax · 54, 62, 170
FICA · 53, 54, 55, 62, 170, 174
Financial planning · 100, 108
Financing · 36, 38, 154, 160, 170
Fiscal policy · 89, 91, 93, 97, 170
Fixed costs · 130
Fixed exchange rates · 44, 170
Float · 106, 108, 170
Floating exchange rates · 166, 170
Focus groups · 130
Forced saving · 51
Foreign currency regulations · 141
Foreign demand for money · 89, 170
Foreign investment · 44
Fractional reserve system · 89
Franchise · 160, 171
Frequent flier miles · 108, 171
Frictional Unemployment · 171
Full employment GDP · 97, 171
Functional organization · 130

G

Gap insurance · 36, 38, 171
GDP deflator · 11
GNP per capita · 28, 30
Gold standard · 44, 171
Golden parachute · 141, 171
Government bond issues · 130
Government securities · 89, 171
Government spending (G) · 97, 171
Gross Domestic Product (GDP) · 7, 8, 9, 10, 11, 14, 28, 91, 93, 97, 136, 138, 166, 169, 170, 171, 172, 173, 174, 175
Gross National Product (GNP) · 8, 9, 10, 14, 25, 28, 30, 171
Gross pay · 62, 171, 173
Guardian · 150

H

Health and accident coverage · 62, 171

Health care representation · 108
Health insurance · 104, 108
Healthcare representative · 145, 147, 150
HMO · 103, 108, 171
Home equity loan · 51, 171
Home insurance · 78
Hospitalization insurance · 108
Hyperinflation · 84, 89, 171

I

Imports (I) · 97, 171
Incentives · 69, 171
Income equality · 164, 171
Income fairness · 164, 171
Indexed mortgages · 51
Individual Retirement Accounts (IRAs) · 57, 60, 61, 62, 63, 66, 68, 104, 155, 171, 174, 175
Inefficient producers · 44, 171
Inelastic demand · 130
Infant industries · 44, 171
Inflation · 10, 14, 46, 89, 97, 171
Infrastructure · 30
Initial public offering (IPO) · 110, 111, 117, 128, 171
Insurance dividends · 108, 172
Insurance Planning · 101
Interest rates · 14, 46, 89
Investment · 30, 55, 63, 97, 101, 108, 166, 172
Investment (I) · 30, 55, 63, 97, 101, 108, 166, 172
Investment Planning · 101

K

Keynes · 83, 88, 89, 172

L

Lease term · 38, 172
Leasing · 37, 38, 172
Less developed country (LDC) · 135, 136, 141, 172
Leverage · 51
Liberal · 69, 172
Line of credit · 130, 172
Liquidity · 58, 62, 172
Listing agent · 78, 172
Livable wage · 70
Living will · 108, 145, 147, 150, 172
Local tax · 62, 172
Loosening the money supply · 89, 172
Loss leaders · 160, 172

M

Macroeconomics · 89, 172
Management recruiter (also see headhunter) · 109, 117, 172
Marginal cost (MC) · 125, 130
Marginal revenue (MR) · 126, 130
Marginal thinking · 130
Market research · 160
Market system · 22
Market testing · 160, 172
Marriage tax penalty · 108, 172
Matching contributions · 62, 172
Means testing · 62, 172
Medical insurance · 62, 172
Medicare · 54, 55, 62, 104, 108, 172
Milton Friedman · 88, 89
Minimum wage · 69, 172
Monetarists · 88, 89
Monetary policy · 83, 89, 92, 93, 166, 172
Money · 57, 62, 85, 89, 116, 169, 172, 173
Money market accounts · 62, 172
Money supply · 89, 173
Multiplier effect · 97, 173
Mutual funds · 108, 173, 174

N

National · 10, 79, 97, 141, 160, 173
National companies · 160, 173
National economy · 97
Net pay · 62, 173
Net worth · 108, 116
Net Worth · 101, 108, 173
Nominal GDP · 11, 173
Nominal interest rates · 51, 173

O

Offer · 78, 173
Open market operations · 89, 173
Open-end lease · 38
Opportunity cost · 78, 81, 173
Ownership · 130, 170, 173

P

Pay yourself first · 62, 173
Payroll deductions · 62, 173
Per capita income · 141, 173
Performance base · 130, 173
Pledge assets · 160, 173
Policy · 79, 91, 108, 173

Population growth · 141, 173
Pork bellies · 164, 173
Power of attorney · 108, 173
Pre-approved mortgage · 78
Precautionary demand for money · 86, 89, 173
Premium · 38, 108, 173
Prenuptial agreement · 108, 173
Price · 126, 130
Prime rate · 51, 173
Private mortgage insurance (PMI) · 74, 78
Pro forma · 160
Probate · 108, 150, 173
Producer Price Index (PPI) · 11, 14, 173
Property taxes · 51, 78, 173
Public company · 130, 174

Q

Quality control · 160, 174
Quotas · 44, 174

R

Real GDP · 11, 14, 174
Real interest rates · 51, 174
Realtor · 78, 174
Recession · 14, 30, 174
Renting · 45, 51, 174
Reserve requirement · 89, 174
Reserves · 89, 174
Residuals · 33, 38, 174
Restructuring · 130
Retainer · 117, 174
Return of premium paid · 108
Risk · 117
Roth IRA · 60, 61, 62, 171, 174
Rule of 72s · 51

S

Scarce resources · 6
Security and damage deposit · 51, 174
Security investments · 62
Selling agent · 78, 174
Shortage · 22
Social Security · 54, 55, 57, 58, 60, 61, 62, 137, 169, 174
Social Security Trust Fund · 57, 61, 62, 169, 174
Solvency · 130
Span of control · 160, 174
Speculative demand for money · 86, 89, 174
Spreading out fixed costs · 38
Staffing · 154, 160, 174

Standard and Poor's 500 (S&P 500) · 46, 49, 61, 104, 174
Startup operations · 160, 174
State tax · 62, 174
Stocks · 130, 174
Structural Unemployment · 174
Sunk cost · 38, 165
Supply · 22, 38, 174
Supply curve · 22
Supply schedule · 22
Supply/demand analysis · 22
Surplus · 22

T

Take-home pay · 97, 174
Tariffs · 44, 174
Task forces · 130
Tax cuts · 69, 174
Tax Freedom Day · 62
Tax policy · 97, 174
Taxes · 68, 101, 108, 175
Technical support · 160, 175
Term life insurance · 62, 108, 175
The Great Depression · 30
Third world country · 141, 175
Tightening the money supply · 89, 175
Time value of money · 49, 51
Title · 108, 175
Total revenue · 130
Trade · 38, 44, 175
Trade deficit · 44, 175

Trade war · 44, 175
Trade-in value · 38, 175
Tradition · 16, 22
Traditional IRA · 62, 175
Transactional demand for money · 89, 175
Trust agreements · 145, 146, 150

U

Unattractive employee · 30
Unemployment · 25, 30, 55, 62, 89, 97, 175
Unemployment insurance · 30, 55, 62, 175
Unlimited wants · 6
Utility · 109, 117

V

Variable costs · 123, 130
Variable rate mortgages · 46, 51
Vesting · 60, 62, 175
Volume · 130
Vouchers · 69

W

Warranties · 51, 175
Welfare · 30
Whole life insurance · 62, 108, 175
Will · 108, 145, 146, 150, 175
Withdrawal penalties · 62, 175

APPENDIX

Written Assignments

Written Assignment 1

Name

Seat No.

1. This spring the crops did not get planted until late because of too much rain. Finally it dried off, and for some reason that made the phone ring while Freddie was studying for his last final. First, he got a call from Dad saying that they could start planting Friday afternoon. The timing was perfect because Freddie could just make it home from his last (F 8-10) exam by about 1:00 p.m. on Friday. The plan was for Dad to start planting and to be sure that all was working right. Then Freddie would take over about 3:00 p.m. and with his Mom's help keep planting until 4:00 a.m. when they would be relieved by Dad and Sis. They would plant 24 hours a day until they got caught up. He said he'd be there. Unfortunately, Sis told Jennifer (Freddie's home-town flame) on the bus that Freddie would be home Friday afternoon. When she heard the news (the last she had heard, he wouldn't be home till Saturday) she called him at WLU and left a message on his machine while he was out photocopying, telling him how thrilled she was that he would be there to go with her to the big special school party Friday night. He noticed the blinking light when he got back, but before he could press the button, the phone rang and it was Shari, the new light in his life, saying that something was wrong with her Mom's car and asking if she could get a ride home with him (it wouldn't be more than a half hour out of his way) but her last exam wasn't until 3:20 Friday afternoon.

Explain what you think Freddie should have done after his exam on Friday and what it would have cost him to do it. As a part of your answer define opportunity cost and show clearly that you understand the concept as it is applied to Freddie's dilemma. (A general statement will be of little value. You must be specific to earn credit.)

3. The Indiana state government is prohibited from going into debt, so hard choices have to be made. When the Indiana legislature voted to fund part of WLU's budget request, there was no money left for State grants to local police departments. Using the opportunity cost concept, explain what it cost Indiana to fund WLU?

3. Define economics:

4. Compare and contrast microeconomics and macroeconomics? Give an example of an economic problem in each area that is important, or at least connected to you.

a. These are alike in that:

b. These are different in that:

c. A microeconomic problem:

d. A macroeconomic problem:

5a. When an economic question is asked, such as, "How will the poor 1995 crop affect the price of corn?", what assumption is made about the demand for corn to make corn sugar, the primary sweetener in soft drinks.

5b. What term do economists use to say that when they look at the effect of one thing on another that all the other things that could cause things to change are held constant?

6. Economic policy decisions are a product of three kinds of information, facts, principles and values. Which of these will this class emphasize?

Which of these will the individuals in this course disagree about the most? Why?

7. List the seven economic policy goals that are common to the folks of most societies:

The following questions cover simple arithmetic and geometric concepts that I will expect you to do easily in problems throughout the semester. Because I am most interested in knowing whether or not you are comfortable doing these problems, I want you to show you work carefully--this means equations and clear substitutions. For most of you these will be very easy. If you have trouble with these, please ask friends for help, because I will expect you to have these skills.

8. Look at Figure 1-A (handed out in class) and answer the following questions:

    a.   As the line goes up (North), what is it that increases?

    b.   As the line goes right, what is it that increases?

    c.   Usually in diagrams the cause is on the (vertical, horizontal) axis and the effect is on the (vertical, horizontal) axis.

9. The value of all the goods and services produced in the US last year was $6900 billion, and consumers bought $4700 of them. What percent of the goods and services produced in the US did consumers buy?

10. You graduate and take a job here in Indiana at an annual salary of $26,000. Indiana income tax is about 5% of your income and the US tax is about 20% of your income. How much tax will you pay Indiana, how much to the federal government and how much in total.

11. Federal law requires that some jugs of farm pesticides must be transported in dual-wheeled trucks. Is how these chemicals are moved from distributor to farmer decided by market, command or tradition? Explain.

Written Assignment 2

Name

Seat No.

1. Economics is a study of how we use our scarce resources to get what we want most. What do we want? We can have almost anything we want, but because resources are scarce, we can't have everything we want. We all have most of life's necessities, or we wouldn't be here. There are some nice things we would like that are in the realm of the reasonable for us. Some things we just obtained, and some we don't have yet, but if everything goes well, we might get them within a year. There are some very nice things that others have but it is not likely that we will get them any time soon. Sometimes we do not do a good job of thinking through what we really want before we spend our money. List not the type of thing, but three specific items from your life in each category.

Necessities that I have had for some time:

Nice things I want that I just got or may get fairly soon:

Very nice things I would like but probably won't get soon:

Some things I used good resources to get, but it was dumb, a waste:

2. Several years ago a massive effort was begun to move the railroad tracks in Lafayette so that they did not interfere with car traffic. The plan involved making a "rail corridor" for all railroad lines along the Wabash River and extending the river bridges over the tracks. The cost of the project is currently estimated to total $160 million, about $1500 for each person living in the Greater Lafayette area. The reason we could afford this is because it could be 90% funded by the federal government; only 10% local cost. It is easy to see work on this project. Completion is not expected for another 5 years. Many other communities made similar decisions with similar reasoning, so the real shift is from local taxes to federal taxes, but the same people pay for it.

Opportunity cost is the value of what we give up in order to get something else. It isn't the value of everything else we considered as an alternative, but the value of the thing we would have chosen instead of what we did. When the decision was made to commit $160 million to Lafayette railroad relocation it meant that we either raised taxes (reduced individual personal expenditures) or we did not do another potential government project.

From your point of view what did we give up, or what would you have recommended that we do, which we did not do because we chose to relocate the railroads.

a. The best personal expenditure possible because of reduced taxes. (If I hadn't had to pay $1500 taxes, what would I have bought?)

Which would your prefer, your suggestion or the railroad relocation?

b. The best new government program or program expansion that was suppressed because of the railroad relocation:

Which would you prefer, your suggestion or the railroad relocation?

3. When WLU wins the Old Oaken Bucket contest we know who loses. For some it is hard to know whether there is more joy in seeing WLU win or seeing those other guys lose. When Martin is chosen to build the new WLU parking garage, the local competitor loses. In some games, for every winner there is a loser. This spring a WLU student's self-employed father lost a major contract and the student was asked to see if he could get a significant part-time job to help with college expenses. A West Lafayette small business owner was fortunate to have his daughter handling the business' computer with the financial affairs and production information on it. Her husband got transferred and the businessman was left without a computer specialist. Through the campus job link, the student and the businessman got together and settled him working for the business 20 hours a week at $10 per hour. Which one was the winner and which the loser in this transaction?

4. There are three ways that tax payments can vary as income is increased. For each define how the tax varies with income, give an advantage of emphasizing this kind of tax and a disadvantage of over emphasizing it. The key to the definition has to do with the percent of one's income that goes to pay the tax as income increases.

a. Progressive Tax:

Definition:

Advantage:

Disadvantage:

b. Proportional Tax:

Definition:

Advantage:

Disadvantage:

c. Regressive Tax:

Definition:

Advantage:

Disadvantage:

5. Taxes are sometimes used to get people to do things that the government thinks are good for society. Sometimes they are used to discourage certain behavior. Below list three favorable kinds of behavior that you think that Congress could (or already has) agreed on, and for each give a kind of tax incentive for encouraging this behavior either that we already have or that we should have:

Behavior to be Encouraged   Tax incentive feature to encourage this behavior

a.

b.

c.

Behavior to be Discouraged   Tax incentive feature to discourage this behavior

a.

b.

c.

6. The grades in this course might average 2.25 this semester. That means that for the 150 people in the class there will be a total of 340 grade points assigned. One way to get this class average would be to assign 40 B's and 110 C's. What grade distribution would you suggest?

Number of Students	Grade	Points	Total Points for Grade
	A	4	
	B	3	
	C	2	
	D	1	
	F	0	
Total 150			340

Did you recommend that everyone get B's and C's? If so, why?

Or did you recommend another grade distribution? If so, why? (You may want to use the ideas of "encouragement" and "incentive" as well as "fear" and "punishment".)

What is the advantage of assigning A's to some people?

What is the advantage of assigning F's to some people?

7. To what extent are the same principles relevant for choosing the best income distribution for the country. Would you recommend that everyone have about the same income, or should there be a possibility of some getting a high income and some getting low? Explain.

Written Assignment 3

Name

Seat No.

1. For each of the situations below:
·   For what product is this the supply and demand?
·   Note the change.
·   If the government changed the price **of this** product, it is a **command change.** If it did not, it is a **market change.**
·   Draw and label the axes and the lines for a supply-demand diagram showing the equilibrium price and quantity.
·   Remember some things change supply, some demand, and some neither. (In this class, never both.)
·   **If the change is a result of a market change:**
·   Decide who is directly and immediately affected; producers or consumers.
·   If producers are affected first, supply changes, if consumers; demand.
·   Is supply or demand increased, decreased or not changed?
·   Draw the new supply or demand curve if appropriate and the new price and quantity. (Increased; to the right, decreased; to the left.) Label each.
·   Report changes in supply, demand, price, and quantity from this change.
·   **If a command system changed the product price:**
·   Neither supply nor demand change--just the price changes.
·   Draw in the new price line.
·   Draw quantity lines down from the intersections of the new price line with the supply and demand curves.
·   Label the quantity from the supply line "Amount available."
·   Label the quantity from the demand line "Amount wanted."
·   Show the surplus or shortage.
·   Report no changes in supply or demand, the change in price, and clearly indicate both quantities available and wanted as a result of this price change.

a. Corn Market
    The crop got planted late, some got drowned out, there was an early frost (all bad) for the 1995 crop.

Supply
Demand
Price
Quantity

b. US Wheat Market
   Crop failures in other parts of the world greatly reduce world wheat availability.

Supply
Demand
Price
Quantity

c. Kiwi Fruit Market
   Many people start to raise kiwi; it takes several years to bring the plants into
   production; now there are many new producers entering the market.

Supply
Demand
Price
Quantity

d. Commercial On-Line Services Market
   Users decide to use direct Internet access providers rather than the on-line services
   companies.

Supply
Demand
Price
Quantity

e. Specialty Grandparent Item Market ("Grandma is like Santa Claus" sweatshirts)
   More young marrieds in their 20's decide to postpone children until their 30's.

Supply
Demand
Price
Quantity

f. Wool Market
   The government is concerned with the declining income of sheep producers and
   raises the price of wool by $0.30 per pound.

Supply
Demand
Price
Quantity

g. Lamb Market (Sheep for Meat)

The government is concerned with the declining income for sheep producers and raises the price of wool by $0.30 per pound.

Supply
Demand
Price
Quantity

h. West Lafayette Apartment Market

The West Lafayette City Government prohibits raising rents on apartments once a tenant has moved in. (Students want more and more apartments.)

Supply
Demand
Price
Quantity

i. WLU Basketball Ticket Market

Even though many are willing to pay more to get good seats, the prices of Mackey tickets are held down.

Supply
Demand
Price
Quantity

j. By-Pass Heart Surgery Market

Federal legislation sets a low price as the maximum that can be charged by hospitals and physicians for this widely needed but expensive treatment.

Supply
Demand
Price
Quantity

2. Define supply:

3. Define demand:

4. What is causing the shortage of onions in Bosnia?

5. Relative to 1 g. where the supply for lamb increased (did you have it right?); what happened to the:

Lamb price in the grocery store?

Lamb price to the farmer?

Lamb production on the farm?

Demand for lamb in the grocery store?

6. Relative to 1 a. where the supply of corn decreased, what happened to the:

Corn price for hog feeders?

Amount of corn hog feeders buy?

Hog feeder's demand for corn?

Written Assignment 4

1. Investment, an important component of GDP, is an increase in the stock of durable, man-made goods and services that are used for production. The most common kinds of investment are:
- Machines and Factories
- Education
- Research and technology
- Infrastructure

a. First give a specific example which shows clearly this kind of investment, and then explain how GDP next year is likely to be affected by an increase in each of these kinds of investment this year.

Machines:

Education:

Research:

Infrastructure:

2. For each draw and label the diagrams and show the changes just as last week.

a. Soybean Market

Soybean producers have long used a chemical to control a particularly troublesome weed, but now that herbicide has been withdrawn.

Supply
Demand
Price
Quantity

b. Milk Market

People are afraid that the BST used to stimulate milk production in dairy cows may not be good for them, even though it cannot be detected in the milk.

Supply
Demand
Price
Quantity

c. Farm Raised Fish Market

New production techniques and feeds dramatically improve the efficiency of fish production on American fish farms.

Supply
Demand
Price
Quantity

d. Peanut Market

The US Department of Agriculture decides to raise peanut prices on the farm by 30% in order to increase the income of the poor southern farmer.

Supply
Demand
Price
Quantity

e. US Car Market

The government requires dual air bags, anti-lock brakes, window glass heaters, and a host of safety equipment on all new cars sold.

Supply
Demand
Price
Quantity

f. US Handgun Market
   The government puts severe restrictions on the purchase of handguns, making it much
   more difficult to own one.

Supply
Demand
Price
Quantity

g. Construction Labor Market
   Indiana passes a law that requires that union wages, well above average, be paid on
   all construction projects financed by state funds.

Supply
Demand
Price
Quantity

h. US Gasoline Market
   After a year of gasoline price controls which substantially lowered gas prices the
   price controls were lifted.

Supply
Demand
Price
Quantity

i. Cream of Wheat, breakfast cereal, Market
   The US starts into a recession, incomes drop and the outlook is bleak.

Supply
Demand
Price
Quantity

j. Rwanda Tapioca Flour Market
   The new government in Rwanda lowers the price of tapioca flour by 30% in order for
   the poor people to be able to afford to eat better.

Supply
Demand
Price
Quantity

k. The Market for Heart-shaped Objects
   Valentines day is approaching ! ! !

Supply
Demand
Price
Quantity

l. The WLU Student Education Market
   The Federal Government institutes a $500 tax reduction for students enrolled in full-time college, and Indiana offers $1000 scholarships.

Supply
Demand
Price
Quantity

3a. In the space below, draw and label a diagram that shows clearly for a wide range of incomes just how much people in the society will spend. Label the axes and label the line "Consumer spending with various levels of income"

3b. On the same axes draw a line showing clearly how much income results from a wide range of consumer spending. Label this line "Income resulting from various levels of consumer spending".

3c. Show the level of income that the people in this economy are likely to have when all settles down. Label it "Equilibrium income".

Written Assignment 5

Name.

Seat No.

1. Unemployment--Looking for and not finding work.

National economic reasons why people are unemployed:

    Cyclical Unemployment--temporary reductions in national spending reduced jobs. After this temporary unemployment, people will be rehired at their old jobs when the economy picks up.

    Structural Unemployment--Jobs are permanently lost because the:

        Product is out-of-date--replaced by something else--job no longer exists

        Production technology is out-of-date--worker replaced by technology or worker with skills needed with the new technology

Personal reasons why people are unemployed:

    Frictional Unemployment--people between jobs who chose to change jobs

    Unattractive Employee--Person can't land or hold a job because of lack of education, character, prejudice, discrimination, attitudes, etc.

    Voluntary unemployment--a person who has job alternatives and chooses not to work, not to look for a job very hard, or to be very picky in the job he will take.

Sad situation, but not a kind of unemployment because the worker isn't looking:

    Discouraged Worker--one with no job but who has stopped looking for work after a long unsuccessful job search resulting from either Structural Unemployment or being an Unattractive Employee.

For each of the situations below, indicate which kind of unemployment from the above list is being described:

a. She was one of the very best typewriter repair people in the business. She had worked for several different models of typewriters through the year and kept up-to-date on new models and features. Women are the direct users of most typewriters and she had an advantage over her male counterparts in that she could understand the complaints better and she knew how to solve most problems. She had seen many of her male co-workers move on and some even lose their jobs, but she thought her job was secure because she was good and she was special. That didn't stop the pink slip from showing up last Friday. They will give two months of severance pay. Whoopee-ding! What to do now?

b. The telephone business is really changing. Ten years ago signal transmissions were an electrical current flowing over a copper wire. But now messages are transmitted as flashes of light passing through a fiber optic cable. Working copper and working glass fibers is very different. He thought that there would always be a place for a good copper wire man, so he had resisted the fiber optic training opportunities presented him. Now without warning, they have given him termination notice.

c. He has been working for five years in the auto assembly plant and has been recognized for his consistent, quality workmanship. He made one of the tree most popular models of cars sold in the US. When interest rates started up and buyers noticed them, it was the less popular model lines that closed down first. Unfortunately, now they have closed his line as well. No one will say when they will start up the line again, but it is easy to see that they build a huge backlog of cars, so it isn't going to be any time soon.

d. He finished college and they got married two years before she graduated. He found a job in a small business, and she decided upon graduation to go ahead and get her MBA. With her good degree and academic credentials, she was one of the first in her class to be offered a management track position with a very prestigious company. After her graduation, they moved and he has hopped from job to job, but nothing seems to satisfy him. He has two offers now, but neither of them are just what he is looking for. On top of that, he has come to enjoy being a full-time daddy to his little girl. Still he is looking, hoping to find a challenging job that really fits.

e. He had changed jobs fairly often after his associate's degree. Mostly it is because the jobs were really quite a bit beneath his capability. Somehow he found himself working for bosses who understood the business far less well than he. He tried to help them, but they didn't seem to appreciate his expertise. His last employer let him go for no good reason. He has been looking, he has been applying, he has been interviewing, but someone else always gets the job. When he asks why he was passed over, he doesn't get good answers. With his "gift of gab", his professional competence, his wide experience and his maturity, he cannot understand why he doesn't get any offers.

f. He was born 150 years too late. He would have been a great pioneer. He liked a couple history courses he took in college, but he really likes driving a beat-up pickup, wearing cowboy clothes, chewing, spitting, whittling, hunting, cogitating and talking slow. He has had worlds of interviews. All of his friends seemed to have set him up for jobs, but the they don't want a common man with wisdom, they want a modem, fast-talking, sophisticate to make sales calls, and he will not do that. The facts are that after he turned down several jobs that didn't fit the kind of man he is, the interviews began to get farther and farther apart. He finally moved in with his grandfather and is finishing a few hogs. It's no fun to get all cleaned up and go out there to an interview just to be shot down. He's given up on most employers who seem incapable or recognizing a good man who was born too late. As long as Gramps pays the bills, he will make it.

g. He earned his associate's degree just before they were married. He found a good job and put her through the rest of her school. She interviewed widely in anticipation of finishing her bachelors degree and even though she thought it would be difficult, she found an excellent position right here in Lafayette. Her good income made it easy for them to live while he finished his degree. His degree is in a pretty specialized area, in contrast to hers, so they planned on him taking the best job he could find. She would find a job wherever his job took him. It sounded like such a good plan, and her first job was surprisingly easy to get, but she has been looking for 4 months and she cannot find a job.

2. The US unemployment statistics show the present percent unemployed to

be _____%. This is (high, medium, low) compared to the last 10 years.

a. In order for a person to be employed, must he have a full-time job?

b. Are all people living in the US either employed or unemployed? What other

category is there?

I personally am in the _____ category because

c.   There are three categories of people in the US with respect to being in or out of the labor force: Unemployed, Employed, and Not-in-the-labor-force. What are the two largest categories?

3. Inflation this last year in the US was _____%. This is (high, medium, low) compared to the last 10 years.

4. Jason's grandmother is living on the pension that his grandfather got when he retired from the railroad. She will receive the same monthly pension payment that they have been getting since he retired 12 years ago. For the next twenty years, would it be in his best interest to have high, medium or low inflation? Explain.

5. In many countries in Eastern Europe inflation has averaged 150% per year. This means that the grocery dollar spent at the end of the month buys many fewer groceries than it did at the beginning. Coping with this high inflation requires strategies that are good only in the short run. High inflation (anything over 25%/year) is maddening for most people.

It is quite possible that a WLU sophomore will live another 70 years. Would it be in the typical sophomore's best interest to have high, medium or low inflation over the next 20 years? Explain.

6. There were three children, born a year apart, to Carl and Carol Cassen, Carrie, Charlie, and Chris. Carl, an administrator with the electric company, told them that if they graduated with a 3.0 or better from WLU, had a job when they graduated and then bought a home when they could afford it, that he would help them their first eight years in their new homes by paying their electricity bills as long as they were reasonable. (He would even pay their electric bills if they bought an all electric home.) Home energy bills are typically about 40% of the home food bills.

Curiously, they each bought their homes during the first six months of 1986.

These children of his, while very alike in some ways, were very different in their eating habits.

Carrie only ate Chocolate Chip Cookies, Bread, Milk, Peanut Butter and T-bone steak.

Charlie only ate ground beef, bananas, ham, chicken and potato chips.

Chris only ate frozen concentrated orange juice, carrots, hot dogs, lettuce, and apples.

Carl paid the electric bills.

(To make the calculations easier, assume that each person ate equal values of each of the items purchased.)

During these eight years, there was inflation such that the consumer price index with 1982-4 = 100 went from 110.0 in 1986 to 148.4 in 1994. Interestingly, when the family met, which they did frequently, and the talk turned to inflation, some people seemed to be much more concerned about it than others. Find how dad and each of the children were affected by inflation from the beginning to the end of this eight year period by finding the average percent change in the real price of each thing they bought. Then average the price changes for each individual to see how they were affected overall. Write a short paragraph explaining the effects on inflations on this family from 1986-1994.

	Price Paid	
Item Purchased	1986	1994
Peanut Butter	$1.47	$1.87
Red Del. Apples	0.84	0.77
Whole Chicken	0.74	0.91
Bananas	0.38	0.42
Choc. Chip Cookies	1.80	2.87
Ham	1.33	1.67
Low Fat Gallon Milk	1.08	1.44
Hot Dogs	1.89	1.78
Carrots	0.42	0.42
Electricity per kWh	0.14	0.09
Bread	0.55	0.80
Fr. Conc. Orange Juice	1.43	1.45
Ground Beef	1.15	1.53
Potato Chips	2.39	2.79
Lettuce	0.57	0.53
T-Bone Steak	3.75	5.41

Hint: To find the percent change in real prices, first find the 1986 and 1994 prices in 1982-4 dollars. To find these real prices, divide the 1986 price by the 1986 price index and multiply by 100 to get the 1986 price in 1982-3 dollars. Repeat for 1994 by dividing the 1994 price by the 1994 price index. These prices are called real prices because they are measured in dollars of the same size. To find what percent the real 1994 price is of the real 1986 price, subtract the 1986 real price from the 1994 real price, divide the difference by the 1986 real price, multiply by 100. Average these price changes for each person, and then write a short paragraph explaining what this means.

Written Assignment 6

Name.

Seat No.

1. Gross Domestic Product (GDP) is the final value of the goods and services produced in the country in a year. When we think of who buys the goods and services produced, there are four major groups of buyers. (We use sales to foreigners less purchases from them in these figures.) List the four "Buyers" in order of purchases from largest to smallest and indicate the percent of GDP each bought.

1995
(In billions of dollars)

GDP = 7,011.8
Personal Consumption Expenditure = 4,838.3
Investment = 1,087.4
Net Exports = - 122.4
Government Purchases = 1,208.5
Compensation of Employees = 4,157.3
Proprietor's Income = 493.6
Rental Income = 25.4
Corp. Profits = 569.7
Interest = 442.4
Indirect Bus. Tax = 631.0
Depreciation = 692.4

Buyer   Share of Purchases 1995

Gross Domestic Product   100%

2. GDP can also be found by adding up income or the payment to the various inputs used in production. List these four major categories of inputs, what the payments are called and the percent each makes up of GDP in order from largest to smallest.

Input   Payment   Share of Income for 1995

Small Business   Proprietor's Income

Government Svs   Indirect Business Taxes

Capital Wearout   Depreciation

Gross Domestic Product   100%

3. If your grandmother sent you an unexpected check for $500 today, how much of it would you spend before semester's end?

What would you buy?

4a. Define Marginal Propensity to Consume:

b. What is yours (based on Q. 3 above)?

5. In adding up the components of this year's GDP we use the term "investment." In this context, what does Investment mean?

Does it mean: (Yes, No)

The purchase of a Port Everglades municipal bond?

The amount spent for WLU tuition in Engineering?

The purchase of a farm combine for grain harvest?

The purchase of word processor software for a business computer?

The purchase of a 1924 Dusenberg car (the basis of "It's a doosey")?

The purchase of a new house?

The cost of a beautifully landscaped five-year-old home?

The purchase of Great Lakes Chemical Stock?

The purchase of farm land?

The purchase of a 1995 semi with a refrigerated trailer

6. To answer these questions, use the national income and expenditure model from Figure 6-A (passed out in class).

To make finding the numbers for the questions below, sketch reference lines on the diagram.

    a.   With an income of $6500, how much will expenditures be?

    b.   With an income of $5500, how much will expenditures be?

    c.   With expenditures of $6500, how much will income be?

    d.   With expenditures of $5500, how much will income be?

    e.   If income is less than $6000, what will happen?

    f.   If income is more than $6000, what will happen?

7. To answer these questions, look at the national income and expenditure model (Figure 6-B) passed out in class.

    a.   If CIG is line A, and Full Employment is $7000, what will happen?

    b.   If CIG is line C, and Full Employment is $7000, what will happen?

    c.   If you could control CIG, which of the CIG lines would represent your economic policy goal?

Written Assignment 7

Name

Seat No.

1. Congress is debating a Constitutional Amendment that would require all spending bills to be linked to revenue provisions (taxes) to stop the Federal Government deficit. This would mean the end of separate taxing and spending bills. Why would a congressman support this Amendment? Why would a congressman vote against this Amendment?

2. If I decide to save an extra dollar, my saving goes up by that amount. But if everyone decides to save an extra dollar, income falls and saving does not rise. Explain.

3. Even today we debate whether the market or the command system is the best way to manage things in our society. Give an example of a discussion that is going on now as we try to decide how to handle a problem in the US today. Give the reasons why some want the market system to solve the problem and why others want the command system to solve it. Use your judgment and values to put the situation in perspective--what should we do?

4. What does Gross Domestic Product mean, and how much is it in the US today? Explain how and why the components of GDP may be organized two different ways? List the components of GDP in each of these two different lists from largest to smallest, and give an example of one individual item that would clearly fit it each of the categories.

5. Explain how, in a market society, when consumer wants change, prices and profit (as well as bankruptcy) work to assure that the products people want more of are available as needed at reasonable prices and the production of products wanted less is reduced. Explain the major problems evident in Eastern Europe now as those economies shift from the command system to the market system, shortages, surpluses, and "exorbitant" profits that some contend some businesses are earning.

6. This winter, a farmer who has had a good year and is bringing a son into the business is planning a major expansion. It is important that the business be big enough to be competitive. List three quite different things that he might buy that will be included as investment, a part of GDP?

a.

b.

c.

7. WLU built a large new parking garage, spending about $11,000,000. If the Lafayette area consumers spend $75 more when their income goes up by a $100, how much will this new garage increase the US GDP? Show clearly how you figured it.

8. Draw and label an income/expenditure model diagram (the one with the 45 degree line) and show equilibrium GDP to be $7200 and Productive Capacity to be $7000. The marginal propensity to consume is = 3/4.

a. What is the problem that this society faces, if any? Explain why this is happening.

b. What fiscal policy actions could the federal government take to solve this problem if half of the problem is to be solved with one tool and the other half with the other? (Show your algebra clearly here and draw and label the new lines on the diagram.)

Government spending:

Taxes:

9. Draw and label an income/expenditure model diagram, and show equilibrium GDP to be $6700 and Productive Capacity to be $7000. In this case, the MPC is 4/5.

a. What is the problem that this society faces, if any? Explain why this is happening.

b. What fiscal policy actions could the federal government take to solve this problem, if it were to be completely solved with the first approach and then completely solved with the second. (Show your algebra clearly and draw and label the new lines on the diagram.)

Government spending:

Taxes:

10. Inflation:

a. What is it?

b. Why do we have it?

c. What can be done about it?

d. How effective will these actions be?

11. Unemployment:

a. What is it?

b. Why do we have it?

c. What can be done about it?

d. How effective will these actions be?

Written Assignment 8

Name.

Seat No.

1. Money is an important part of our culture and history. Below give three sayings, parables, attitudes, etc. about money that you brought with you to this class:

a.

b.

c.

2. On a separate sheet of paper, list the major expense categories in your life from March of last year through of this year, such as food, clothing, tuition, car, soft drinks, etc. Estimate and sum the amount of expenditure that it took to support you. Estimate what annual level of income is associated with your expenditure level. On another sheet of paper, estimate how much money you have today. Which is greater, your money today or your annual income? How many times greater? I do not want you to tell me or anyone else how much money you have. To preserve your confidentiality, multiply or divide your income and money by a factor of 1.7 (raise or lower them both, whichever way you prefer), but use the same coefficient to adjust both and report them and the income/money ratio below. Include the adjusted income and money information for another family member whose income is substantially higher than yours. Put in the national income and money figures for comparison.

What are the various kinds of money that you have?

_____, _____, _____

Your Annual Income _____, Money (_/_/_) _____;

What is your ratio of Income/money? _____

Other person's annual income_____, Money _____

What is their ratio of Income/money? _____

US Income _____ , Money _____

For the US in total, what is the ratio of Income/money? _____

3. The car we choose to buy is often influenced by our budget--how much we can pay per month for the car. The size of our monthly payments is determined by the car price and the interest rate. To see the effects of the interest rate on monthly car payments, lets look at three cars and three interest rates, keeping the repayment period at 60 months. To find the monthly payment, multiply the price of the car times the Monthly Pay Coefi shown below. To find the coef. use the following approach (the same the bank uses):

Information wanted M = monthly payment for 60 month loan

Information needed:

r = annual interest rate charged (use 0.05 for 5%)
p = price paid (and borrowed) for the car

$$M = \frac{r}{1 - \frac{1}{(1+r)^{60}}}$$

Steps to find the monthly payment:

1. Divide r by 12 to get monthly interest rate (r/12) =   ___ (a)___
2. Add 1 to (a)   (1 +a) =   ___ (b)___
3. Raise (b) to the power of 60 (b^{60}) =   ___ (c)___
4. Invert--divide 1 by (c)   (1/c) --   ___ (d)___
5. Subtract (d) from 1   (1-d) =   ___ (e) ___
6. Divide (a) by (e)   (a/e) =   Month. Pay Coef. (f)
7. Monthly payment = (f) times (p) =   ___(M)___

Find the monthly payments over five years for the three cars at the three interest rates shown below:

	Interest Rates		
	18%	12%	5%
Monthly Pay Coef.	.025393	.022244	.018871
Car; Price	Monthly Payments over Five Years		
Cobra; $17,500	_____	_____	_____
Probe; $14,850	_____	_____	_____
Escort; $13,000	_____	_____	_____

If you could afford an Escort at 18%, which car could you afford at 12%?

If you could afford a Cobra at 5%, at 18% you would have to buy what car?

A-38

Written Assignment 9

Name

Seat No.

1. What are the three principal tools of Monetary Policy? When the economy has problems, what action should be taken for each tool?

	What should be done to correct:	
Mon. Policy Tool	Unemployment	Inflation

2. Monetary policy has the goal of

Monetary policy is done by the "Fed"; who is that:

Fiscal policy has the goal of:

Fiscal policy is done by:

3. To show that you understand clearly that your money and your income are not the same thing, describe a situation in which the amount of income you have changes but the amount of money you have moves in the opposite direction.

4. Below on the left draw and label an income expenditure model with Equilibrium GDP more than Productive Capacity, and on the right draw and label an income expenditure model with Equilibrium GDP less than Productive Capacity. Below each tell what problem the society would be experiencing. Below each list the three principal monetary policy actions that would be appropriate to solve the problem. Step by step on the lines 1-9 below, tell how the policies would help to solve the problem. With a contrasting pencil, draw on the new CIGX line which your prescription would produce.

Problem =   Problem =

Appropriate Monetary Action:

This monetary action would set in motion the following string of changes: (enter UP, DOWN, NO EFFECT

Figure above   Figure above
Steps: **Steps:**
1. Money Supply   1. Money Supply
2. Interest Rates   2. Interest Rates
3. Consumption Spending   3. Consumption Spending
4. Investment Spending   4. Investment Spending
5. CIGX   5. CIGX
6. Equilibrium GNP   6. Equilibrium GNP
7. Potential GNP   7. Potential GNP
8. Unemployment   8. Unemployment
9. **Inflation**   9. **Inflation**

Fiscal Policy Actions

_____   _____

_____   _____

Add appropriate fiscal policy actions in the last blanks of the lists above.

5. The quantity theory of money says that the money supply (M) times its velocity (V) equals the GDP just as the real output (Y) times the price level (P) equals the GDP.

$$M \times V = GDP = P \times Y$$

Define Velocity:

6. For relatively small changes in M, V, P, or Y, the percent change in M plus the percent change in V will equal the percent change in GDP. Similarly, the percent change in P plus the percent change in Y will equal the percent change in GDP. Using this principle, we can see that if Y increased 4%, V doesn't change (and it usually changes very little in any short period), an increase in M of 5% would result in a P increase of 1%. Now you try it. If real output (Y) increased by 3% and the desired rate of inflation is 2%, how much should the Fed increase M?

Explain what will happen if the money supply is increased more than you recommend.

Explain what will happen if the money supply is increased less than you recommend.

7. So far this year, how has the US economy been doing?

What was the Fed concerned about and what was been the nature of monetary policy?

Written Assignment 10

Name

Seat No.

1. Draw an Aggregate Supply curve similar to that in Figure 10-A (passed out in class) showing a vertical section at the top, a curved section in the middle and a horizontal section on the lower left part of the AS curve. Label the aggregate demand curve that intersects the AS curve in the range where it is sloped about at forty-five degrees "Demand B". Draw another "Demand A" that intersects AS in the vertical range, and a third, "Demand C" that intersects it in the horizontal range. Now beside each of these demand curves, draw three new demand curves that show small increases in demand at each of these three levels of demand. For each tell what would be the consequences (big, medium, small) and (increase, decrease) to Inflation and Unemployment from an increase in demand.

	Demand Increase Effect on:	
Small Demand Increase at:	Inflation	Unemployment
Demand A:		
Demand B:		
Demand C:		

2. In a few years, primarily because of your reputation for being economically astute, a direct result of an outstanding Economics class taken at WLU, you are elected State Senator in Washington. Given your vast understanding of fiscal policy, what would you recommend as appropriate governmental actions in these areas of constituent interest under these conditions.

Condition	Constituent Interest	Recommended Action
Recession	Community health programs	
Recession	Income taxes	
Recession	Youth Job Programs	
Inflation	Community health programs	
Inflation	Income taxes	
Inflation	Youth Job Programs	

You are likely to be remembered more for the legislation you propose and get implemented than for the general level of the economy while you were in office. When your constituents consider what you have done during your first term as they consider whether to reelect or replace, if you were a politician, (one who looks out for his own welfare) in contrast to a statesman, (one who looks out for the well-being of the country) what would be the great advantage of being in office during recessionary rather than boom times?

3.a. If the economy began to suffer from increased unemployment as a result of a feeling of general discouragement among businessmen and consumers, what change in the money supply would seem appropriate to you?

b. Explain clearly how or if your suggestion would help the following people:

1. Cousin Rupert who has been building Chevy S-10's for six years now without a break. He manages the computer controlled spot welders that build the truck box. Now the inventory of these trucks has grown so that they have decided to close the plant till the inventory is reduced by 75%.

2. Rupert's brother, Clyde, who has been hand welding the frame-strut support-fender-wheel well front assembly for the S-10's. His work has been steady, too. He won't touch a computer and knows that hand welding is basically superior to computer welds. Welding the truck box is real easy and so the computer welds are OK, but the front end is much more difficult and requires special skills. Clyde has always been a better welder than Rupert. While the plant is down waiting for this inventory reduction, rumor has it that they are going to install a new robotic upgrade that can do all that front end welding.

If you didn't discuss the role interest rates play in how monetary policy affects unemployment, you were barking up the wrong tree.

4. If it began to look as if we were sliding into another depression like that of the 1930's, what would/should/could be done?

One agency who is supposed to do something:

What would they do?

Another agency who is supposed to do something:

What would they do?

Put a W by those items above that the agency would be likely to do. Put an N by those items above that would be unpopular with the public.

In your judgment, how likely are we to have another depression in the next thirty years while you are establishing yourself professionally and financially?

5. The output of goods and services in the country tends to vary from year to year. It is fairly easy to see the variation in the grand total, GDP. Are there segments of the economy that vary more or less than the GDP varies? What would some sectors that vary lots more; lots less, and why?

Written Assignment 12

Name   Seat No.

Name   Seat No.

Name   Seat No.

I encourage you to do this assignment in groups of up to three.

A simple economy with GDP made up of only Consumption and Investment has been stable for years with GDP of $7055. Investment is at 8.1% of GDP, or $571. Investment is an increase in the stock of man-made goods and services used for production and provides the basis for increased production in the future. For a long time an average of 1000 people have been dying of starvation annually because the economy is not producing enough to support them.

As a Senator, you can influence policy for the proportion of GDP that goes into investment. Investment, at least in the short run, is competitive with consumption, yet is the basis for economic growth in the long run. Babies are easy to save. An increase in GDP of $10 annually will save one child from starvation. Your job is to establish the best investment policy for your economy and promote it.

1. Choose two national investment policies, and show their effects by making a table for each policy which continues the table started below. It's easiest to use a spreadsheet. To do the analysis, change the percent of GDP that goes into investment starting in 1997, leaving it at the changed level through 2050. One policy will be to have more than 8.1 percent of GDP that goes to investment, and the other will be to use less than 8.1 percent of the GDP that goes to investment. Evaluate the consequences of your policy alternatives over much of your expected lifetime by continuing the tables through 2050.

The numbers in the columns are found as follows:
- Year--Consecutive years from 1995 through 2050
- GDP--GDP this year equals GDP last year plus 21% of last year's investment, less $120
- % Investment--8.1% in 1995 and 1996 but in 1997 it ought to be raised and kept the same for 53 years, and in a second table lowered and kept constant for the next 53 years.
- Economic Growth--The percent increase in GDP from one year to the next (assume constant population)
- Investment--GDP times the % Investment
- Consumption--GDP less Investment
- Starvation-- 1648 less one for each $10 of Consumption

There will be a small prize given to each student who finds an investment rate that correctly does any of the following:

        a. Has the minimum 1997 starvation level.
        b. Can eliminate starvation by 2050.
        c. Minimizes total starvation deaths 1997-2050

2. Write a half page news release supporting one of your policy positions that you, a Senator, who is up for re-election this fall will use as a part of your economic policy in your campaign. Your opponent is recommending a 9% rate of Investment. In your release recognize the weaknesses of your proposal. Use this assignment page as the cover page when you submit your assignment and staple your news release and tables to it.

Year	GDP	Econ Growth	% Invest.	Investment	Consumption	Starvation
1995	$7055		8.1%	$571	$6484	1000
1996	7055	0.00%	8.1%	571	6484	1000
1997	7055	0.00%	8.1%	571	6484	1000
1998	7055	0.00%	8.1%	571	6484	1000
1999	7055	0.00%	8.1%	571	6484	1000

Written Assignment 13

Name.

Seat No.

1. Suppose that the US and China can both produce shirts and CD's. The US has 70 units of resources and China has 90. The production from one unit of resources in each country is as follows:

Product	US	China
Shirts	8	7
CD's	10	6

a. China has a comparative advantage in producing:

   I can tell that China has this comparative advantage because:

b. The US has an absolute advantage in producing:

   I can tell that this is true because:

c. If each country divided its resources equally between the production of both products, how much of each product would be produced in each country and in total?

Product	US Resources	Production	China Resources	Production	Total Prod'n.
Shirts					
CD's					
Total	70		90		

d. If each country produced only the product in which it had a comparative advantage, how much of each product would be produced in each country and in total?

Product	US	China	Total
Shirts			
CD's			

e. Now suppose the US produces only the good it has a comparative advantage in and China also produces only the good in has a comparative advantage in. The US keeps 40 more of the product it produces than it had when it split its resources evenly, and traded the rest of its production to China at the rate of one unit of Shirts for one unit of CD's. How much of each product would each country end up with?

Product	US	China	Total
Shirts			
CD's			

f. Bring forward the amount of product available when each country split its resources evenly between the two products (Q1.c.). Also bring forward the amount of each product in each country available with specialization and trade (Q1.e.)? In the table below find what percent better (or worse) off each country is in each product with the trade option compared to the no trade option. (Divide the trade option availability by the no-trade production, subtract 1, and multiply by 100 to get the percent change.)

Product	United States			China		
	50-50	Spec & Trade	% better	50-50	Spec & Trade	%Better
Shirts						
CD's						

2. Do countries gain or lose by trade? In the above analysis we made some unrealistic assumptions like ignoring the costs of shipping and that the CD's from one country might be different quality from the other, so that it is easy to see that there is more to trade than this analysis. What we can learn from this analysis?

a. Which country gains from trade?

b. How is the larger country affected by trade?

c. How is the smaller country affected by trade?

d. How is the more productive country affected by trade?

e. How is the less productive country affected by trade?

3. The argument has been made that a country can be hurt by trading. If a country were free to trade if it wished and it was clear that it would lose by trading with this partner on these terms, would it do it? Explain why a country can or cannot be hurt by trade.

4. Based on the situation in Question 1, the producers of what products in what country will lose jobs?

5. Based on the situation in Question 1, the producers of what products in what country will gain jobs?

6. If Pat Buchanan asked you to write his opening speech in a debate on whether to produce for ourselves or to trade with Japan, what would be the most important economic arguments that you would make to support his opposition to trade?

7. If Bob Dole asked you to write his opening speech in the trade debate, what would be the most important economic arguments that you would make to support his pro-trade position?

8. What is happening to the volume of world trade?

Written Assignment 1

Name _____ Seat No._____

1. Prof. Taylor is a woodworker who enjoys turning--using a wood lathe. A few years ago he became frustrated with the all the vibration when he turned big pieces on his small lathe. In the Lafayette *Journal and Courier* want ads, he found an advertisement for an old 650 pound wood lathe, just what he had been dreaming about. He called on the owner of the big lathe and found that he often needed to move the lathe in his small shop in order to use some other machinery and he was looking for a small lathe that would be easier to move. They quickly arranged a trade with Taylor giving $300 to boot. With an additional expenditure of $250, Taylor now has a lathe that would have cost $4000 to buy new--he feels like one lucky guy! Explain how much better or worse off the former owner of the big lathe is?

_____

_____

_____

2. In economics we deal with large money values. Sometimes it is hard to get our minds around the size of the values. Here are the answers to the questions that follow; you choose the best answer for each question. The answers are:

If a dollar were spent every second, it would take this long to spend this amount:

Three hours

One month

As long as your grandmother has been alive

Twenty-five times longer than water has been going over Niagara Falls.

a. It costs about **ten thousand dollars** a year to keep a student at Purdue. That number is written (Put the correct number of zeros and commas and a decimal where it ought to be) $10,000_____ It takes about this time to spend this amount of money if it were spent a dollar a second: (3 hours, 1 month, grandmother's age, 25 times Niagara)

b. A Purdue senior returns to farm with his father on a cash-grain farm who owns 1100 acres, an investment of **three million dollars** in land. (Put the correct number of zeros and commas and a decimal where it ought to be) $3,000_____ It takes about this time to spend this amount of money if it were spent a dollar a second: (3 hours, 1 month, grandmother's age, 25 times Niagara)

c. The United States Federal Government spends about **2 billion dollars** a week more than it collects in taxes. That number is written (Put the correct number of zeros and commas and a decimal where it ought to be)$2,000 _____ It takes about this time to spend this amount of money if it were spent a dollar a second: (3 hours, 1 month, grandmother's age, 25 times Niagara)

d. The final value of goods and services produced in the United States in a year is about **eight and a half trillion dollars**. That number is written (Put the correct number of zeros and commas and a decimal where it ought to be) $8,500 _____ It takes about this time to spend this amount of money if it were spent a dollar a second: (3 hours, 1 month, grandmother's age, 25 times Niagara).

3. Check all that apply:

Microeconomics deals with:

_____ Problems that a business faces

_____ Problems faced by government

_____ Scarce resources

_____ Unlimited wants

_____ Having to say "No" to some very important things

_____ Whether to make a major investment in the nation's interstate highway system

_____ Whether to make a major investment in a new big farm machine

_____ Whether to order Domino or Papa John's pizza

_____ Whether to raise taxes or cut government spending

_____ Whether to cut taxes for businessmen or middle income American

Macroeconomics deals with:

_____ Problems that a business faces

_____ Problems faced by government

_____ Scarce resources

_____ Unlimited wants

_____ Having to say "No" to some very important things

_____ Whether to make a major investment in the nation's interstate highway system

_____ Whether to make a major investment in a new big farm machine

_____ Whether to order Domino or Papa John's pizza

_____ Whether to raise taxes or cut government spending

_____ Whether to cut taxes for businessmen or middle income American

This course will emphasize? (macroeconomics, microeconomics)

4. List the seven economic policy goals that are common to the folks of all societies:

_____   _____

_____   _____

_____   _____

_____

5. A year ago the price farmers received for hogs was $0.37 per pound and now it is $0.12. How much has the price changed?

___-68%   ___-32%   ___3.2%   ___-3.0%   ___-308%

6. A year ago the wholesale price of butter was $1.15 per pound and now it is $1.47. How much has the price changed?

___32%   ___78%   ___28%   ___-32%   ___-78%

Written Assignment 2

Name_____ Seat No._____

1. Julie has been invited to spend the weekend of February 13 & 14 with her friend Mark at Ball State. She has known Mark since high school and she has enjoyed their few dates. Julie works a few hours a week for her favorite biology professor and he asked her last week if she would look in on his lab that same weekend since he plans be out of town. This afternoon the neat guy that has been sitting by her in English class asked her to go to his fraternity Valentine dance that Saturday night.

What should she do?

_____

What will it cost her? (An application of the opportunity cost concept.)

_____

If she were to choose to go to the dance, what would it cost her?

___ The joy of spending the weekend with Mark and the income from the biology job.

___ The joy of spending the weekend with Mark or the income from the biology job.

2. In every business there are four main types of inputs; complete the table below by naming the inputs beside the payments made for these inputs. The inputs are land, labor, capital and management.

Input	Term describing the payment for the input
_____	Interest
_____	Profit
_____	Rent
_____	Wages or Compensation to Employees

2. List the four biggest expenditure items by the US Federal Government.

_____   _____

_____   _____

3. List the four biggest revenue items, or taxes, of the US Federal Government.

_____   _____

_____   _____

B-5

4. What is a government transfer payment? What is the fundamental difference between a transfer payment and a national defense expenditure?

5. The first exam will have an essay question "Explain what the basic economic questions, "What", "How" and "For Whom" mean." The following help you to see what these questions mean and the issues associated with them.

What to produce:

In the Market system, consumers buy what they like that they can afford, so whatever sells well gets produced. From the following pairs of purchases, circle which you would choose to buy and briefly explain why.

One Choice	Other Choice	Why this choice?
Red and white sweatshirt	Gold and black sweatshirt	_____
Ford pickup	Honda car	_____
Country music concert	Jazz concert	_____
Salad	Steak	_____
Coke	Coffee	_____
Rolls Royce ($88,000)	Dodge ($15,000)	_____
Cigarette	Candy bar	_____
Fitness club membership	Sam's club membership	_____

The market system says that consumers can buy what they want that they can afford, but some governments pass laws that prohibit their consumers from buying some products freely. For each item below check whether you feel it should be freely available to anyone who can afford it in the US, or whether its purchase or use should be restricted by law. Briefly explain why you chose as you did.

Consumer Good or Service	Freely Available	Use Restricted by Law	Why
Reese's Pieces	_____	_____	_____
Beer	_____	_____	_____
Brown chicken eggs	_____	_____	_____
Bald eagle eggs	_____	_____	_____
Car without a muffler	_____	_____	_____
Penicillin	_____	_____	_____
Slot machines	_____	_____	_____
Abortion	_____	_____	_____
Ride a bicycle in the road	_____	_____	_____
Ride a bicycle on PU sidewalk	_____	_____	_____
Drive a power boat	_____	_____	_____
Fly an ultra-light aircraft	_____	_____	_____
Drive without a seat belt	_____	_____	_____

How to produce:

In a market society, producers are free to use the lowest cost way of production that produces a product that they can sell profitably. In some societies, the government has chosen to restrict the use of some production methods by law. For each production method below check whether you feel it should be freely used by anyone who chooses to in the US, or whether its use should be restricted by law.

Production Method	Free Choice	Use Required or Restricted by Law	Why
Replace woman with robot	_____	_____	_____
Wearing hard hat on hot day	_____	_____	_____
Roll-over protection on farm tractor	_____	_____	_____

Choice of corn or barley for hog feed   _____   _____   _____

Choice of corn or garbage for hog feed   _____   _____   _____

Respirator use in a paint room   _____   _____   _____

Fire extinguisher presence   _____   _____   _____

Choice of gasoline or diesel tractor   _____   _____   _____

Door knobs on classroom doors   _____   _____   _____

Use of guards on pulleys   _____   _____   _____

Use of hearing protection   _____   _____   _____

Food irradiation   _____   _____   _____

Listing of nutritional characteristics on food   _____   _____   _____

For whom:

In a market society, consumers can buy whatever and however much they can afford, depending on their income. But how much should an individual's income be? How much more should some earn than others? For each of the pairs of earners listed below indicate what percent more or less the income of the earner in the second column should be compared to the income of the person in the first column. Suppose, for example, that you thought that the coach of the men's basketball team at Purdue University should earn a third (33%) more than the president of Purdue University, put +33% to show that Gene Keady should earn 33% more than Steven Beering earns. Suppose that you thought that the president of Ball State should earn 20% less than the president of Purdue, put -20% to show that the Ball State president should earn 20% less. If you think that a professional basketball coach should earn five times what a college coach earns, put +500%.

First Earner	Second Earner	Second earns this % more
Steven Beering	Gene Keady	+33%
President of Purdue	President of Ball State	-20%
College Basketball Coach	Professional Basketball Coach	+500%
Car salesman	Auto mechanic	_____
College teacher	High School teacher	_____

Line worker at Wabash National	Vice President of Wabash National	_____
Janitor of Ben and Jerry's	Ben Cohen (CEO, Ben and Jerry's)	_____
Male pharmaceutical salesman	Female pharmaceutical salesman	_____
Really strong roofer	Ordinary roofer	_____
Really fast, accurate typist	Ordinary typist	_____
Really good teacher	Ordinary teacher	_____
Man	Woman	_____
Spectacularly beautiful hostess	Ordinary hostess	_____
Teacher: a wonderful speaker	Teacher: an ordinary speaker	_____
Young salesman	Old salesman	_____
Top 20% salesman	Bottom 20% salesman	_____
President of Microsoft	President of United States	_____

In some societies, the government has chosen to take away purchasing power from some by taxing. Some governments develop welfare programs for providing extra purchasing power to some.

a. Beside each group listed below indicate the percent of the last dollar of income that should be taxed away:

_____% 1999 Purdue Graduate in the year 2000

_____% Parents of current Purdue students in 1999

_____% 2000 Purdue Graduate in the year 2020 when she is CEO of her own business

_____% 1999 income of the top 20% of the US income earners

_____% 1999 income from stock market speculation

_____% 1999 income from construction work

b. Beside each group listed below indicate at what level the US government should support their income. How much should their welfare benefits be? Express the level as the percent of the level of the income of the average US wage earner:

_____% US citizen with disabilities who cannot find work

_____% US citizens who choose not to work for any reason

_____% Young, single, US citizen with two small children without a high school diploma who is going to school

_____% Young, single, US citizen, with two small children without a high school diploma and who is sexually active

_____% Older US citizen, abandoned by his family

6. The syllabus says how the grades are going to be determined in this class this semester but other grading options were considered. One option is to give everyone B's. Explain whether or not you favor this approach? You may want to use the terms, "incentive"," reward"," fear" and "punishment".
A. Would you recommend giving everyone a B in this class?
___Yes, or ___ No; why?

_____

_____

_____

What is the advantage of assigning A's to some people?

_____

_____

What is the advantage of assigning F's to some people?

_____

_____

7. To what extent are the same principles relevant for choosing the best income distribution for the country. Would you recommend that everyone has about the same income, or should there be a possibility of some getting a high income and some getting low? Explain.

_____

_____

_____

_____

Written Assignment 3

Name_____ Seat No._____

Market Price Problems:

a. US Corn Market (Basic Market Price Situation ___)

Foreign buyers of our corn to feed to livestock so that their people can improve their diets by adding more meat find themselves in a recession, unable to buy our corn.

Supply   _____

Demand   _____

Price   _____

Quantity   _____

b. The US Corn Market (Basic Market Price Situation ___)

The price of soybeans falls a great deal and farmers can plant either corn or beans on the same land with the same machinery.

Supply   _____

Demand   _____

Price   _____

Quantity   _____

B-11

c. Beef Market. (Basic Market Price Situation ___)

The price of pork falls sharply and many consumers are indifferent between beef and pork.

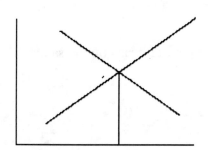

Supply   _____

Demand   _____

Price   _____

Quantity   _____

d. Butter Market (Basic Market Price Situation ___)

Consumers decide to splurge and satisfy their craving for dessert by eating super-high-quality high fat ice cream.

Supply   _____

Demand   _____

Price   _____

Quantity   _____

e. Cheese Market (Basic Market Price Situation ___)

Cheese is made from milk solids and butter fat and these are much more expensive as consumers splurge on fancy ice cream desserts.

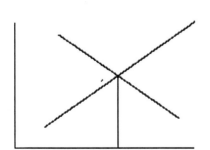

Supply   _____

Demand   _____

Price   _____

Quantity   _____

f. Coffee Market (Basic Market Price Situation __)

Coffee growing weather improved making a much larger harvest of excellent coffee beans.

Supply   _____

Demand   _____

Price   _____

Quantity   _____

g. Hog Market (Basic Market Price Situation ___)

Many new, large producers enter the market.

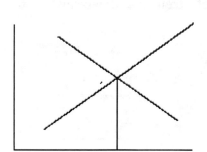

Supply   _____

Demand   _____

Price   _____

Quantity   _____

h. Wool Market (Basic Market Price Situation ___)

New fabrics are available that can do what wool has done and do it better and cheaper.

Supply   _____

Demand   _____

Price   _____

Quantity   _____

B-14

i. Corn Market (Basic Market Price Situation ___)

Farmers get access to seeds that allow them to use a cheaper, more effective weed control chemical.

Supply   _____

Demand   _____

Price   _____

Quantity   _____

j. Copper Market (Basic Market Price Situation ___)

The data of the information revolution is transmitted more and more by fiber optics and less by copper wire.

Supply   _____

Demand   _____

Price   _____

Quantity   _____

2. Define supply:

_____

_____

3. Define demand:

_____

_____

4. What is causing the shortage of rice in Ethiopia?

_____

_____

5. Relative to 1 a. where the demand for corn decreases (do you have it right?); what happens to the:

Price Staley pays for corn to make into corn syrup? _____

Corn price to the farmer? _____

Corn production on the farm? _____

Supply of corn? _____

6. Relative to 1 b. where the supply of corn increases, what happens to the:

Price Staley pays for corn to make into corn syrup? _____

Corn price to the farmer? _____

Corn production on the farm? _____

Demand for corn? _____

Written Assignment 4

Name _____ Seat No. _____

Basic Market Price Situations:

1. **Increase Supply**--Producers decide to produce more at each price.

2. **Decrease Supply**--Producers decide to produce less at each price.

3. **Increase Demand**--Consumers decide to consume more.

4. **Decrease Demand**--Consumers decide to consume less.

5. **Government Raises Price Above Equilibrium**--They are trying to help someone.

6. **Government Removes Supports that held Price Above Equilibrium**--Trying to help someone.

7. **Government Holds Price Below Equilibrium**--They are trying to help someone.

8. **Government Removes Controls that held Price Below Equilibrium**--Trying to help someone.

a. US Corn Market (Basic market price situation number ___)

The President, in order to get farmers on his side, decides to raise the corn price 25%.

Supply   _____

Demand   _____

Price   _____

Quantity   _____

b. Corn Belt Farmland Market (Basic market price situation number ___)

To raise the income of Indiana farmers, the Indiana legislature decrees that 1999 land rents must be reduced 15% from 1998 rent.

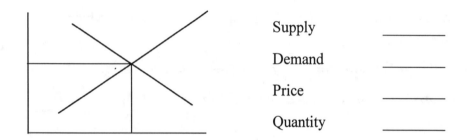

Supply   _____

Demand   _____

Price   _____

Quantity   _____

c. Cotton Market (Basic market price situation number ___)

Price supports that have been in effect for sixty years are removed.

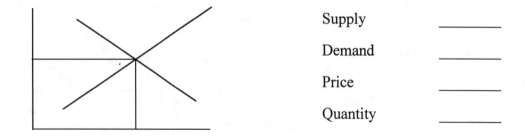

Supply   _____

Demand   _____

Price   _____

Quantity   _____

d. Thailand Rice Market (Basic market price situation number ___)

To fight inflation Thailand announces a rollback in rice prices to last December 31st levels.

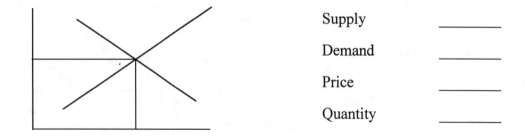

Supply   _____

Demand   _____

Price   _____

Quantity   _____

e. Furby Market (Basic market price situation number ___)

Retailers hold the line on prices even when many more people wanted them than was expected.

Supply _____

Demand _____

Price _____

Quantity _____

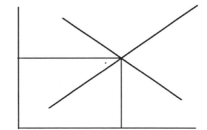

f. US Body Piercing Market (Basic market price situation number ___)

Body piercing becomes the thing to do among a large group of people.

Supply _____

Demand _____

Price _____

Quantity _____

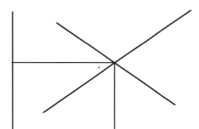

g. Gasoline Market (Basic market price situation number ___)

Crude oil producers (the raw material of gasoline) find more, low-cost was of getting crude oil.

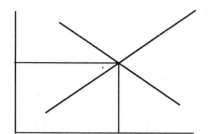

Supply   _____

Demand   _____

Price   _____

Quantity   _____

h. Labor Market (Basic market price situation number ___)

The federal government raises the minimum wage.

Supply   _____

Demand   _____

Price   _____

Quantity   _____

i. Labor Market (Basic market price situation number ___)

Effective unions raise wages.

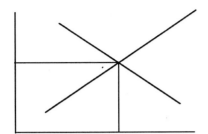

Supply   _____

Demand   _____

Price   _____

Quantity   _____

j. Residential Housing Market (Basic market price situation number ___)

The interest rate on home mortgages falls.

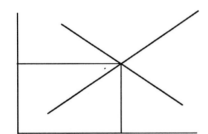

Supply   _____

Demand   _____

Price   _____

Quantity   _____

3. Explain why for years there was a long waiting list for Purdue Basketball Season Tickets and now the waiting list no longer exists:

4. Why was there a shortage of Furbies last Christmas?

Written Assignment 5

Name_____ Seat No._____

1. For each of the situations below, indicate which kind of unemployment it is from the above list (a couple Discouraged Worker examples are included also):

a. She got her Purdue masters degree and married a Purdue Ph.D. student the same month. She has seen this coming and has been sending out resumes and reading and responding to want adds for the last four months, but nothing comes up. She's pleasant, pretty, bright, well-educated and unemployed. She can't seem to get past the first screening--she doesn't even get an interview.

_____

b. He told everyone since Junior High that he would work for Lilly after Purdue. He had whiled away his summers helping his semi-retired dad on his small "farm". He watched the job postings and knew the dates Lilly was interviewing. He bought a new black double-breasted suit and signed up--his only interview in college. Lilly's ding letter didn't even hint at why he was not offered a second interview, but they did say they would keep his application on file. He is puttering around at home waiting for a call from Lilly. It has been over a year now.

_____

c. It must have been a very toxic something (nobody knows what) that his mother got into early in her pregnancy, but Paul has a bent back, severe learning disabilities and a small speech defect. With accommodations, he has been successful at Purdue and he has had lots of job interviews, many resulting in second and a few third interview trips, but none resulting in a job offer. He has an engaging personality, a positive spirit and an intense desire to be a successful professional but he can't get a job offer.

_____

d. Paul got his MS in civil engineering and had a challenging and rewarding job for a consulting company. He liked being out on assignment and working with the client's engineers. Then he found a client's engineer he really liked, and Joan agreed to marry him. There was no official, signed, prenuptial agreement, but Paul knew that Joan would continue to keep her good job--he'd commute. Then two big unexpected things happened, first little Emily was born and a few months later Paul got RIFFED (that is "Reduction In Force"--he got fired as a part of downsizing). Paul couldn't see sending Emily to the day-care on days he was between interviews so he played Mr. Mom. He has had three offers for jobs he would have been glad to have before, but each of them has its problems. Besides the whole family seems to be happier now that he is taking care of things at home. He is still interviewing, but the job has to be right.

_____

e. Their small town had known tough times, then Charlie the Auto-Fix-it manager came up with a great idea for making the ten foot satellite dishes better and cheaper. He hired people, skilled and unskilled, paid good wages for good work, built a modern factory that with the good local workers could out-compete everyone, sold satellite dishes nation-wide and soon people from miles around were coming here for good jobs. And then along came the small plastic disc system that took practically all of the satellite dish market. Making them takes an altogether different technology, and with dried up sales and returned dishes pouring in, Charlie just closed the plant. Four hundred employees are without work, and the town is in a great depression.

---

f. He graduated from Purdue in Building Construction Technology and began to work for his father-in-law in the steel-framed home construction business. He found he was good at helping young families to develop plans for houses that were within their budget yet had the features that they really wanted. The advantages of steel framing resulted in trouble-free homes buyers could be proud of. He knows that this is the quality-home construction material of the future. Business boomed, and then interest rates climbed over two percent and that translates into about $200 per month increase in payments for the same house. The last house they built was completed a month ago and he can't even find a potential buyer to talk to. Last night his father-in-law with moist eyes told him to up-date his resume and start the job search because the bank is not going to let him pay even one more month's salary. No job; no warning; no severance pay; this is the real world! Tomorrow he'll find out how to get eligible for unemployment compensation.

---

g. John found a good job in Lafayette to support his wife, Joyce, and their son while she worked on her Ph.D. In the final stages of her degree program, she got a good offer from Texas A&M. The market is a little tight. She had six interviews and one job offer, but it is just the kind of job she wants. With her dissertation complete, he quit his job, loaded the U-Haul and moved to Texas. Now he is struggling to find a job. With the job market so tight there, he wishes they had negotiated for a job for him with the University as a part of Joyce's job package.

---

h. She's done everything right; she's bright, she has a Purdue degree, she has good grades, she's pretty, she's charming; but she's unemployed. It's not that she hasn't had a job, she had several, but every job she has held has ended up being an awful experience. They have asked her to do things she had neither the experience nor the training to do, they treated her like a dumb blonde, the work environment was demeaning, the jobs were either impossible or boring and her supervisors were uniformly insensitive and uncaring. She keeps interviewing and is using a HeadHunter to help find a job. She doesn't have any trouble getting interviews and the interviews seem to go well, but the offer never comes.

---

i. She was one of the very best typewriter repair people in the business. She had worked for manufacturers of several different models of typewriters through the years and kept up-to-date on new models and features. Women are the direct users of most typewriters and she had an advantage over her male counterparts in that she could understand the complaints better and she knew how to solve most problems. She had seen many of her male co-workers move on and some even lose their jobs, but she thought her job was secure because she was good and she was special. That didn't stop the pink slip from showing up last Friday. They will give two months of severance pay. Whoopee-ding! What to do now?

_____

j. He has been working for five years in the auto assembly plant and has been recognized for his consistent, quality workmanship. He made one of the three most popular models of cars sold in the US. When interest rates started up and buyers noticed them, it was the less popular model lines that closed down first. Unfortunately, now they have closed his line as well. No one will say when they will start up the line again, but it is easy to see that they built a huge backlog of cars, so it isn't going to be any time soon.

_____

k. He finished college and they got married two years before she graduated. He found a job in a small business, and she decided upon graduation to go ahead and get her MBA. With her good degree and academic credentials, she was one of the first in her class to be offered a management track position with a very prestigious company. After her graduation, they moved and he has hopped from job to job, but nothing seems to satisfy him. He has two offers now, but neither of them are just what he is looking for. On top of that, he has come to enjoy his woodworking hobby. He has built some really nice furniture, but this woodworking doesn't even come close to providing a regular income. All his income goes into buying tools. Still, he is interviewing from time to time, hoping to find a rewarding job that really fits.

_____

l. He had changed jobs fairly often after his associate's degree. Mostly it is because the jobs were really quite a bit beneath his capability. Somehow he found himself working for bosses who understood the business far less well than he. He tried to help them, but they didn't seem to appreciate his expertise. His last employer let him go for no good reason. He has been looking, he has been applying, he has been interviewing, but someone else always gets the job. When he asks why he was passed over, he doesn't get good answers. With his "gift of gab", his professional competence, his wide experience and his maturity, he cannot understand why he doesn't get any offers.

_____

m. He was born 150 years too late; he would have been a great pioneer. He liked a couple history courses he took in college, but he really likes driving a beat-up pickup, wearing cowboy clothes, chewing, spitting, whittling, hunting, sometimes line-dancing, cogitating and talking slow. He has had worlds of interviews. All of his friends seemed to have set him up for interviews, but they don't want a common man with wisdom, they want a modern, fast-talking, sophisticate to make sales calls, and he will not do that. The facts are that after he turned down several jobs that didn't fit the kind of man he is, the interviews began to get farther and farther apart. He finally moved in with his grandfather and is finishing a few hogs. It's no fun to get all cleaned up and go out to an interview just to be shot down. He's given up on employers who seem incapable or recognizing a good man when they see one. Gramps pays the bills; maybe times will change again.

---

n. He earned his associate's degree just before they were married. He found a good job and put her through the rest of her school. She interviewed widely in anticipation of finishing her bachelor's degree and even though she thought it would be difficult, she found an excellent position right here in Lafayette. Her good income made it easy for them to live while he finished his bachelor's degree. His degree is in a pretty specialized area, in contrast to hers, so they planned on him taking the best job he could find. She would find a job wherever his job took him. It sounded like such a good plan. He got a good job, but even though her first job was surprisingly easy to get, she has been looking for four months and she cannot find a job.

---

2. Unemployment is looking for and not finding work. It is expressed as the percent of the labor force, those working and looking for work, that are looking and haven't found a job.

The January US unemployment rate was _____%.

How often is a new rate announced in the US?_____

About half of the people living in the US are in the labor force. US population is 272 million.

How many people in the US are:

Not in the labor force _135 million_

Employed _____

Unemployed _____

3. Draw and label an income/expenditure model. This time we will use the diagram to see how it describes individuals. Label the vertical axis as Spending, the horizontal axis as Income and the sloping line that intersects the 45 degree line as Consumption Spending. This diagram shows the relationship between income and spending. For each person below, draw a vertical line showing his income, label it, and for each individual show how his income compares with his spending and therefore his saving or dissaving. The key factor in locating the individual's income is to decide whether it is to the right of, left of, or at the intersection of the 45 degree line and the

Consumption Spending line.

College **student** with a part time job

Professional **grandfather** in his last five years before retirement

Established young **professional** who is enjoying and spending his income

4. Draw another income/expenditure model. This time we will use it to represent the total income and spending of all the people in the US. Label the:

Vertical axis	Aggregate Expenditures, CIGX
Horizontal axis	Aggregate Income, GDP (including employee compensation, profits, rent, interest, etc., and indirect business taxes)
Sloping line that intersects the 45 degree line	Aggregate Expenditures, GIGX

This diagram shows the relationship between total national income (Aggregate Income) and total national spending (Aggregate Expenditures). Draw a vertical line showing how much GDP (Income) will be. This level of income is called: _____

(Circle the correct word in each pair.)

If GDP is more than Equilibrium GDP for any period, then instead of people spending all/only their income they will (save, dissave) which will (add to, subtract from) spending,

B-27

and income will (rise, stay the same, fall) back to (a higher, a lower, equilibrium) GDP.

If GDP is less than Equilibrium GDP for any period, then instead of people spending all/only their income they will (save, dissave) which will (add to, subtract from) spending, and income will (rise, stay the same, fall back) to (a higher, a lower, equilibrium) GDP.

5. Reproduce another diagram like that of Figure A. Again we will use it to represent the total income and spending of all the people in the US. Label it as you did the diagram above. Now add Equilibrium GDP and a level of GDP, Productive Capacity, which is 20% less than Equilibrium, and label them.

A. Under these circumstances, the level of GDP will be at (Equilibrium, Productive Capacity).

B. The problem this economy will experience is (unemployment, inflation).

6. Reproduce another labeled diagram like that above, representing US aggregate income and spending with Equilibrium GDP drawn and labeled but place and label Productive Capacity GDP 20% more than Equilibrium.

A. Under these circumstances, the level of GDP will be at (Equilibrium, Productive Capacity).

B. The problem this economy will experience is (unemployment, inflation).

Written Assignment 6

Name_____ Seat No._____

(Please tear off the last page and get answers to these questions from your grandparents and/or any other people with lots of experience you come in contact with. There will be a place for this information on the next assignment.)

1. Investment, an important component of GDP, is an increase in the stock of durable, man-made goods and services that are used for production. To be "investment" the item must be:

>A new good or service
>
>Man-made
>
>Last more than a year
>
>Be used for production

The word "investment" is also used to describe the activity of buying things with the hope that they will earn income for us as we hold them. "I am investing in mutual funds, Ford stock and antique cars." reflects this use of the "investment" word. In this class when we say investment, we are referring to "investment" a part of GDP, not to buying assets with the hope of gain. The four key kinds of investment are listed below. Only the first category is included in the I of CIG, but the others are also investment and are very important to economic growth.

M   Machines and Factories

E   Education

R   Research and technology

I   Infrastructure--ways of
       improving transportation,
       communication, and/or
       doing business.

Below find a list of activities, some of which are investment. By each indicate the type of investment using the letters above or put an N if it is not investment.

____ A 1994 combine to harvest this fall's crop

____ A new computer to keep better farm business records

____ A purchase of new 4WD pickup for hauling livestock to market with a goose-neck trailer

B-29

___ Research leading to the cloning of high producing dairy cows

___ Lafayette railroad relocation

___ The purchase of 40 acres of flat, black Benton County land

___ The construction of farm machinery storage

___ The purchase of a new punch press at Wabash National

___ The purchase of a new airliner by United from Boeing

___ The purchase of a Monet masterpiece painting

___ The purchase of some General Motors stock as a basis for saving for a college education

2. Draw and label an income-expenditure model showing an Equilibrium GDP of $8600 and a Full Employment or Productive Capacity GDP of $8700. The marginal propensity to consume is 2/3.

What problem will this economy face and why? _____
_____

To solve this problem does the CIGX line need to be raised or lowered?
_____

How much does it need to be changed? Show your algebra clearly.

Who is responsible for changing it? _____

What is the action to prevent the problem mentioned above from happening called?

_____

3. Draw and label an income-expenditure model showing an Equilibrium GDP of $8700 and a Full Employment or Productive Capacity GDP of $8650. The marginal propensity to consume is 3/4.

What problem will this economy face and why? _____

_____

To solve this problem does the CIGX line need to be raised or lowered?

_____

How much does it need to be changed? Show your algebra clearly.

Who is responsible for changing it? _____

What is the action to prevent the problem mentioned above from happening called?

_____

4. Inflation means generally rising prices and it is usually expressed as the percent increase in prices over the last 12 months.

The US inflation rate from February 1998 through January 1999 is _____%.

How often is a new rate announced in the US?_____

5. Papa Cusamano retired January 1, 1999 at age 65. He earns an annual pension of $36,000 as long as he or his wife lives. His life expectancy today is about 23 years. That is longer than your life expectancy because he has already made it past many of the things that can get you between now and age 65. Today his pension is a little more than the average total compensation for working people in the US. From it he will have to pay all his bills. His monthly pay will be $3000 and that is the purchasing power of his pay today, but inflation will influence how much it will buy in the future. If we have 4% inflation as long as he lives, (just under the average over the last 20 years), how much will his $3000 check buy over time in today's money value. To find the price index, start with this year's index and multiply by 1 plus the inflation rate to get next year's index (1.04). To find the purchasing power of future income with inflation, divide the nominal income ($3000) by the price index divided by 100.

(Note that the step between the lines below sometimes is one year, but not always.)

Year	Price Index	Purchasing Power of Papa Cusamano $3000 in 1999 Dollars
1999	100	$3000
2000	104	$2885
2001	108.2	_____
2002	_____	_____
2009	_____	_____
2019	_____	_____
2029	_____	_____

In short, the effect of inflation on Papa Cusamano is:

_____

_____

B-32

These questions will be repeated on next week's assignment. Get the info now.

6. Inflation affects people differently. Some people are really helped and others are really hurt by inflation. Real prices are the current prices divided by the price level, so that the real price stays the same if the price on the item doubles while the price level doubles. The real prices of some things go up rapidly over time and the real price of some things go down.

a. Name an item, important to your grandparents, whose real price has gone up dramatically during your lifetime: _____

b. Name an item, important to your grandparents, whose real price has gone down during your lifetime: _____

c. Who in your family or community has really been hurt by inflation?

Who? _____

When?

_____

How?

_____

d. Who in your family or community has really been helped by inflation?

Who? _____

When?

_____

How?

_____

Written Assignment 7

Name _____ Seat No. _____

1. Inflation affects people differently. Some people are really helped and others are really hurt by inflation. Real prices are the current prices divided by the price level, so that the real price stays the same if the price on the item doubles while the price level doubles. The real prices of some things goes up rapidly over time and the real price of some things actually goes down.

a.　　Name an item, important to your grandparents, whose real price has gone up

　　　dramatically during your lifetime: _____

b.　　Name an item, important to your grandparents, whose real price has gone down

　　　during your lifetime: _____

c.　　Who in your family or community has really been hurt by inflation?

　　　Who? _____

　　　　　　When? _____

　　　　　　How? _____

d.　　Who in your family or community has really been helped by inflation?

　　　Who? _____

　　　　　　When? _____

　　　　　　How? _____

2. If, when you check your mail, you find a letter from Grandmother with a check for $300 and a note saying that you may spend it any way you wish, how much of it would you spend by Thanksgiving? $_____ (Avoid answers of either $0 or $300 to make answering questions below easier)

3. Marginal Propensity to Consume (MPC) means how much more a person will _____ as a result of an increase in income of $1.

4. Based on questions 2 and 3, my MPC is _____.

B-35

5. The multiplier tells us how many times more the (GDP, CIG) changes than the change in (GDP, CIG).

6. The multiplier is the reciprocal of, or the number found by dividing the number one by,

_____.

7. If the change in CIG is -$15 and the Multiplier is 4, then GDP will go (up, down) by

$_____.

8. If the GDP needs to be increased by $75 and the Multiplier is 3, then CIG must be increased

by $_____.

9. If the Multiplier is 5 and Consumption spending is +$17, CIG is (up, down) by $_____, and GDP is (up, down) by $_____.

10. Create a carefully labeled income-expenditure model with equilibrium income $8600, MPC of 3/4 and full employment GDP or potential GDP of $8550.

a. The GDP that represents how much the people in the country want to buy is:

_____

b. The GDP that represents how much the country can produce is: _____

c. What problem will the country in this situation face? _____

d. If you were to prevent the above problem using Government spending, how much would be needed? Show your algebra here and draw the new line on the diagram.

e. If you were to prevent the above problem using Taxes, how much would be needed? Show your algebra here and draw the new line on the diagram.

11. Create another diagram such that the equilibrium income is $8700, MPC is 2/3 and full employment GDP is $8800.

a. The GDP that represents how much the country can produce is: _____

b. The GDP that represents how much the people in the country want to buy is:

_____

c. What problem will the country in this situation face? _____

d. If you were to prevent the above problem using government spending, how much would be needed? Show your algebra here and draw the new line on the diagram.

Written Assignment 8

Name _____ Seat. No. _____

1. Monetary Policy is a deliberate change in the money supply to affect Equilibrium GDP, much as Fiscal Policy was a deliberate change in incomes to affect GDP. Often people make little distinction between changes in their money and their income, but this difference is important as we contrast Monetary Policy and Fiscal Policy. Below clearly explain situations where the amount of money a family has and the amount of income they have move in opposite directions. What happens to the amount of **money** a person has and the amount of **income** when the following occurs:

a. During the first year after a Purdue student graduates, moves to a new town, takes high paying job and starts to repay his student loans.

_____

_____

_____

b. During the first month after a ten year employee has been fired and given four months severance pay.

_____

_____

_____

2. What are the three principal tools of Monetary Policy? When the economy has problems, what action should be taken for each tool?

What should be done to correct:

Monetary Policy Tool:	*Demand Pull Inflation:*	*Cyclical Unemployment:*
_____	_____	_____
_____	_____	_____
_____	_____	_____

B-39

3. Monetary policy has the goal of:

_____

Monetary policy is done by the "Fed"; who is that:

_____

Fiscal policy has the goal of:

_____

Fiscal policy is done by:

_____

4. Below on the left draw and label an income expenditure model with Equilibrium GDP less than Productive Capacity, and on the right draw and label an income expenditure model with Equilibrium GDP more than Productive Capacity. Below each tell what problem the society would be
experiencing. Below each list the three principal monetary policy actions that would be appropriate to solve the problem. Step by step on the lines 1-9 below, tell how the policies would help to solve the problem. With a contrasting pencil, draw on the new CIGX line, which your prescription would produce.

Problem = _____   Problem = _____

Appropriate Monetary Action:

_____   _____

_____   _____

_____   _____

This monetary action would set in motion the following string of changes: (enter UP, DOWN, NO EFFECT)

<table>
<tr><td>Figure Above</td><td>Figure Above</td></tr>
</table>

Steps:

1. Money Supply _____

2. Interest Rates _____

3. Consumption Spending _____

4. Investment Spending _____

5. CIGX _____

6. Equilibrium GDP _____

7. Potential (Full Employment) GDP

_____

8. Unemployment _____

9. Inflation _____

Add appropriate fiscal policy actions.

_____

_____

Steps:

1. Money Supply _____

2. Interest Rates _____

3. Consumption Spending _____

4. Investment Spending _____

5. CIGX _____

6. Equilibrium GDP _____

7. Potential (Full Employment) GDP

_____

8. Unemployment _____

9. Inflation _____

_____

_____

5. The car we choose to buy is often influenced by our budget--how much we can pay per month for the car. The size of our monthly payments is determined by the car price and the interest rate. To see the effects of the interest rate on monthly car payments, lets look at three sport/utility vehicles (SUV) and three interest rates, keeping the repayment period at 6 years. **Find the monthly payment to the closest dollar by multiplying the price of the SUV times the Monthly Pay Coefficient shown below.**

Find the monthly payments to the closest dollar over six years for the three cars at the three interest rates shown below:

Interest Rates:

	12%	*9%*	*4%*
Monthly Pay Coefficient	.019550	.018026	.015645

SUV; Price	*Monthly*	*Payments*	*over Six Years*
Plain Blazer; $21,550	_____	_____	_____
Loaded Blazer; $24,800	_____	_____	_____
GMC Suburban; $26,900	_____	_____	_____

You had planned to buy the Escort when it looked like you would have to pay 12%, but interest rates dropped to 4%, so now which car can you afford? _____

Your cousin thought he could afford a Taurus as he planned with 4% interest rates, but when rates jumped to 9%, which car could he afford? _____

When interest rates changes, consumer purchases change:

When interest rates drop, purchases (increase, decrease).

When interest rates rise, purchases (increase, decrease).

Written Assignment 9

Name_____ Seat No._____

1. The quantity theory of money says that the money supply (M) times its velocity (V) equals the GDP just as the real output (Y) times the price level (P) equals the GDP.

$$M \times V = GDP = P \times Y$$

Define Velocity:

_____

_____

2. For small changes in M, V, P, or Y, the percent change in M plus the percent change in V will equal the percent change in GDP. Similarly, the percent change in P plus the percent change in Y will equal the percent change in GDP. Using this principle, we can see that if Y increased 4% and V doesn't change (and it usually changes very little in any short period), an increase in M of 5% would result in a P increase of 1%. Now you try it. If real output (Y) increased by 4% and the desired rate of inflation is 3%: (put the percent change on the lines below.)

_____ x _____ = _____ = _____ x _____

a. How much should the Fed increase the money supply? _____%

b. If the money supply is increased half as much as you recommend above: (check all correct)

___ V will be less than expected

___ GDP will be less than expected

___ Y will be less than expected

___ P will be less than expected

3. Explain what Monetary and Fiscal Policies are, who does them, and what their goals, tools and effectiveness are both in normal and in extreme times.

4. As a Senator in Washington, check whether you would vote to expand or reduce each program as you use wise fiscal policy in these areas of constituent interest under these economic conditions.

		Recommended Action (check one)	
Economic Condition	*Constituent Interest*	*Expand*	*Reduce*
Recession	Extending Unemployment Insurance Payment Period.	___	___
Recession	Tax Credits (refunds) for Parents of College Students.	___	___
Recession	Cancer Research Programs	___	___
Inflation	Extending Unemployment Insurance Payment Period.	___	___
Inflation	Tax Credits (refunds) for Parents of College Students.	___	___
Inflation	Cancer Research Programs	___	___

You are likely to be remembered more for the legislation you propose and get implemented than for the general level of the economy while you were in office. When your constituents consider what you have done during your first term as they consider whether to reelect or replace, if you were a politician, (one who looks out for his own welfare) in contrast to a statesman, (one who looks out for the well-being of the country) what would be the great advantage of being in office during recessionary rather than boom times?

_____

_____

5. Explain whether it would be easier to explain the more popular programs to your constituents during times of budget surplus or budget deficit.

_____

_____

6.a. If the economy began to suffer from increased unemployment because the market for exports dried up as result of a recession in Asia, what change in the money supply would you suggest?

(Increase, Decrease)

b. Explain clearly how or if your suggestion would help the following situations:

I. Karl really enjoyed the Computer Aided Design (CAD) classes in Agricultural Engineering at Purdue. Purdue has the best CAD training facility in the world and Karl is one of ABE's good students. He wants a job in the construction machinery industry and they just aren't hiring because business is slow. Several said they would keep his resume on file, but no offers. He is discouraged.

II. Susan was runner-up for Purdue Homecoming Queen and has well-above-average grades. She wants a fashion design job and has done well in her design classes. The only reason she doesn't have higher grades in her design classes is that she felt she knew better than the teacher what went into modern design, and she didn't take correction very kindly. She has always been a little temperamental and some find her abrasive. She has an interesting portfolio and she can be charming, but she does not get second interviews. She thinks Purdue lied to her about job prospects, and she is angry.

(If you didn't discuss the role interest rates play in how monetary policy affects employment, you were barking up the wrong tree!)

7. If we begin to slide toward another depression like that of the 1930's, who should do what?

One agency who is supposed to do something: _____

What would they do?

_____

_____

 Another agency who is supposed to do something: _____

What would they do?

_____

_____

_____

Put a **W** before those items above that the agency would be likely to do. Put an **N** before those items above that would be unpopular with the public.

In your judgement, how likely are we to have another depression in the next thirty years while you are establishing yourself professionally and financially?

_____

_____

_____

8. How would your answer be different if the Senate had passed the constitutional amendment requiring a balanced budget and it had gone on to become law?

_____

_____

_____

9. The output of goods and services in the country tends to vary from year to year. It is fairly easy to see the variation in the grand total, GDP. Are there segments of the economy where output varies more or less than the GDP varies?

What business or product would have a booming market in good times and business would just dry up when the economy slowed down? List two and explain why business varies so.

_____

_____

_____

_____

_____

_____

What business or product would be about the same whether there were boom times or a recession? List two and explain why business activity doesn't change much from when times are bad to good.

_____

_____

_____

_____

_____

_____

10. Explain what the Great Depression was:

When it happened:

_____

_____

Why it kept getting worse:

_____

_____

What was done at first to get out of it:

_____

_____

What was done that seemed to work to get us out of it?

_____

_____

Explain how likely we are to have another depression in your lifetime.

_____

_____

How might the adoption of the budget balancing amendment change that?

_____

_____

Written Assignment 10

Names: _____ Seat No. _____ % Contribution _____

                     _____   _____   _____

                     _____   _____   _____

Do this assignment in teams of up to three. The team members may come from either section. If a fourth wants to join your group, divide into two groups of two. <u>Submit only one assignment for the team</u> with team members' names on the top. The purpose of this assignment is to find the wisest ways to cut the deficit from its current $128 billion. The plan for eliminating the deficit would be to cut out the foolish ways the federal government spends money, keeping the wise programs, and increasing the taxes as indicated in the list below, while reducing taxes in the final list.

1. List the kinds of federal programs that you know about. You are making a list of the ways that the federal government spends money. You may include ways you or your families benefit from federal expenditure. (One tremendously important expenditure of federal funds is for Pell grants to students who attend Purdue, making possible large tuition payments, the basis for Prof. Taylor's generous salary.) You may think of things the federal government spends money on that are foolish. **Each person brings to the first meeting a list of federal programs or expenditures he knows about.** The lists are then divided into wise uses for federal funds and questionable or unwise uses of federal funds. These are then pooled and two lists are created and presented in priority order with the ten wisest and the ten most foolish expenditures listed below.

Before you make your lists, you must decide the criteria you will use for evaluating the wisdom of the expenditures. We used the same criteria for evaluating all expenditures, and chose and rejected all ideas based on what appears to be best for:

_____ The country as a whole over the next 40 years.

_____ Us as individuals over the next three years

a. Our list of wise federal expenditures starting with the wisest expenditure follows:

1. _____

    _____

2. _____

    _____

3. _____

_____

4. _____

_____

5. _____

_____

6. _____

_____

7. _____

_____

8. _____

_____

9. _____

_____

10. _____

_____

b. Our list of foolish federal expenditures starting with the most foolish expenditure follows:

1. _____

_____

2. _____

_____

3. _____

_____

4. _____

_____

5. _____

_____

6. _____

_____

7. _____

_____

8. _____

_____

9. _____

_____

10. _____

_____

2. **Each person brings to the first meeting a list of the sources of federal revenue (taxes) he knows or has thought about.** This may be a list of the things that ought to be or are taxed (excise taxes on auto tires), it may be a list of the different kinds of income that ought to be or are taxed (gambling income, income above $100,000) or it may be a list of income or expenditure that is currently and shouldn't be exempt from tax (save-the-whales contributions). The lists are then divided into the expandable sources of federal funds and the already overtaxed sources of federal funds. These are then pooled and two lists are created and presented in priority order with the ten best sources of increased tax income and the ten taxes that should be eliminated or reduced.

Use the same criteria for evaluating all taxes and choose and reject all ideas based on the same criteria used for expenditures, as indicated above.

a. Our list of things the federal government taxes which ought to be taxed more, starting with the one which should have the greatest tax increase follows:

1. _____

_____

2. _____

_____

3. _____

_____

4. _____

_____

5. _____

_____

6. _____

_____

7. _____

_____

8. _____

_____

9. _____

_____

10. _____

_____

b. Our list of things the federal government taxes that ought to be taxed less or not at all, starting with the tax that ought to be eliminated or reduced most follows:

1. _____

_____

2. _____

_____

3. _____

_____

4. _____

_____

5. _____

_____

6. _____

_____

7. _____

_____

8. _____

_____

9. _____

_____

10. _____

_____

B-54

Written Assignment 11

Name_____ Seat No._____

Name_____ Seat No._____

Name_____ Seat No._____

I encourage you to do this assignment in a group of up to three.

A simple economy with GDP made up of only Consumption and Investment has been stable for years with GDP of $8791. Investment is at 6.5% of GDP, or $571. Investment is an increase in the stock of man-made goods and services used for production, and provides the basis for increased production in the future. For a long time an average of 1000 people have been dying of starvation annually because the economy is not producing enough to support them.

As a Senator, you can influence policy for the proportion of GDP that goes into investment. Investment, at least in the short run, is competitive with consumption, yet is the basis for economic growth in the long run. Babies are easy to save. An increase in GDP of $10 annually will save one child from starvation. Your job is to establish the best investment policy for your economy and promote it.

1. Choose two national investment policies, and show their effects by making a table for each policy, which continues the table, started below. It's easiest to use a spreadsheet. To do the analysis, change the percent of GDP that goes into investment starting in 2000, **leaving it at the new level through 2060**. One policy will be to have more than 6.5% of GDP that goes to investment, and the other will be to use less than 6.5% of the GDP that goes to investment. Evaluate the consequences of your policy alternatives over much of your expected lifetime by continuing the tables through 2060.

The numbers in the columns are found as follows:

- **Year--Consecutive years from 1998 through 2060**

- **GDP--GDP this year equals GDP last year, less $120, plus 21% of last year's investment,**

- **% Investment--6.5% in 1998 and 1999 but in 2000 it ought to be raised and kept the same until 2060, and in a second table lowered and kept constant until 2060.**

- **Economic Growth--The percent increase in GDP from one year to the next (constant population)**

- **Investment--GDP times the % Investment**

- **Consumption--GDP less Investment**

- **Starvation--1822 less one for each $10 of Consumption (S = 1822 - .1*C, but never less than zero)**

When creating your spreadsheet, enter the information from the table below for 1998 and 1999 as data. Then add the 2000 row as formulas. Start with the 6.5% investment level to test your formulas. Copy the 2000 row until you have lines through 2060. If all the numbers in each row 1998 through 2060 except the date year are the same, you have the correct formulas. If not repair them until they are the same. Then change the percent investment for 2000-2060 to see its effect on growth and starvation. Try the 7% of your opponent to be sure that your recommendation is superior to his.

In the event that you cannot get access to a spreadsheet for this assignment, do the tables by hand, seeing the effect of your investment changes only for 20 years and draw your conclusions from that information.

> For a small amount of extra credit, find an investment rate that correctly does any of the following:
>
> a. Has the minimum 2000 starvation level. (Investment rate ____%)
>
> b. Can eliminate starvation by 2060. (Investment rate ____%)
>
> c. Minimizes total starvation deaths 2000-2060 (Investment rate ____%

2. **Write a half page news release** supporting one of your policy positions that you, a Senator who is up for re-election this fall will use as a part of your economic policy in your campaign. Your opponent is recommending a 7% rate of investment. In your release recognize the weaknesses of your proposal. Use the first assignment page as the cover page when you submit your assignment and staple your news release and tables to it.

Year	GDP	Econ Growth	%Investment	Investment	Consumption	Starvation
1998	$8,791	0.00%	6.5%	$571	$8,220	1000
1999	$8,791	0.00%	6.5%	$571	$8,220	1000
2000	$8,791	0.00%	6.5%	$571	$8,220	1000
2001	$8,791	0.00%	6.5%	$571	$8,220	1000

Written Assignment 12

Name_____ Seat No._____

1.   Suppose that the US and Japan can both produce steel and soybeans. The US has 50 units of resources and Japan has 90. The production from one unit of resources in each country is as follows:

Product	US	Japan
Soybeans	5	2
Steel	4	3

a.   Japan has a comparative advantage in producing: _____

I can tell that Japan has this comparative advantage because:

_____

_____

b.   The US has an absolute advantage in producing: _____

I can tell that this is true because:

_____

c.   If each country took its total resources and used half of them for producing one product and half for producing the other, how much of each product would be produced in each country and in total?

	Product Available with 50-50 Resource Split				
Product	US		Japan		Total
	Resources	Production	Resources	Production	Prod'n.
Soybeans	_____	_____	_____	_____	_____
Steel	_____	_____	_____	_____	_____
Total	50		90		

d.   If each country specialized and used all its resources to produce only the product in

B-57

which it had a comparative advantage, how much of each product would be produced in each country and in total?

Production with Specialized use of Resources

Product	United States Resources	United States Production	Japan Resources	Japan Production	Total Production
Soybeans	_____	_____	_____	_____	_____
Steel	_____	_____	_____	_____	_____
Total	50		90		

e.   Now let's evaluate specialized production and trade. Suppose the US and Japan both produce only the good in which they have a comparative advantage (Q1.d.). The US produces and keeps 10 more of its product than it had when it split its resources 50-50 (Q1.c.). The rest of its production it trades to Japan at the rate of one unit of soybeans for one unit of steel. How much of each product would each country end up with?

Availability with Specialization and Trade

Product	US	Japan	Total
Soybeans	_____	_____	_____
Steel	_____	_____	_____

f.   Bring forward the amount of product available when each country split its resources evenly between the two products (Q1.c.). Also bring forward the amount of each product in each country available after trade with specialized production (Q1.e.)? In the table below find what percent better (or worse) off each country is in each product with the trade option compared to the no trade option. (Divide the trade option availability by the no-trade production, subtract 1, and multiply by 100 to get the percent change.)

Product	United States 50-50	United States Spec & Trade	United States % better	Japan 50-50	Japan Spec & Trade	Japan % better
Soybeans	_____	_____	_____	_____	_____	_____
Steel	_____	_____	_____	_____	_____	_____

2.   Do countries gain or lose by trade? In the above analysis we made some unrealistic assumptions like ignoring the costs of shipping and that the products from one country might be

different quality from the other, so that it is easy to see that there is more to trade than this analysis. What we can learn from this analysis?

a. Which country gains from trade? _____

b. How is the larger country affected by trade?_____

c. How is the smaller country affected by trade? _____

d. How is the more productive country affected by trade? _____

e. How is the less productive country affected by trade? _____

3.   The argument has been made that a country can be hurt by trading. If a country were free to trade if it wished and it was clear that it would lose by trading with this partner on these terms, would it do it? Explain why a country can or cannot be hurt by trade.

_____

_____

4.   Based on the situation in Question 1, the producers of what products in what country will **lose** jobs? Will these people be helped or hurt a little or a lot?

_____

_____

5.   Based on the situation in Question 1, the producers of what products in what country will **gain** jobs? Will these people be helped or hurt a little or a lot?

_____

_____

6.   How will the citizens of Japan and the US be affected by free trade compared to each country producing for its own citizens? Will these people be helped or hurt a little or a lot?

_____

_____

7.   If you were asked you to write a speech on trade, what would be the most important economic arguments that you would make to support expanded trade?

_____

_____

8.   If you were asked you to write a speech on trade, what would be the most important economic arguments that you would make to argue against expanded trade?

_____

_____

9.   What is happening to the volume of world trade?

_____

_____